TALENT

ALSO BY TYLER COWEN

Big Business

Stubborn Attachments

The Complacent Class

Average Is Over

The Great Stagnation

An Economist Gets Lunch

The Age of the Infovore

Discover Your Inner Economist

TALENT

HOW TO IDENTIFY ENERGIZERS, CREATIVES, AND WINNERS AROUND THE WORLD

TYLER COWEN
AND DANIEL GROSS

ST. MARTIN'S PRESS

NEW YORK

First published in the United States by St. Martin's Press,
an imprint of St. Martin's Publishing Group

TALENT. Copyright © 2022 by Tyler Cowen and Daniel Gross. All rights
reserved. Printed in the United States of America. For information, address
St. Martin's Publishing Group, 120 Broadway, New York, NY 10271.

www.stmartins.com

Designed by Meryl Sussman Levavi

Library of Congress Cataloging-in-Publication Data

Names: Cowen, Tyler, author. | Gross, Daniel, 1967– author.
Title: Talent : how to identify energizers, creatives, and winners around the world /
    Tyler Cowen and Daniel Gross.
Description: First Edition. | New York, NY : St. Martin's Press, [2022]
Identifiers: LCCN 2022000900 | ISBN 9781250275813 (hardcover) |
    ISBN 9781250275820 (ebook)
Subjects: LCSH: Employment interviewing—Psychological aspects. | Employee
    selection. | Employee retention.
Classification: LCC HF5549.5.I6 C689 2022 | DDC 650.14/4019—dc23/eng/
    20220203
LC record available at https://lccn.loc.gov/2022000900

Our books may be purchased in bulk for promotional, educational, or
business use. Please contact your local bookseller or the Macmillan
Corporate and Premium Sales Department at 1-800-221-7945, extension
5442, or by email at MacmillanSpecialMarkets@macmillan.com.

First Edition: 2022

1 3 5 7 9 10 8 6 4 2

To finding each other

CONTENTS

TALENT

1

WHY TALENT MATTERS

This book started with a conversation.

We search for talent—obsessively—as part of our jobs. After we met a few years ago, we started to talk about our approaches to hiring, and how, for both of us, the search for rare, transformative talent is so important. This started as a workplace fascination, but over time it morphed into a way of seeing the world—we were constantly searching for hidden talents in people we met in all parts of our lives.

During that first meeting we quickly began to trade tips and generate new hypotheses. We set up a WhatsApp channel to pursue the dialogue, which was punctuated by periodic visits and a few joint trips, all motivated by a mixture of fun, obsessive mischievousness, and the desire to learn something of practical value. What happens if you take two very opinionated people, both working on talent search, and let them tease each other, prod each other, hack away at each other, challenge each other's prejudices, and bicker with each other for a few years, all on how to spot talent?

This book is the product of those exchanges.

Tyler remembers one of his early chats with Daniel. Daniel stressed the importance of hobbyists and "weirdos," noting that many major mainstream internet revolutions started with products that appeared to be niche. It is the people who work intently on pleasing a narrow fan base, but pleasing them intensely, who end up with the skills and networks to market the product to broader audiences. So very often, if you are looking for a start-up that will hit it big, do something counterintuitive by seeking out people aiming, at least at first, to please smaller and weirder audiences.

Daniel recalls that he first learned from Tyler this question for prospective hires: "What is it you do to practice that is analogous to how a pianist practices scales?" You learn what the person is doing to achieve ongoing improvement, and perhaps you can judge its efficacy or even learn something from it. You also learn how the person thinks about continual self-improvement, above and beyond their particular habits. If a person doesn't practice much, they still might be a good hire, but then you are much more in the world of "what you see is what you get," which is valuable information on its own. If the person does engage in daily, intensive self-improvement, perhaps eschewing more typical and more social pursuits, there is a greater chance they are the kind of creative obsessive who can make a big difference.

If those two anecdotes focus on outsiders, it is because we are each outsiders in our own ways. Daniel started with gaming and did not pursue higher education, while Tyler began his career ascent in the early days of blogging. Both of us think of ourselves as examples of initially hidden talent, and that is part of the reason we wish to help you find other outsiders for your ventures.

Daniel Gross once wrote a self-description starting with "I spent most of my youth feeling like an outsider looking in." Before his foray into the tech world Daniel was an obsessive gamer, but he decided to bring his competitive experience from gaming to address bigger and more socially relevant problems. He began his tech career with a company called Cue, which he ended up selling to Apple when he was twenty-three, becoming a director at Apple at a time when Apple experienced some of its most dynamic growth. Daniel next served as a partner and founder at Y Combinator, an esteemed Silicon Valley start-up incubator with an aggregate market cap of over $100 million. There he helped build and then institutionalize what is perhaps the most influential systematic approach to venture capital and talent search in the world. He also became an angel investor, seeking out promising companies and creators in their very early stages, an exercise in talent search, of course.[1]

In 2018 Daniel founded Pioneer, an upstart venture capital firm based in San Francisco. Pioneer is devoted to finding new talent around the world, using online methods and gaming in addition to the usual techniques of referrals and interviews. Daniel and Pioneer are committed to the view that there is *much* more talent to be found out there, including in new and unusual places. They want to find the creators that everyone else is failing to see in the first place. Daniel mostly is looking to find and fund company founders, but of course he hires for Pioneer as well, for a variety of roles at all levels of the company. But don't think of Daniel as a practitioner alone: in his spare time he cruises Google Scholar for research articles on talent, and then sends them to Tyler.

Tyler is a professor of economics at George Mason University, where he has been involved in academic hiring and graduate admissions for over thirty years. He is the head of the Mercatus

Center, a research center with nearly two hundred employees. Within Mercatus he directs a philanthropic fund devoted to spotting and funding talent—typically young talent—called Emergent Ventures. He has written a daily blog, *Marginal Revolution*, for eighteen years, runs an online economics education site, Marginal Revolution University, and hosts a podcast, *Conversations with Tyler*. Tyler remains an academic, but he is involved in personnel selection and project management almost every day.

One of his blog commentators, Alastair, described him as follows: "Tyler is contrarian in method. His superfast reading speed, various professional roles, constant podcasting and networking, obsessive learning, perpetual travel, and sheer stamina enable him to take in many more and different inputs, which allows him to have many more and different outputs. But it's what's in between where he shines. He sees the world as an economist, philosopher, psychologist, sociologist, anthropologist, liberal and conservative, globalist and nationalist, foreigner and native, art critic and artist, employer/administrator and employee, grant provider and grant recipient, interviewer and interviewee, teacher and student. There is almost no one who views the world like Tyler because almost no one has a comparable number or variety of inputs or mental models. Even if his conclusions were conventional, his reasoning and perspectives wouldn't be."[2]

We might seem pretty different based on our jobs; furthermore, Daniel is in his late twenties and Tyler is in his late fifties. Daniel was born in Israel (to American parents) and moved to San Francisco, and Tyler was born in New Jersey and ended up in northern Virginia. Daniel can come across as a little grumpy, while Tyler seems detached. Daniel seems surprised each time that Tyler actually teases him. Daniel goes scuba diving and listens to EDM, while Tyler plays basketball and listens to Beethoven and Indian classical music. Daniel hated high school and rebelled against it, but Tyler mostly ignored it. Still, we share a stubborn curiosity, a love for ideas, and the willingness to persist in hacking away at tough problems. Thus, once we started talking we never stopped.

This dynamic started right away when Daniel and Tyler first met on February 1, 2018, at a group dinner, a kind of informal salon in a private room at a San Francisco restaurant. Tyler was visiting friends, and he was invited along to an event that was fascinating in its own right for its insights into British politics. But Tyler also noticed Daniel, whom he had not previously met. Daniel was sitting in a corner seat at a large table and was reasonably quiet, but Tyler perceived immediately just how quickly and thoroughly Daniel was taking everything in. "Who is this young guy?" he was thinking. "What should I be making of that wry smile?" Tyler also noticed right away how much the other people at the dinner, some of them eminent Silicon Valley founders and venture capitalists, listened carefully whenever Daniel did speak.

One of the first things Daniel noticed about Tyler was his now-iconic tote bag. This simple accoutrement, filled with an iPad and a few books, speaks to the aesthetic of Mr. Cowen: whimsical, down-to-earth, and nontraditional. People from "old money" do not lug around such things. After everyone was seated, the game of dinner discussion began. Events like this, in which ideas are shotgunned out at a rapid pace, often provide a quick window into whether a person's true interests lie in status or in ideas. They allow you to catch a glimpse into a person's creative talents. Status-seekers focus on maximizing attention from the perceived elite. Idea-seekers, on the other hand, want to advance knowledge and stimulate curiosity, speaking to the entire room and holding the attention of the group. Intrigue is their reserve currency, and conjectures are often framed as questions, not statements. Daniel felt Tyler embodied the latter kind of creative spark. In group conversations the two usually managed to catch each other's attention and to follow up on each other's points and themes, a good sign they ought to be talking further. By the end of the evening, each felt the other had understood the ongoing dialogue in the same general terms.

Each meeting led to another, and it was while having lunch at a San Francisco Chinese restaurant in 2019 that we decided to write this book. The plan flowed quickly, and we both agreed that the key was to get started and to allow the gains from intellectual trade to flow. Tyler recalls feeling very guilty during this conversation, as he had to report to Daniel that he could not start work on the project for several months because he first had marketing obligations for his previous book (Tyler *hates* it when people cannot start on their work right away). Still, Daniel noticed that Tyler hated this fact, and that pleased him just enough to keep the momentum going.

We then discussed how such a book should offer (among other topics) a high-level treatment of intelligence, personality traits, and how to interview, blending the oral lore of the venture capital tradition with newer perspectives on how to search for diverse talents. Such a book should apply those insights to both start-ups and to the plain ol' regular economy.

It is evident that a lot of people want to find talent, but they do not always succeed. According to the Conference Board Annual Survey, hiring talent is the top concern of CEOs and other senior business executives. Furthermore, the unavailability of needed skills and talent is judged to be the number one threat to businesses. When we speak to CEOs, nonprofit directors, or venture capitalists, lack of proper talent—and how to go about finding more of it—is an obsessive concern of theirs.[3]

That is all the more true today as individuals have been leaving jobs in record numbers and reevaluating their futures, in part due to the COVID-19 pandemic. We are entering a brave new world where remote work is far more common, which means a great deal of talent needs to be repriced for a world where connections and meetings so often are made over Zoom.

Of course, talent search isn't just about jobs and business. It's about handing out scholarships, allocating auditions, choosing the right athlete in the draft, opting for the right co-author, and even choosing your friends and partners. Talent search is one of the most important activities in virtually all human lives. Elon Musk personally interviewed the first *three thousand* employees at SpaceX because he wanted to make sure the company was hiring the right people.[4]

Don't just think of talent search as a problem faced by "the boss" or by human resource departments. If you are hoping to be discovered, one of the most valuable things you can learn is how other people are thinking about talent (or how they should be thinking about talent), in case you can showcase exciting and valuable traits that potential employers otherwise might miss. You have to worry about talent judgments at least as much as the boss does.

Just about everyone is on a quest to find talent in others or to show off their own. Surely you care about how talented your boss and co-workers are, as you want to work with the most talented people possible, *especially* if they are your bosses. That is one good way to grow more talented yourself. The decision to take a job or pursue an opportunity is almost always a decision about other people—namely, those you will be working with and answering to, no matter what your place in the hierarchy.

The practical value is that identifying underrated talent is one of the most potent ways to give yourself a personal or an organizational edge. Large companies can afford to overbid for the "obvious" talent, but if you are in a smaller institution you might not be in a comparable position. Screening correctly for the overlooked late-career woman, the non-obvious misfit producer, or the hidden genius is your best bet at building a unique, motivated, and loyal team. If you work for an established large institution, perhaps you have seen a descent into excess credentialism and highly bureaucratic hiring procedures rather than the quest for inspired talent that made the company great in the first place. You might like to get your institution taking more chances again—good chances, of course.

Most of all, we oppose and seek to revise the bureaucratic approach to talent search, which is poorly serving the American economy—and many American and global citizens. The bureaucratic approach, as we define it, seeks to minimize error and loss, and it prizes consensus above all else. It demands that everyone play by a set of overly rigid rules, that individualism be hidden or maybe even stamped out, and that there is never any hurry, so another set of procedures can be applied, virtually without end. At the end of all this you have a hiring process full of "kludge" and "sludge," to cite two terms coming into fashion in political science, and you will attract candidates of comparable temperament. Virtually all of you are familiar with the standard bureaucratic interview setup. A bunch of people show up in a room, armed with scripted questions (and answers), often bored by the process and hoping for the best; they are trying to find someone who seems "good enough" and capable of commanding consensus by being decent but most of all sufficiently unobjectionable.

We are realists, and we recognize the world is never going to eliminate these approaches, if only because bureaucracy is so widespread. Still, we are revolutionaries when it comes to hiring, and we think that a lot of you really can do much better than the typical approach. When it comes to talent, *we will try to teach you how to think past the bureaucracy.*

We focus on a very specific kind of talent in this book—namely, talent with a creative spark—and that is where the bureaucratic approach is most deadly. In referring to the creative spark, we mean people who generate new ideas, start new institutions, develop new methods for executing on known products, lead intellectual or charitable movements, or inspire others by their very presence, leadership, and charisma, regardless of the context. Those are all people who have the gift of improving the world by reimagining the future as a different and better place. And because they are often hard to spot, such people can turn up at all levels of an organization. It might be the CEO or a high-level executive, but it might just as well be a new marketing director who overturns your longtime approach to advertising or even an intern who wonders whether you should start a new kind of podcast. If you are trying to hire talent "on the way up"—as we think you should be—you will need to hone your skills to find that creative spark, rather than just looking for people with a long track record of achievement.

Doing better on the talent question really is critical. When we—Daniel and Tyler—read the project proposals that cross our respective desks, so often we see that talent and not money is the truly scarce variable. Tyler reads a proposal for a think tank in Indonesia, but who exactly will be the director and fundraiser? Daniel sees a company pitch asteroid mining in outer space, but rarely does one meet an individual with the perfect mixture of chutzpah and gravitas to execute on such an interplanetary idea. "Who is going to be the project driver on this one?" is a question that recurs again and again, and perhaps you see it in your work as well. Far too often there is no really good answer, not because the talent doesn't exist somewhere, but because it is hard to find and mobilize. There is a shortage of workers and leaders who can make things happen. That is true whether the question is building a new church, writing a hit pop song, or starting a successful company, thereby creating sustainable jobs for many other talented workers.

The scarcity and importance of talent are such major issues that they show up at the level of the macroeconomy. In essence there is a scarcity of talented labor relative to capital, as evidenced by the relative plenty of venture capital and what economists call "the savings glut." The Japanese conglomerate SoftBank, with its stash of billions, has become the world's largest venture capital firm, but it can't always find the right opportunities, and it has made many mistakes, such as funding WeWork and its CEO and founder, Adam Neumann. Sovereign wealth funds, in nations as diverse as Singapore, Norway, and Qatar, are looking for new and ever broader ways to invest their growing surpluses. They have the money and are looking for the always-scarce talent.[5]

If we look at the growth in U.S. output since 1960, by the best available estimates at least 20 to 40 percent of that growth has stemmed from the better allocation of talent. Circa 1960, the United States was doing a stunningly bad job at allocating talent, in part due to sheer prejudice and misconception. For instance, 94 percent of doctors and lawyers were white men. In 1952, when Sandra Day O'Connor graduated third in her class from Stanford Law School, she could only get a job as a legal secretary. In earlier times, *and still today*, we are not always putting the most productive people into the jobs they would best be suited for; in other words, we were and are underusing, indeed wasting, human talent. This is bad for our economy, but it is also a human tragedy for those who cannot rise, and it harms our national spirit and morale.[6]

When we think of discrimination, we often think in terms of race, gender, and sexuality. Those remain very real problems, and the issue is so deeply rooted that there are many other areas in which American society has made mistakes in allocating talent. Circa 1970, were we really using nerds and introverts to the greatest and most productive degree possible? How about people with disabilities, or recent immigrant arrivals, or short individuals? Prejudices were—and still are—distorting many of our talent allocation decisions.

The data on American incomes reflects how talent is increasingly the binding constraint. If you look at the years 1980–2000, the main driver of rising income differences—which explains 75 percent of the variation—is whether a person has a college degree, no degree, or a graduate degree. But for 2000 to 2017, when we look at the rise in income inequality, amount of education explains only 38 percent of the variation. (For the time being it suffices to know that explaining 100 percent of the variation is explaining all of it, while lower numbers indicate a weaker connection, zero percent being no connection at all. The contrast between 75 and 38 percent is a big drop in explanatory power.) In the latter period, most of the increases in income inequality are seen in people *within* the same educational groupings. In other words, simply being educated only gets you so far; the real returns are to your talent above and beyond your educational level.[7]

Globalization also has boosted the relevance of the talent question, because there is more talent to be found than ever before. Take Nigeria. Thirty or forty years ago, rates of malnutrition in that country were so high and school systems were so bad that most of the talent and potential talent there didn't have much of a chance. Today, Nigerian living conditions are highly uneven and often miserable, but there is nonetheless a sizable middle (and upper) class. Nigerian entrepreneurs are starting businesses at a rapid clip, both in Africa and in the larger global community, and there is plenty more to come. In England, many of the kids with the strongest math scores have Nigerian backgrounds, and in the United States, Nigerian Americans are climbing the income ladder. Yet by no means have all Nigerians found their proper place in the world—again, a sign that talent search and evaluation could do far better, and furthermore, that you as a talent searcher have some very real opportunities.

Excess credentialism, one of the worst instantiations of the bureaucratic approach to hiring, is also a problem of talent search. Many jobs that decades ago required only a high school education now require a bachelor's or even an advanced degree. *The New York Times* has reported that the master's degree has become the new bachelor's. Does a worker in law enforcement or construction management really need to have a master's degree, as is currently a trend? Another way of asking the question: By requiring a master's degree for those positions, are we potentially overlooking people with more relevant skills and talents who might be better for the job? Credentialism plays an important role in helping us narrow down who is best for the job. But when it misses the mark, it hurts the candidate and employer, limits the economic and social mobility of those who can't afford an advanced degree, and encourages overinvestment in formal education. If we wish to combat excess credentialism and restore America as a land of true opportunity, we have to get better at talent search.[8]

Keep in mind that the venture capital or "Silicon Valley" approach to talent search worries much more about "sins of omission" than "sins of commission." That is, if you're a venture capitalist and miss one of the year's big founders, you are out a lot of money and possibly out of your job as well. Thousands of people are trying to climb the heap with their start-ups, yet only seven or eight will truly hit it big, and in a given year, perhaps only one or two of those hits will be transformative companies. So missing out on the next big thing is a surefire way to lose money. By no means do venture capital or tech dominate our economy, but we can glean from them some useful ways to look beyond credentials and find hidden sources of transformative talent.

Talent search is a fundamentally optimistic endeavor, based on the premise that there is always more value to be found in our world. But finding this talent is itself a creative skill, akin to music or art appreciation. It cannot be done by boilerplate interviews, groupthink, algorithms, studying PowerPoints, or simple formulas.

Everyone talks about being impressed by a candidate. But in venture, one odd emotion Daniel focuses on is fear—specifically those moments when a founder launches their pitch and Daniel begins to feel a subtle fear, brought on by the person's brazen ambition and drive, that they will do *anything* to succeed. It's not that the founder is trying to scare him; rather, they ooze ambition, and Daniel picks up on that. If Daniel feels subtly afraid of them, he will pay attention. The twenty-first-century founder is akin to the pirate of the sixteenth century—an outsider overflowing with energy and brazen charisma. Sometimes Daniel anchors his investment conviction in the market: it was easy to see how Opendoor could become a large business. But sometimes he anchors it in the founder: Instacart, Cruise, and Embark come to mind as extremely profitable investments with non-obvious paths to profitability but very fearsome founders.

For all the importance of talent, we find it striking that there is not a single go-to book on talent search akin to, say, Dale Carnegie's *How to Win Friends and Influence People* for sales,

Andy Grove's *High Output Management* for CEOs, or Robert Cialdini's *Influence* for marketing and personal relationships. There are, however, extensive literatures on talent and talent search in psychometrics, management, economics, sociology, education, art and music history, and sports, among other areas. We will give you the best of these insights, as filtered through our judgment and practical experience, in easy-to-digest, readily interpretable form.

Any book on discovering this kind of talent must fundamentally engage with larger questions about humanity and human behavior—specifically, which traits are correlated with creativity and predict a person's ability to use their creativity to make a difference in whatever sphere they operate in. Which traits make people good or bad at working with others or at coming up with new ideas? To what extent can we predict human creativity with correlated personality traits and intelligence quotients? Or is human creativity irreducible, perhaps something we can glimpse through intuition but is unique each time it appears? Which kinds of people actually can get things done? The art and science of talent search get at those questions and thus offer a new way to understand the world around us.

In our many conversations, we have come to see the world's inability to find and mobilize enough talent as one of the most significant failures of our time, and so this is also a book about how to fight for social justice. A world of rampant inequality and insufficient opportunity is, among other things, a world failing to recognize and mobilize talent. At the end of the day, too many potentially highly productive individuals are underutilized, to their detriment and to the loss of society as a whole. The idea that "talent search is one of the main things we are bad at" is a radical reconceptualization of the way so many parts of our world have gone astray. The traditional bureaucratic approach to finding talent doesn't typically *intend* to be discriminatory, but the focus on credentials, hierarchies, and consensus is far from ideal for giving better chances to outsiders. Therefore, we will focus on how you, within current structures, can make the world better at giving other people—the otherwise overlooked ones—their justly deserved opportunities. It is now commonly recognized that diversity and inclusion efforts are based on structural failures in our institutions, so improving your ability to spot talent is another way to have a direct and positive impact.

Before proceeding, we'd like to lay out four core perspectives that inform our approaches. You will find these themes recurring throughout the book, and they are general lessons worth carrying through any talent search problem, and indeed they apply to many other life dilemmas as well.

Talent Search Is an Art and a Science

Performing better at talent search really is possible if you put in enough study and practice, just as the experienced basketball watcher understands a game better than does a novice, and just as music and art and cinema appreciation repay careful study even if you don't always find fixed rules for quality. You invest in skills of pattern recognition that come in handy in the field, even though most of your individual decisions cannot be boiled down to a simple principle. "Red paintings are always good" is a silly rule, but if you study how Titian and Mondrian deployed the color red, it will help you recognize other artistic talents and other effective ways of painting with red. And the same is true of talent spotting more generally. One must understand both the science and the art of talent spotting, and the art side means looking for general regularities that are not rules and seeing how they manifest themselves in particular instances of individual talent. This helps you develop your intuitions so that you can spot yet another individual with potential.

The most famous and successful talent spotters process a phenomenal amount of data, but they also inject their intuition into the process. Peter Thiel found and helped to mobilize the talents of Elon Musk, Reid Hoffman, Max Levchin, Mark Zuckerberg, and others, including Steve Chen, Chad Hurley, and Jawed Karim (all behind YouTube), and Jeremy Stoppelman and Russell Simmons (behind Yelp). His approach is not well described by any kind of mechanical formula, and Peter's own background is in the humanities—philosophy and law—rather than science or tech. Many of his current interests concern religion, as he studied the Bible under French anthropologist and philosopher René Girard, who was a professor of Peter's at Stanford. We understand Peter as applying a very serious philosophical and indeed even moral test to people. This isn't a point about whether you agree with Peter's approach to politics or, for that matter, with his morality. In a venture capital context, Peter realizes that our moral judgments are some of our most penetrating and motivated sources of insight, and that helps him bring extra faculties to bear on talent judgment issues. In our view, Peter actually asks whether you deserve to succeed, as he understands that concept, and he derives additional information from that interior and indeed deeply emotional line of inquiry. It is often moral judgments that call forth our deepest and most energetic intuitions.

Michael Moritz is another remarkable judge of talent. From Stripe to Google to PayPal, Mike has had a remarkable eye for talent and is regarded by many in the industry as the best. Prior to joining Sequoia Capital, he spent his whole career as a journalist, and we believe this helps him suss out who has talent and who does not. Whereas we understand Thiel's mind to be more philosophical, Moritz seeks a story of authentic, raw energy in the individual, and his art is in spotting such backgrounds. A tale of exceptional endurance, especially during childhood, will spark Moritz's interest. People who have had to endure hardships have a chip on their shoulder and thus a need to prove themselves, and he has found this to be correlated with success. It is no accident that Moritz worked with famous soccer manager Alex Ferguson on the latter's autobiography, and in that book Ferguson explains how the very top players in the game, such as Ronaldo and Lionel Messi, have an extra obsession with self-improvement that puts them above the rest. Moritz realizes that the most important prospects do not always arrive with big successes under their belts, but rather are determined to work harder than anyone else to reach the top.

The scientific side of talent search is most relevant when you have lots of data on preexisting performance capabilities. Sports has seen a lot of progress in identifying and recruiting talent, mostly through measurement. Are you trying to evaluate a young baseball pitcher? Well, you can start with the speed of the kid's fastball, but these days you also should measure his spin rate and the kind of rotation he imparts to the ball.

The revolution Billy Beane brought to baseball, documented in Michael Lewis's book *Moneyball* and then in a hit movie starring Brad Pitt, started with the Oakland Athletics early in this millennium, and it brought that initially mediocre team to the playoffs in 2002 and 2003. The Moneyball philosophy, in a nutshell, uses statistics to spot players and strategies that are being undervalued by the baseball establishment. At least for a while, the Oakland Athletics were able to find and develop talented players that other teams could not. A similar emphasis on data followed in most of the other major sports—for example, the NBA moved to more three-point shots, and teams began drafting and then playing more good three-point shooters. Numbers are great when you can use them, but we also recognize they aren't relevant in many cases.[9]

Developing the Talent-Spotting Mindset

We hope to spark your interest and curiosity in talent in all parts of your own life, and that you will think and talk about talent as much as you possibly can, not just at work. Try to figure out the people you encounter and to analyze the situations you find yourself in, even when there is no evident practical value to that obsession. Pay attention to talent in fields unrelated to your job, such as sports, entertainment, politics, or even celebrity gossip, and try to figure out who really has it and who does not. When you happen to meet other talent evaluators, take advantage of it by striking up conversations about talent. Getting better at talent evaluation really does require continuously testing and honing your skills by observing the natural experiment that is everyday life. Make talent evaluation one of your hobbies.

Scientific Research Matters, but Read Your Sources

We have learned a great deal from the academic research on talent search, but we've also found that some writers make overly strong claims. Many results cannot be replicated, or they are not convincing in the first place, or they apply only to a very particular context. For instance, we will see that the quality called "grit" matters, but when you look at the numbers, perseverance is a personality feature that matters much more than passion taken alone. We have made a pact to not rely on the mere possibility of an academic footnote to leap to a conclusion—we look carefully at the methods, the depth of the surrounding literature, the quality and specificity of the data, and whether it accords with the testimony of practitioners, among other issues. There are times when we rely primarily on our intuition and experience rather than research results, and we also make this clear.

Similarly, we encourage you to be skeptical of the hyperbolic pronouncements in many management and tech books, particularly those that claim to have identified the one (or three) things that will make you better. Always ask: In which areas might this work? Might this not work? When does this work or not work? We call that last question "looking for the cross-sectional variation." If you don't understand when and where a particular claim is wrong, you probably don't understand the claim in the first place, and you probably shouldn't be relying on it so heavily. It is the understanding of context that breeds alertness to talent.

We are both "fallibilists," to use a term that has been revived by Irish tech entrepreneur and Stripe CEO Patrick Collison. That means we're also going to tell you about things you might think you know but that aren't true. For instance, for a large swath of jobs, intelligence and IQ are far less important than many smart people believe. Discarding faulty knowledge and being open to surprise are two of the most important things you can do to discover previously unknown talent.

There Is an Ethics of Judgment

Finally, we recognize that spotting talent can be a morally uneasy enterprise. For most jobs or posts, there are many more applicants than winners, and so often you are making only one person feel good about the outcome. Most of the time, you are saying no to most of the people. Furthermore, to the extent you are a good assessor of talent, you're essentially saying to people, "No, we are not rejecting you because of your bad shoes or the school you went to. The real problem is *you*." It is hard to feel entirely comfortable with issuing that kind of judgment, even if it is your responsibility and even if it is better in the long run for those who are rejected.

If your goal is to found or lead a company, you will need to get over any potential butterflies and lean into that. What is the practical alternative? Not everyone can be a CEO, and, both practically and morally, it is better to judge individuals as individuals than to rely on group stereotypes, even if that means a brutal pinpointing of a person's weaknesses. You can help the world a great deal by being a better judge of talent. That said, we are not going to pretend that this is only a feel-good book. Any move to become a better appreciator of the talents and virtues of others probably also will improve your skills at ruthlessly identifying the causes of human failure. Such is the burden of knowledge.

Proper use of this book thus requires you to deploy a kind of dialectical perspective. You should try to hold in your mind, at the same time, both the marvels of human achievement and the causes of human failure, without fear of contradiction. The marvels should come through more strongly (the world is on net a very good thing), but with this balance you will be able to deploy multiple perspectives on talent to maximum positive effect. You will then be able to simultaneously find people who can help you further your mission, help those people take the next step to wherever they are trying to go, and avoid doing them the harm of taking them down the wrong path only for them to have to go back and start again.

2

HOW TO INTERVIEW AND ASK QUESTIONS

These days, our very favorite interview question is this one:

- "What are the open tabs on your browser right now?"

In essence, you are asking about intellectual habits, curiosity, and what a person does in his or her spare time, all at once. You are getting past the talk and probing for that person's demonstrated preferences.

Especially for higher-level jobs, the question of spare time is a critical one. The very best performers don't stop practicing for very long, and if you hear or sense that a person doesn't do much practicing and skill refining in his or her spare time, they probably are poorly suited to assume a top position or to meet very high expectations. The browser-tab question gets at this, but it is not as awkward or exaggeration-inducing as "How hard do you work anyway?" or "How much do you try to improve your skills in your spare time?"

(If you are wondering, Tyler's open browser windows at the moment of writing are his blogging software, two email systems, Twitter, the Google Doc for writing this book, another Google Doc for another writing project, WhatsApp, his calendar, a friend's blog, an article on quantum computing, his RSS feed, a podcast on chess, an article on progress in the life sciences, an article on online interviewing, a French radio station [Fip] that plays Jamaican dub, and an article on in-migration to Poland. Daniel's open browser windows include his email, calendar, WhatsApp, Slack, two psychology studies, Spotify [rock], the Advanced Running subreddit, a new Pioneer feature, and an article from Stack Overflow on fixing an elusive programming bug. Hire or fire us accordingly!)

We both find during interviews that "downtime-revealed preferences" are more interesting than "stories about your prior jobs." So for instance, "What subreddits or blogs do you read?" usually is better than "What did you do at your previous job?" We very much like the title of the research paper by Mohammed Khwaja and Aleksandar Matic, "Personality Is Revealed During Weekends," and in that piece the researchers attempt to measure how people use their smartphones outside of work hours. If someone truly is creative and inspiring, it will show up in how they allocate their spare time.[1]

Just to repeat that wonderful title phrase once again: "Personality Is Revealed During Weekends."

There is a striking study of violinists and how they excel — namely, through practice. But do you know what kind of practice is most predictive of success? No, it is not teacher-designed practice; rather, it is practice alone, driven and directed by oneself. Think of practice habits as one path toward continuously compounding learning and performance. Try to learn the practice habits of the person you are interviewing, as it will reveal one aspect of their approach to work. You also should try to learn just how self-conscious a person is about what he or she is doing for self-improvement. And if they give you a fumbling or bumbling account of their practice habits, as we have heard numerous times, you can help them out very easily by suggesting they think about practice a little more systematically.[2]

Another way of measuring time allocation and actual behavior is to look at what Sam Altman, former head of venture capital firm Y Combinator (YC), describes as *speed of response*. Here is an excerpt from Tyler's 2019 dialogue and podcast with Sam:[3]

COWEN: Why is being quick and decisive such an important personality trait in a founder?

ALTMAN: That is a great question. I have thought a lot about this because the correlation is clear, that one of the most fun things about YC is that, I think, we have more data points on what successful founders and bad founders look like than any other organization has had in the history of the world. We have that all in our heads, and that's great. So I can say, with a high degree of confidence, that this correlation is true.

   Being a fast mover and being decisive—it is very hard to be successful and not have those traits as a founder. *Why* that is, I'm not perfectly clear on, but I think it is something . . . about the only advantage that start-ups have or the biggest advantage that start-ups have over large companies is agility, speed, willing to make non-consensus, concentrated bets, incredible focus. That's really how you get to beat a big company.

COWEN: How quickly should someone answer your email to count as quick and decisive?

ALTMAN: You know, years ago I wrote a little program to look at this, like how quickly our best founders—the founders that run billion-dollar-plus companies—answer my emails versus our bad founders. I don't remember the exact data, but it was mind-blowingly different. It was a difference of minutes versus days on average response times.

In essence, this quality of speed of response is picking up on how much the individual is focused on being connected to the world and responding to plausibly important queries. If *your* queries are not a priority for the person, then perhaps that individual is not the right match. And no matter what your level, give further thought to responding more quickly to at least some of your interlocutors, especially if you wish to continue your dialogues with them.

Why Are We Intrigued with Interview Questions?

Hiring experts often draw a distinction between "structured" and "unstructured" interviews. By structured we mean a situation where a set of common questions is determined in advance, often at the organizational level, and the answers are collated and judged by common standards applied to many candidates across the organization. Those are important methods for large institutions and they underpin bureaucratic methods of hiring, but they are not what we teach in this book. In similar fashion, in some areas testing and examining credentials and reading letters of recommendation may be important; for instance, eye tests and reaction tests for military pilots may be critical. But again, our potential value added and expertise are about exercising individual judgment, so we will, in this chapter and the next, focus on talking to people and asking them questions on an individual basis (in later chapters we will consider how you might modify these strategies for people with different cultural, racial, or disability backgrounds).[4]

Unstructured interviews flow more naturally and are more like normal conversation, albeit with a specific purpose. In practice almost every interview has unstructured segments, no matter how it is classified, and that is where most of our advice is targeted. The higher the level you are hiring at, or the more creative the job under consideration, the more likely the interview will have a significant unstructured component. If you are hiring a cashier, the needed skills are pretty standardized, but if a CEO is hiring his or her chief of staff, personality mesh will matter more; that individual may need to have idiosyncratic talents and understand the full scope of the business, requiring a more in-depth and also a freer-flowing interview style.

So let's say you find yourself in a room with a job candidate and half an hour to chat. How can you discover if the candidate is the right hire, the best business partner, a deserving recipient of a fellowship? The interview is fundamentally about how to engage with people, and if you cannot engage with people, you cannot break through the combination of bravado, nerves, and possibly even deceit that people bring to their interviews. During an interview, you can ask anything (legal) in the known universe and explore any angle you wish. What a splendid but also baffling position to be in.

Before proceeding, let's look at some of the arguments against the use of interviews at all, to get a sense of both their strengths and limits.

Do Interviews Matter?

Yes, interviews very much do matter.

You may have read articles like the one that Sarah Laskow wrote a few years ago in *The Boston Globe*, "Want the Best Person for the Job? Don't Interview," or the one Jason Dana published in *The New York Times*, "The Utter Uselessness of Job Interviews." These and other stories make the all too familiar claim that interviews do not boost your ability to spot the better job candidates. You might then wonder whether interviews, or trying to improve your interview skills, are worth your while.

This common myth of interview impotence misses the point. At the very least, interviews can help you rule out some candidates quickly. But the main reason why virtually all top companies stick with doing interviews is that interviews yield useful information.[5]

Most importantly, many of the research studies pessimistic about interviewing focus on unstructured interviews performed by relatively unskilled interviewers for relatively uninteresting, entry-level jobs. *You can do better*. Even if it *were* true that interviews do not on average improve candidate selection, that is a statement about *averages*, not about what is possible. You still would have the power, if properly talented and intellectually equipped, to beat the market averages. In fact, the worse a job the world as a whole is at doing interviews, the more reason to believe there are highly talented candidates just waiting to be found *by you*.

In most of the studies on this subject, interviews were more effective for higher-level jobs. So if you wish to hire an economist, Tyler believes that asking a person substantive economics questions during an interview is a good way to start assessing their competence, though to our knowledge this never has been proven or disproven in study form. Daniel believes that if you wish to fund an applicant for venture capital, it is worth asking about the business plan to see how well the basic idea is presented and defended. If they can't make a case for it to you, they'll probably have trouble attracting talent to help them. The anti-interview crowd, many of whom are centered in academia, overlooks these obvious truths.

Interviews also play a crucial role in recruiting candidates and helping spread a positive impression of you and your company, even in cases where you don't end up hiring the person. So put aside any inclination to skip or devalue this part of the process. Interviews are essential, and, because so many organizations rely on mindless bureaucratic approaches, the bar is low and the payoff high.

The First and Most Important Rule: Be Trusted and in Turn Be Trustworthy

Don't approach interviewing as a process where you are trying to trick or trip up the other person. First, that is intrinsically a bad way to behave. Second, once the person realizes what you're doing, they'll stop trusting you and, in most cases, become guarded. That will make it harder for you to determine whether the person is a good match for your job or assignment, not to mention harder to land them should you decide they are.

Our approach is to begin by trying to establish common ground. How to do this obviously depends on context, but you could talk about a shared regional history, hobby, or interest, or start with a question about the kind of job or task at hand. Another approach is to ask the person a substantive question, based on your knowledge of his or her previous employment history. Most importantly, it should be a question *you really want to know the answer to*. So if the person worked in a ball bearings factory in Cleveland, ask yourself if you care more about ball bearings or more about Cleveland. And your follow-up questions should also reflect real interests of yours.

Caring about their answers will put the other person at ease, but more importantly, it will often put you at ease too. It will get them—and you—into the mode of inquiry, the mode of curiosity, the mode of conversation, and the mode of learning. It will signal that you feel you can learn from them, and encourage them to feel comfortable responding in kind. Most importantly, it will take you out of the realm of the dull, obvious, phony job interview.

Nature has equipped most humans with the ability to sniff out phoniness and perfunctory interest. There is only one real and credible protection against those phoniness-spotting abilities: to be actually worthy of someone's trust. When we are genuinely curious it draws people out, and as we show interest, they begin to trust us. This doesn't mean you shouldn't ask hard questions and challenge answers that don't add up—it's simply that you must be genuine.

Getting into the Conversational Mode

As noted, a key benefit of avoiding phoniness from the start is that it helps you get the candidate into the conversational mode as quickly as possible, and this is a critical principle of interviewing. By this we mean how people relate to each other directly, outside of interview settings, when they just say things. It sounds spontaneous, and indeed it is spontaneous. In the conversational mode, you are getting a much better look at how that person will interact with others on a daily basis on the job. We're not saying that it shows "the real person," whatever you might take that to mean. The conversational mode still involves a lot of conscious and subconscious presentation of the self to the outside world. It reflects that person's signaling, airs and affectations, feints, and conditioned social habits. Still, at the very least, you are getting "the real version of the fake person," and that is still more valuable than trying to process prepared interview answers.

How exactly can you get people into the conversational mode? Here are our main suggestions, starting with a particular favorite of Daniel's.

Get Candidates Telling Stories About Themselves Rather than Reciting Facts or Canned Answers

A simple question designed to elicit a story, such as "What did you do this morning?," is a good way to begin to get to know a person without being threatening. The stories you hear will reflect how the candidate organizes ideas, adds emotional valence, drives a narrative arc, and selects what is important. Telling a story also forces the candidate to demonstrate a sense of audience—namely, their sense of you and the others in the room, and what kinds of understanding or context you might be bringing to the interaction. Having a sense of an audience is an important skill for virtually any kind of job involving human interaction, and even if there is a certain phoniness to storytelling, for most jobs a certain amount of phoniness is necessary. You also are testing how well the candidate understands the nature of the interview itself.

It is hard to fake an entire story on the fly, so when you ask for a story, maybe some relevant details are being censored, but you are likely to hear some version of the truth. If you ask, "Tell us a detailed story about how a co-worker expressed appreciation for you," virtually everyone will tell a version of what actually happened. Precisely because the storytelling mode occupies us with so many details and particular structural features of the story itself, the storyteller cannot lie so easily, as that would involve juggling too many balls at once. It is much easier for the candidate to lie in response to a merely factual question, such as "Were you loved at your last job?" If you hear in response "Oh, yes, absolutely, everyone loved me there," as both Daniel and Tyler have heard versions of, what exactly are you supposed to do with that?

In some cases, you will be talking with a "survivor" who experienced trauma in the realm you've asked about. For instance, perhaps they were sexually harassed in the job you asked them about. Tyler once asked a job candidate about previous experience and received a series of tense, nervous answers that hinted at a history of harassment. He will never know the real story, but at the very least, you should be aware that for these individuals, the proffered stories are not and maybe cannot be about the full truth. So look for intelligence and sensitivity in their reactions, rather than just simple evasiveness, especially if you sense that something might be lurking beneath the surface or if you intuit a certain awkwardness in presentation. And rather than pounding again on the topic of the original question, think what you might ask to defuse the tension. Try to figure out what topic this person actually might want to talk about and move in that direction— for instance, try an open-ended question about which problems the job candidate enjoys working out in her head.

Dullness is catching. The main problem with obvious questions is that they tend to elicit obvious answers. Try not to ask for stories that are likely to be canned. Don't ask for a story about something the person did right or wrong on the previous job. Don't ask whether a person is easy or hard to work with. Every interviewee has an answer at the ready for questions like these. Testing for preparation is fine and to some degree necessary, but it is one of the easiest things to do and relatively easy to judge. Our whole purpose, as we've said, is to help you test for other qualities.

Here are some questions that not only will elicit stories but also might yield relatively interesting answers:

- "How did you spend your morning today?"
- "What's the farthest you've ever been from another human?"
- "What's something weird or unusual you did early on in life?"
- "What's a story one of your references might tell me when I call them?"
- "If I was the perfect Netflix, what type of movies would I recommend for you and why?"
- "How do you feel you are different from the people at your current company?"
- "What views do you hold religiously, almost irrationally?"
- "How did you prepare for this interview?"
- "What subreddits, blogs, or online communities do you enjoy?"
- "What is something esoteric you do?"

Buyer beware: when asking these uncommon questions, you'll often get a long silence, followed by an unrelated answer. This is a great sign! It means the candidate wasn't prepared and needs time to think. You'll want to give the candidate, who may well be nervous, time to contemplate before blabbering. One strategy is repeating the question: "That's great. What's another reason you want to work here?" Another is to be explicit about the situation: "Now, you might not have an answer prepared. That's fine! While you think, let me tell you about something esoteric I do. . . ."

Once the words are streaming out of their mouth, your real task begins: assessing their response and what it reveals. And to do that you need to draw on a broad variety of knowledge about cognition and personality as well as on your own trained intuition.

One good place to start is to consider their general quality of resourcefulness, which is obviously of use in any job, especially in crises or in difficult times. And when testing for resourcefulness, whether or not you are disappointed in particular answers, keep on asking yourself whether the candidate is successively able to draw upon intellectual and also emotional resources in his or her answers. They might just keep on showing innovative responses, no matter how far or how hard you push them. That is a sign of the broader stores of intellect and energy that the individual will be able to bring to the job.

Daniel's company creates tournaments to select recipients of their investments. A group of potential founders is asked to play a series of online games, and their progress and commitment are tracked over the course of weeks. This tests technical skill, dedication, and competitiveness, all important qualities in the world of tech start-ups. Daniel also likes to ask interview candidates to share their criticisms of the Pioneer tournaments he runs to select eventual recipients of Pioneer's investments. He is looking for a specific approach to their critique, as much as the substance of their response. He gets especially worried when they ramble on vaguely rather than providing a focused approach to feedback, or when they choose to unload their gripes on the broader world of tech (a common response that suggests a lack of focus). He seeks specificity and frankness that focus on how Pioneer's tournaments can be improved.

Daniel also places candidate answers in a very specific framework. As the candidate tells their story, Daniel continuously asks himself: *Whom is this person responding to or used to performing for? Whom do they view as important to impress? Their parents? A particular peer? High school friends? A former boss?* This is revealed at moments when they disclose some angles of their past successes and failures rather than others. You might be surprised how often this information comes through in the context of an interview. For instance, a person may refer to college teachers who scorned her or did not appreciate her innovations, or a person may still be wrapped up in how he was viewed as a child by his parents. Thinking about this question can give you the context people are speaking from and, more generally, a sense of their ambitions and worldview. If they are still trying to impress their high school peers, for instance, they might have focus but they are unlikely to understand the broader picture behind your company or grasp its global ambitions. Most importantly, be alert for the distinction between those who are stuck in their past and those who learned from it but are moving forward and seeking to expand the sphere of people they can impress. Daniel sold Tyler on the importance of this approach early in their discussions and debates.

Most of us have a bias toward well-spoken and articulate storytellers. But make sure you keep an awareness of this at the front of your mind, for it can cause you to hire glib but unsubstantial people and overlook rare creative talent. *Do not overestimate the importance of the person's articulateness.* Focus instead on the substance and quality of the answers to your questions. Many very qualified candidates are not that quick on their feet, nor do they speak off the cuff in well-formulated, smooth-sounding sentences, but if they have good content, notice it. Perhaps you have seen how some Americans are impressed by the accents of British people. Well, nothing against hiring British people, but in the workplace the accent probably isn't worth much, just as what Americans might consider a "clumsy" German accent or "effete" French accent should not be used as stand-ins for particular assessments of personality or intelligence. We too often correlate accent with linguistic fluency, or sometimes intelligence. Similarly, it is fine to notice if someone's voice has an unusual pitch or their speech has unusual prosody, but don't leap too quickly to conclusions about the person being "a weirdo," because you probably cannot draw reliable inferences from that data; furthermore, "weirdos" may end up as some of your best performers.

You may encounter candidates who at times do not seem able to pass a Turing test, or in other words, they will not make enough sense to prove that they are a human rather than an imperfect software program, such as Siri given a question too difficult for it to handle. If a candidate fails the Turing test that is relevant information, as many jobs require a baseline of a particular kind of verbal fluency. Still, try to develop a deeper understanding of what is going on rather than just dismissing that person. The brilliant Alan Turing did not himself seem convinced of his own articulateness or quickness on his feet, and yet he was one of the leading mathematicians, computer scientists, logicians, and cryptographers of his time. He was very good at processing information at levels that did not correspond to the skills we use to generate charming casual conversations.[6]

Daniel has also found it useful to pay attention to any particular strategies candidates seem to use in order to maintain focus and generate good answers (he calls these strategies "triggers," analogizing to the way athletes, for instance, prime themselves with mental triggers to maintain good form during a performance—a weightlifter, for example, might think "Chest up" before performing a lift). Sometimes these can be seen in a small physical gesture—say, the person sits up a bit straighter, they take a slightly deeper breath, or their voice takes on a more commanding tone. Alternatively, you might see a negative trigger—you might hear a change in voice or excessive repetition when a candidate loses focus. Ask yourself what kind of impression this person seems to be trying to make in the interview and how they are trying to do that. How well is that strategy working? This will help you build out a more insightful image of the person you are talking to.

In order to obtain the best sense of a candidate, it is important not only what you ask but also how you ask it. End at least some of your questions on a note of surprise. Do not be afraid to let a question hang in the air after you ask it; hold the tension as a way of making it clear that you expect an answer, and a direct answer at that. Do not reduce that tension with a nervous laugh, with too noticeable a blink, or by turning away—anything that would reduce the focus on the matter at hand. Don't be afraid to keep on looking at the candidate, though don't do this in an unfriendly or overly challenging way. Be relaxed but attentive. If the candidate avoids the question, ask it again.

This insistence on an answer is one strategy that makes many interviewers feel uncomfortable or even a little mean. When it's obvious that a candidate is avoiding giving an answer, many people feel a great temptation to ease the tension by allowing the topic to be changed. By maintaining or even heightening the focus on the substance of the responses, you will see how the candidate responds to pressure, but most of all, you will ensure that every question generates a maximally informative answer.

As you present your questions and listen to the candidate's stories in response, note whether the interviewee uses unusual expressions, seems to be coining their own phrases, explains basic concepts in a way different from what you might hear in the mainstream, speaks as if they are developing useful memes, has unusual rhythmic patterns to their speech, or conjures up a unique worldview. There are some people who, when they speak, no matter what the topic, seem to draw you into their own worldview, almost like an act of magic, like you are stepping into a movie, TV show, computer game, or graphic novel of their making. This can be a sign of their energy and creativity.

The first time each of us met Peter Thiel, for instance, we noticed how engrossed he was in his explanations and, furthermore, how quickly and effectively he pulled people into his worldview, introducing and applying concepts such as "technological stagnation," "the inability to imagine a future very different from the present," "Georgist economics," and "the Girardian sacrificial victim." Maybe you don't know what all of those concepts refer to, and maybe Peter's audience doesn't always either, but that is not the point. There is a logic to his argument, and Peter communicates that logic with the utmost conviction; the audience correctly senses a coherent underlying worldview, involving themes of lost dynamism, pessimism, and the all too human desire to copy other people and their habits. When Peter, in a public dialogue with Tyler, referred to the "Straussian interpretation of Christ," everyone basically went along with it and kept on listening with extreme attentiveness, even though probably few of them understood the reference.

Demonstrating a language of one's own is not always a positive sign, especially if you are hiring for a job requiring low creativity and high conscientiousness. But if you are looking for a founder, an entrepreneur, a maverick, or a highly productive intellectual to lead a venture to the next level, creating and commanding one's own language may be an important positive feature. It may suggest that you have found a truly creative, charismatic, and generative individual, one of the 1 or 2 percent of people who are capable of creating something grand. It's not that having a special language always translates into successful results; if someone creates and opens up their own world with language, there's no guarantee that such a new and original world is a good one, or a good match for what you want to achieve as an employer or backer. But it is a sign that further investigation into the person is warranted, for there's a chance that they might be an earth-shattering, pathbreaking genius.

As an aside, this point about language is one reason knowledge of the humanities, reading fiction, and being bilingual or trilingual can help you locate creative talent. If you are going to recognize what new personal languages look like, it helps to have been exposed to them in the past. It helps to know the sound of Shakespeare, whose language is like no one else's, of his time or any other. It helps to be fluent in French, Spanish, Hindi, Chinese, or whatever other language you may have learned. And don't neglect popular culture; shows such as *Seinfeld*, *The Simpsons*, *Game of Thrones*, and *Rick and Morty* have rhythms and languages all their own, just like the high-culture masterworks from the past. Tyler is a big advocate of learning as many different such "languages" as you can, not only to boost your understanding of the world, but also so you can recognize and better evaluate the languages and cultural codes of other people.

Change the Physical Setting of the Interview

Go to a coffee shop or restaurant. Take a walk or sit on a park bench. This can happen mid-interview, or you can hold the entire interview there. In any case, the different setting allows you to see how the candidate responds to unexpected change and can ease the move to a more conversational exchange. It also makes it harder for the candidate to keep up the protective interview mode. The candidate can't speak to the server or cashier in interview mode, so you get to see a different side of the person. Besides, once the candidate has spoken more naturally to the server, it is harder for the candidate to switch back into protective interview mode with you.

The new setting also gives you the chance to ask the candidate more questions for which they won't have a stock answer: "What do you think of the service here?" Or "Do you usually find rooms to be so noisy?" You are giving the candidate a chance to express emotions, register grudges, and evaluate new and unexpected settings, all in relatively unfiltered form. It's just not possible for the candidate to fall back entirely on prep in addressing such questions.

New physical settings also introduce the possibility of random and surprising events, in a way you probably won't get just sitting in an interview room. Maybe there won't be an open seat at Starbucks, so how will the candidate react and what will they suggest as a next course of action? *Does* the candidate decide to suggest the next course of action, or do they rely on you? If the checkout line is interminably slow, when will they start to exhibit frustration? Best yet, how do they respond if a server spills something onto their shirt (though we do not recommend arranging this in advance—remember: be good).

If time or circumstances don't allow this kind of change, you can switch rooms for a while. At the very least, that is likely to rearrange the seating positions, even if all the same people are involved, and that too will change the nature of the dialogue.

The key point here is that the best interviews are not formal interviews at all. We're sure you can think of other creative ways to take the candidate out of interview mode and into their everyday self. This is important, because the everyday self is what you'll get if you hire them. Furthermore, non-work settings often lead to more revealing conversations. Try seeing a basketball game together—most likely you will end up talking about work issues during halftime and time-outs. Or go running with the person. The old-school approach here was to suggest a round of golf. In any case, be very open to doing something that might stand outside of the normal hiring routine.

Be Specific and Use Forcing Questions

A good rule of thumb is this: if you found your question in a job interview book or on a website, it is likely you are simply testing the candidate's preparation level. Again, that is fine up to a point, but don't confuse it with additional insight.

Here are a few somewhat more unusual questions we recommend—again, depending on context—with more questions coming in the section on how to get "meta":

- "What are ten words your spouse or partner or friend would use to describe you?"
- "What's the most courageous thing you've done?"
- "If you joined us and then in three to six months you were no longer here, why would that be?" Or ask the same question about five years down the line as well and see how the two answers differ.
- "What did you like to do as a child?" This gets at what they really like to do, because it harks back to a time before the world started bossing them around.[7]
- "Did you feel appreciated at your last job? What was the biggest way in which you did not feel appreciated?"

You'll notice that these questions ask for some very specific pieces of information. They also ask for stories and for the candidates to reveal something of their true natures.

Regarding the last question, the one about not feeling appreciated: many people cannot hold in their emotions here. In general, be wary of candidates who use a lot of negative words; it is a sign of possible future troubles and lack of cooperativeness in the workplace. Even if the negative experiences at the person's previous job were not at all their fault, you wish to assess the extent to which they can move on from bad experiences. Negative words can be less of a bad sign if you are interviewing a potential boss or founder, as in that case you may be looking for a kind of revolutionary disagreeableness; even then, users of negative words can be trouble. Be wary of curse words, excess deployment of the word "hate," and too much talk about whose feelings got hurt and why and whether the complaint is justified or not.

Another way to keep the focus on specifics is to test how well the candidate understands your institution. Anyone who is serious about the job will have learned basic information about your key products or services, so questions about them are unlikely to reveal very much. We're big believers in asking questions designed to see how well they can zero in on the key conceptual challenges we face in our chosen fields. So you might ask instead:

- "Who are our competitors?"

Reed Hastings, the Netflix CEO, once famously said that his biggest competitor was sleep, and furthermore, that he was winning. At the Mercatus Center, a research center with an emphasis on studying markets, Tyler argues to his co-workers that their competitor is often Google, not some other research center. If people want to know things, they might just go to Google rather than to any particular research center. So you had better place your work well on Google—or, better yet, induce people to go to you before they go to Google. For Daniel's Pioneer, the biggest competitor is not another venture capital firm but rather the risk that top prospects might prefer to take a steady salary at a good company and forget about any bigger plans. (Is it so bad to live out a comfortable but less challenging life?) Daniel understands that the mystique and thrill of building a new company have to outweigh the inertia of the status quo and its easier defaults, and that he is in part responsible for articulating that vision of creating something new.

Which Clichéd Questions Should You Avoid?

Peggy McKee's 2017 book *How to Answer Interview Questions* lists more than a hundred common questions. Here are just a few examples:

- "Give me an example of a time that you felt you went above and beyond the call of duty at work."
- "How can you apply your specific skills to help the organization achieve sustainable growth and generate revenue?"
- "How do you handle stress and pressure on the job?"
- "What did you like or dislike about your previous jobs?"[8]

You might escalate your quest for questions and Google "15 Favorite Interview Questions to Completely Disarm Job Candidates," in which case you would end up with an article by Jeff Haden and a list that includes the following, which are snoozers:

- "What are the failures you most cherish?"
- "If you could go back five years, what advice would you give your younger self?"[9]

There is a whole class at Stanford, for engineers, on how to best prep for interviews and answer interview questions.[10] Their paradigmatic example of a question to be prepared for is:

- "What is your greatest weakness?"

Again, by now most people are ready for that one, especially when you are interviewing at higher levels, where you encounter better-prepared candidates. Both of us have heard (in joint interview sessions, where we were not the ones asking the questions) answers like "Sometimes I feel I am just too committed to my job." We are not sure what to make of such responses, other than perhaps the respondent read someone else's book on interview strategy.

If you are going to ask achievement-oriented questions, avoid the ordinary by continuing to ask for successive instances of candidate success until the respondent can't come up with any more. So don't just ask "Give me an example of a time that you felt you went above and beyond the call of duty at work" one time, because there you are just testing for basic prep. Ask it again. And again. And again, until the candidate can't come up with any more answers. And don't look away, break the tension with a chuckle, or give the candidate a chance to divert attention and halt the questioning process.

The first time you ask this question, most candidates will draw upon their preparation. Sustained repetition, however, will get the person out of prep sooner or later, usually sooner. The previously cached answers will be exhausted, leaving time for the real meat. You will then see the depth of the candidate's intellectual resources and emotional resilience. How does the person respond when being challenged continually? How many instances can the person come up with? If the respondent feels stymied and truly has no further responses, how readily and how poorly is he or she willing to resort to BS? Finally, if the candidate really does have seventeen significant different work triumphs, maybe you do want to hear about what number seventeen looks like.

For a creative job, you can repeatedly ask the candidates for their best idea. As with their work triumphs, plenty of people will have prepared one or two answers to this kind of question, but how does a person respond when asked five times? Eight times? How does the candidate handle the arrival of the moment when the honest and right answer is: "Those are all the good ideas I've had that I can think of." Or maybe the candidate should say: "I can tell you about some other ideas I've had, but I'm not sure how good they were." Then you are likely in uncharted territory, out of candidate prep, and you will learn more about how the person really thinks and responds to unusual situations, how well that person thinks about the quality of what he or she is doing, and also about that person's self-evaluation more generally.

With that idea of uncharted territory in mind, you also might ask, "What have you achieved that is unusual for your peer group?" But again, don't just ask it once. Keep on asking to elicit as many answers as possible. And if you encounter a candidate who has achieved twenty-three different things unusual for his or her peer group, well, that is worth knowing. Even a simple, one-tiered answer like "I started a successful company at the age of seventeen" has the power to impress.

Who wants to hear about the boring management or career success book the person came prepared to talk about? But if books come up naturally in the conversation, or music, movies, or most other art forms, by all means pursue the topic. One of Daniel's strongest initial bonds with Tyler—which boosted the prospects for our collaboration on this book—was discovering we both had a love of Orson Scott Card's science fiction novel *Ender's Game*, which is in fact about a series of talent competitions for young children. As we discussed it, we found that we appreciated the same things: its directness, its engagement with questions of meritocracy, and its sense of just how early talent can blossom or be revealed. The book embodies precisely the right mix of competitiveness, playfulness, empathy, gamification, and the stakes really mattering, which is what a great book about talent search should offer. By the end of that conversation, Tyler and Daniel had a much better sense of their shared interest in those topics. If a person seems to have a good grasp of a book or other artistic or aesthetic object, by all means be willing to let the conversation flow in that direction, because you will end up staring right into that person's soul.

The Cycle of Interview Questions

Many interview questions have a limited period of usefulness, and so they eventually need to be discarded or modified. Consider one of the most renowned interview questions of all time: "What is it you believe to be true that other smart people you know think is crazy?" There are other versions of this question, typically of a contrarian bent, such as "What is your most absurd belief?" This type of question is often attributed to Peter Thiel, although it seems it first came from a blog post by Tyler in 2006, and it is part of a broader philosophic tradition of critical self-examination.[11]

In its early days, this question was magnificently effective. It caught respondents by surprise, and at the very least you could observe how they responded to an unexpected situation, which was a plus for gathering data about their performance abilities. Furthermore, their answers revealed a good bit about how they understood the world. You had a chance to learn "What kind of kook is this person?"—and really, what would you rather know? That kind of information usually isn't contained on a resume. You could see how quickly they could put together an argument, and how quickly they could make it sound plausible (or not).

Alternatively, some people will confidently answer the question with a totally ordinary, orthodox belief, convinced they have stated something highly unusual. Those individuals may be good hires for their reliability and conformity, but don't expect them to shake up any internal systems that need reforming. If they think "globalization extended too far" is their weird, radical, absurd belief, whether or not you agree, the proper conclusion is that they are not exposed to many truly radical, weird ideas at all and wouldn't know one if it hit them on the head.

When Tyler first put the absurd beliefs question out there, his favorite (written) answer was: "I believe that if you go to the beach, but you do not give the ocean a chance to taste you, she will come take her taste when she chooses." He later met the person who wrote that, and she turned out to be remarkably smart and productive, and she was underplaced in her job at the time.

Part of what made this question work was its unpredictability. Most interviewees are working hard to please the interviewer, and that includes answering all of the questions. But when confronted with this question—well, if you had never thought about it before, it is hard to come up with a decent answer . . . other than the truth. A lie is too risky, would be too hard to articulately defend, and could make you seem entirely insipid—"I think apple pie has too much sugar." Besides, many of the possible lies you might tell would make you look even crazier than you really are. So most people struggled to reach for some version of the truth, even if it was a partially sanitized version.

That interview question, for a while, was very effective at identifying true contrarians. Tyler recalls seeing some respondents utterly baffled because they couldn't think of any nonconforming view they held. He checked the mental box "Not a contrarian" on them.

But the question was too good, and thus, it became widely used.

Over time, interviewees came, if not to expect it, at least to show up prepared for it. After all, if you interview for a bunch of jobs, you might end up being asked the question at least once, and you would be alerted for the next time. And a canned answer to that question, while it revealed skills of preparation, just wasn't that revealing anymore. The interviewee would prep to demonstrate just the level of contrarianism that he or she thought the interviewer was looking for. And suddenly the question now was rewarding a perverse kind of conformity—conformity to the proper level of contrarianism—rather than the true contrarianism it was supposed to ferret out.

Tyler also has experimented, with success, with an inverted version of the question. This one is useful only for limited purposes, but here goes:

- "What is one mainstream or consensus view that you wholeheartedly agree with?"

Let's think through what this question does and does not do. First, it does not so strongly select for intelligence or analytic acuity, since enough elements of the status quo are defensible even if they are not entirely ideal. It is hard to totally whiff on the question, since it is not demanding a specific answer or even a non-corny one. Second, it does not cause the person to feel extremely threatened or challenged.

What does the question do, then? First, it contains an element of surprise. Reactions to surprising questions usually have some intrinsic informational value, no matter how easy the question. Second, it is not really a question a person can brush off or refuse to answer without looking excessively grumpy. Third, it probes how a person interacts with the authority of mainstream institutions. Fourth and most importantly, it gives the person a chance to signal his or her values and orientation in a way that is nonthreatening. No one is worried that their answer to this question might be used against them on Twitter. At the same time, the respondent can signal his or her real priorities. Is it faster innovation? Poverty reduction? Patching the holes in democracy? With the question, you have created a nonthreatening way of eliciting where the person really stands in the world—where and how they fit in—and which values he or she assigns high weight to. For values-based jobs and applications (as you frequently find in the nonprofit world, for instance), that can be highly useful.

Another set of interview questions that is now outmoded is sometimes called "the Google questions." Google is famous for the highly analytical questions it once posed to potential hires, especially for software and engineering jobs. These are best illustrated by example:

- "How many golf balls can you fit into an airplane?"
- "How many gas stations are there in Manhattan?"

Or maybe you would like a longer, more complicated one:

- "You are given two eggs. . . . You have access to a hundred-story building. Eggs can be very hard or very fragile, which means they may break if dropped from the first floor or may not break even if dropped from the hundredth floor. Both eggs are identical. You need to figure out the highest floor of the hundred-story building an egg can be dropped from without breaking. The question is how many drops you need to make. You are allowed to break two eggs in the process."[12]

You can think of these questions as good tests of one very particular kind of analytical ability, especially designed to distinguish very, very smart people from those who are only quite smart. Smart in a particular mathematical sense, that is.

As it happens, Google itself has moved away from using these questions. Laszlo Bock, formerly Google's Senior Vice President of People Operations, announced, "We found that brainteasers are a complete waste of time." That is perhaps an overstatement, as there are still successful quantitative hedge funds that seem to find such questions useful for testing analytical abilities. Still, for most jobs, you probably are better off asking a direct analytical question about the actual job in question. You could investigate the candidate's knowledge of economics, programming, mathematics, and so on. For the most part, these Google-linked questions should be ushered into a dignified retirement.[13]

Keep in mind that the person actually has to become understandable to you, and the brainteaser questions don't help very much in that regard, unless the job in question has an extremely specific set of technical requirements.

Going Meta: The Best Ways

Rather than trying to go small with your questions (e.g., "How many ping-pong balls fit into a Volkswagen?"), it is often more useful to look for the larger picture. For instance, how well do your applicants understand themselves and their place in the world? Toward that end, how about these questions?

- "Which of your beliefs are you least rational about?"
- "What views do you hold almost irrationally?"

These questions ask the respondent to give an account of their own self-awareness. In essence, you are trying to learn how many cultural and intellectual worlds an individual is master of, and how much perspective they have on their own perspectives. That is what we mean by "meta"—that the person is considering their own thought world from a viewpoint one level higher, more general, and more distant. You are testing their facility with ideas and also how readily they can identify with alien viewpoints.

It is hard to stonewall when asked these questions. Surely *everyone* has some pretty irrational views, maybe a lot of them. But presenting your irrational views almost necessarily requires an awkwardness or revelation of weakness since you are forced to explain *why* you are so irrational on these questions. It is hard to be purely mechanical on the response here, because the irrational reasons typically are quite human ones. By asking this question, you are pulling the person into the human mode, into the self-awareness mode, into the awkwardness mode, and into a bit of weakness. When you can do all of that at once, useful interview information is likely to be forthcoming.

A related and decent interview question is:

- "Which of your beliefs are you most likely wrong about?"

The most brutal of all the meta questions is:

- "How do you think this interview is going?"

An even more brutal version of it is to have two separate people ask the same question at different points throughout the day, and later compare notes. We don't recommend it for most settings, but let's pause for a moment and think through what this question does. You are in essence asking the candidate how much weakness he or she wishes to disclose. Should the candidate give an articulate account of her weaknesses so far, thereby impressing you with her insightfulness but also confirming your negative impressions? Or should the candidate stonewall and instead give an account of everything that has gone well? If nothing else, you will confront the candidate with a surprise situation and put her in a difficult position, but one that gives her a chance to shine in confronting a challenge.

But here's why we are not entirely enamored of this one. Let's say the candidate opts for the risk-averse choice and simply stonewalls it on the negative, offering a strong positive account of what went well. How much should you hold this risk aversion against the candidate? Is it a true and reliable signal that the person actually is too risk-averse? The answers here are not obvious to us. The candidate just might not trust you enough to give the full answer, and so you cannot distinguish the "insufficiently strong trust" hypothesis from the "candidate is too risk-averse" hypothesis. If you ask the candidate to perform too risky a task, as might be the case here, you can end up with too little information being revealed. So while we can think of particular situations where this question might work very well, deploy it with caution and don't get too caught up in its cleverness.

Finally, here is another useful question used by Peter Thiel:

- "How successful do you want to be?"

Or this variant favored by Tyler:

- "How ambitious are you?"

Offhand, this one might sound a little silly, but it can be useful to ask an individual to put his or her cards on the table. If the essence of the answer is "I wish to ensconce myself as a mid-level manager in a secure company," well, that is probably the truth. You would then be ill-advised to invest in that person as an ambitious entrepreneur or a founder. You might want to invest in them as a midlevel manager, but even then be aware that promotion incentives may not motivate the person very much. When Tyler posed this question to one potential academic hire, the candidate simply responded: "I would like to publish some papers and get tenure." ("That's it!?" Tyler wanted to shriek.) Alternatively, a potential fellowship recipient might have the ambition to cure cancer; a person who actually has such an ambition will be able to articulate it pretty clearly and with some degree of conviction.

Upon reflection, this question is surprisingly difficult to fake. If you really don't have the ambition to cure cancer, it isn't so easy to claim in an interview that you do and defend the reality of your vision. It will sound like mere bragging, not backed up by analysis or details about the planned execution of the vision. On the other hand, people with truly ambitious goals often are eager to tell this to the world, and often they have some plans already worked out. Of course, in some cases you will immediately sense that a person's ambitions are set implausibly high, and that is reason for doubting their judgment and self-knowledge, however sincere their answer might be. World peace would be a wonderful thing, but we're not sure you should hire the candidate who pledges to bring it about.

The degree of a person's ambition is pretty valuable to know, and it gives you a clear sense of their potential upside. It also offers you a sense of a person's self-knowledge and of how they present and defend that self-knowledge when they are in an unexpected situation. We have found that hardly anyone is expecting this question. It is somehow too direct, too probing, and it touches too deeply upon a person's inner thoughts. Most people are used to settings where the default is to fake some mix of ambition, lack of ambition, or both, and where everyone else goes along with the faux presentation.

Two caveats about using this question. First, it may become less useful over time as it becomes known and expected. If the respondent has a prepped, fine-tuned answer to the question, they may be presenting exactly the level of ambition they think you are looking for. The question would become correspondingly less valuable. Second, there may be gender, cultural, or racial differences in the answers, a topic we will return to in later chapters. Suffice it to say, for example, that for a variety of reasons, women may be less willing to express extreme ambition — or maybe even visualize it to themselves. So if you ask a woman this question, the answer you receive may well be affected by some measure of social inhibition in addition to a sense of ambition, and that may render the answer correspondingly noisier in terms of information. Be aware of this potential distortion. The same problem may exist with some minority and immigrant groups, again, a topic we will return to. Even if the person is extremely ambitious, he may, for cultural reasons, view the interviewer as higher in status and may thus be unwilling to voice an ambition that is greater than, say, the current status of the interviewer, fearing that might be viewed as a kind of improper aggrandizement or insubordination. As always, be aware of your cultural context.

Another set of meta questions reverses the tables. Try this one: "What criteria would *you* use for hiring?" Again, you are testing an individual's understanding of the job, of him- or herself, and of the interview process itself.

It can be very instructive to ask, "What questions do you have for me?" or "What questions do you have about us?" or similar variants on this theme. The goal is to get the candidate to voice information about what he or she really cares about, and it also tests how well the candidate knows the job or project under consideration. On top of all that, it is testing for whether the candidate has penetrating insight into things you know about and, furthermore, whether the candidate might someday be in a position to insightfully interview, and perhaps hire, other people.

Still, this question only works some of the time, in part because so many people prep for it. It works best when you've already covered what they might have asked about from their prep, or when you can phrase the query in such a specific way that they can't fall back on their prep. Something like: "During the middle of this discussion, we chatted about [a very particular project]. What questions do you have about that project?" Then you are testing their engagement in the conversation and how much their understanding can evolve rapidly on the fly. If you simply ask them to present you with questions and they come back with "What does your benefits package look like?," then you have tested only for prep. That is an entirely reasonable comeback on their part, but usually you are looking for a greater revelation of information.

Interviewing the Person's References

We are big fans of interviewing a person's references, especially for higher-level jobs. Here are some basic tips for doing that effectively:

1. The person you are calling probably wants to get off the phone quickly, help or not harm the candidate, and also not lie too badly. However, they are probably willing to bend the truth.

2. As with the interview itself, the key is to move out of the realm of the bureaucratic and into a more conversational mode.

Their limited time means you need to rapidly create an atmosphere where the reference giver feels criticism can be given safely, without violation of confidence or without a single negative comment being turned into a case for the prosecution. That can be done by simply mentioning the nature of this problem, showing understanding for the complexities of job candidates, and signaling (honestly, one hopes!) that you do in fact keep an open mind about people with flaws.

3. Ask questions about specific quantitative comparisons, because in those instances, even a truth-bending reference is unlikely to lie. "Will this person be a better COO than John Smith?" may not get a completely honest answer, but if the reference does not immediately answer "Yes, the candidate will be a better COO," you should take that as some form of negative information. In the academic hiring market, it usually works to ask the recommender to compare the potential hire to another student they have tried to place on the market or perhaps to another tenured professor with a reputation.

4. If the candidate's reference list doesn't contain leaders (or at least links in the chain of direct reports) of the prior organization, that's a bad sign.

5. Keep the person talking, in part by being interesting yourself. And if you don't come away from those conversations with a sense of the candidate's drawbacks, know that you have failed in your investigation so far.

Finally, we are struck by these three questions for interviewing that Stripe CEO Patrick Collison presented to Reid Hoffman in their public interview from 2019.[14] Patrick doesn't seem to have intended these as "for references only questions," but nonetheless we find them useful in that context. Here goes:

1. Is this person so good that you would happily work for them?
2. Can this person get you where you need to be way faster than any reasonable person could?
3. When this person disagrees with you, do you think it will be as likely you are wrong as they are wrong?

Those are all very good forcing questions; ask them of the references but also of the job candidates as well.

In sum, conversing well with potential hires or award winners is one of the most important things you can do. Keep in mind that it not only brings you talent, but it helps you retain talent and mobilize those individuals to use their skills better. If you cannot relate to your talent at a conversational level, you will learn less, you will build less trust, and you will end up relying too heavily on direct monetary incentives to motivate people. If you are looking for something to practice, practice your own skills of conversing.

3

HOW TO ENGAGE WITH PEOPLE ONLINE

We've noticed that evaluators often make incorrect assessments when real-world conversational models are accidentally applied to online interactions. Someone with whom you're conversing online might come across as "obnoxious" because they're loud. But of course, loudness may just be an artifact of people's uncertainty about how sound is reproduced in virtual meetings. One must also be careful not to allow frustration at the *medium* to seep through to a judgment of the *participant*. When calls hang or meetings lag, subsequent discussion might suffer extra scrutiny, much as bad handwriting might cause readers to disbelieve its contents. Keep your cool, and realize that you are looking at distorted filters, so to speak.

By the way, these questions are sufficiently complex that they can provide an interesting interview question:

- "Why are person-to-person interactions often more informative than Zoom calls?"

That will test rather quickly a person's understanding of a product's limitations and advantages ("How does Zoom really work anyway?" "What makes a personal meeting a good one?") and also a person's introspective abilities and social abilities. The candidate likely has been doing numerous online and in-person interviews. How did those go? How did they feel, and how did the types of interview feel different? How would the candidate articulate those differences? These questions test self-awareness and articulateness and also a person's ability to focus on a task they need to excel at—in this case, the interview process.

Or try this tougher one:

- "In which ways might a Zoom call be *more* informative than a person-to-person interaction?"

Not only are we suggesting that question, but we'd like to spend the rest of this chapter answering it. The online medium is different from face-to-face interactions. But how? And how can you turn those differences to your advantage, or at least minimize their disadvantages?

Even before COVID-19, people were using virtual meetings with increasing frequency, and it's safe to say that this will continue when the crisis passes. Daniel's company, Pioneer, interviews and advises people around the world, mostly online, and the same is true for Tyler's Emergent Ventures. Well before the pandemic, we had Skype and, later, Zoom calls virtually every day. These days there is also "virtual lunch" persisting as a thing, webinars replacing many public talks, university classes moving fully or partially online, Zoom dating, Clubhouse, BlueJeans, Houseparty, and much more.

Furthermore, talent search has become more global, and so if you are speaking to a possible hire in Mumbai or Lagos, that will likely be done online, at least for the early rounds of the process and, as is increasingly common, perhaps for the entire process. Even if the person is merely across town, traffic congestion, office bookings, or scheduling constraints all might favor online contact.

How to do an online interview is one of the questions we receive most often, and unfortunately there is not yet a solid body of research on the best methods. Nor do most books on talent search and management reflect the new realities of how humans now communicate. Because of the lack of research or years of established best practices, this chapter is necessarily more speculative than the others, but we feel confident that our basic conclusions are useful.

What Is Similar and What Is Different Online

Some fundamental truths remain the same for online connections: you need to be trustworthy, and to establish trust you need to start a natural conversation. As you know from the previous chapter, this requires finding a way to *engage* with the interview subject. But what in the online format is different? Why does this work differently than in an in-person meeting?

For one thing, with an online interview it is much harder to use body language and eye contact to bond and to establish trust. With a Zoom call, for instance, you see the person's face and background in two dimensions, but usually not more.

Among other limitations, you cannot easily tell exactly where the person is looking, since your frame of reference and their frame of reference are not the same. Even if you superficially feel you are "looking right at the other person," you are not, just as you do not receive true eye contact when watching your favorite star on television. Nor is the eye tracking of two callers synched in the same way that it might be face-to-face. (Having multiple callers only heightens these problems.) If you stare at the screen, it is difficult for the other party to tell if you are engaging with their eyes (provided the angle of your head signals some limited kind of attention) or gazing into space or past the countenance of the other person. In this regard, screen calls can be relatively impersonal.

So all other things being equal, online trust will be lower. Consequently, edgy interview questions are harder to pull off in these settings. As an interviewer, you are more likely to appear obnoxious, or overly pushy, or simply "off," and in any case your intentions will be harder to read. So you may be forced to use fewer such questions or to blunt their hard edges. That is one reason online interviews tend to be less informative, and it is also a factor you need to respect when choosing your angle of approach.

That said, you can compensate for this greater difficulty. You can try to establish greater trust up front. You can deploy more bonding over common interests, or use self-deprecating humor more, if only to blunt your own harder edges later on. You can use more assuring rhetoric throughout the interview as a whole. All that takes time, and it can limit your own effectiveness; still, those approaches can give you greater leeway for pushing harder in other directions for more specific information.

It's likely that the interviewee will find it harder to take risks in the online setting. When interviewed, often we start an anecdote or story and rely on implicit visual feedback to encourage or discourage us from proceeding further. But when most of that feedback is absent or delayed, we are less likely to go down that particular route to begin with. So interviewees will often be more boring, risk-averse, and homogenized, and as the interviewer, you will need to adjust your expectations accordingly.

To consider the information poverty problem more generally, when you use distance communications you are missing out on at least three distinct sources of knowledge: social presence, information richness, and the full synchronicity of back-and-forth. By social presence we mean your understanding of how the person interacts with others and projects a self-image. Information richness refers to the ability of the in-person interaction to indicate more about how a person walks, shakes your hand, greets others entering the room, and so on. And synchronicity concerns the rhythm and patter of your interactions, the nature of the pauses, the speed of the convergence of understanding, how well you coordinate on who is due to speak next, and so on.

For a particular interview, it is worth thinking through which of these you really need to make up for, and which you are willing to do without. Don't just mentally compare Zoom to "real life"; rather, disaggregate and break down the exact problem you are facing. Missing out on social presence, for instance, is probably important if you are trying to hire a salesperson or a team leader. It could be less important if you are looking for someone who will telecommute and largely work solo, such as a writer or copy editor.

Very often, online interactions are fine for specific, focused discussions based around a concrete problem or issue or point of contention. They seem to function much less well as a way of generating spontaneous interaction or as a means of eliciting non-goal-specific information, and thus—compared to in-person interviewing—you don't get a sense about things you would have never thought to ask about in the first place. If someone visits your office for a chat, they might note a common bond because of something in a photo, a piece of artwork, or a poster on the wall. That kind of observation is much less likely to happen over Zoom, both because the cue is less likely to be seen in the first place and also there is less "space" in the more focused conversation for raising it. So if that kind of background information is important for the job in question—for instance, by getting a sense of the broader social context a person is coming from—by all means compensate by asking about such matters directly.

By breaking down the deficiencies of online communication in this fashion, you get a better sense of how you might need to generate more information elsewhere. You could make up for the deficiencies of the online interview by asking a person more direct questions about the information-deficient area or adding questions when talking to references.

Online interviews also bring greater coordination problems when it comes to discerning whose turn it is to speak. Due to various technical glitches, there still may be delays in transmitting messages (perhaps some of those problems will be fixed by the time you are reading this; at the moment, about half of Tyler's podcast guests have this problem at least once during the dialogue). Truly high-speed, uninterrupted internet access still is not the norm in the United States. Online conversations still often have short lags, or worse yet, the system can freeze up, if only temporarily. That harms the general flow of the conversation, even if a freeze or lag is not happening at a particular moment, because the discussants are never sure how their information is being transmitted, and they are never sure how well and how swiftly they are reading the signals of the other party to the conversation. There is a much greater disconnect—sometimes literally as well as figuratively—between the parties to these online interactions. Again, that is going to make a lot of interpersonal signals harder to read.

Status Relations Online

Another notable feature of online interaction is that it drains away many of the traditional markers of status.

Think of how many aspects of status relations are blurred or obliterated by the online setting. For instance, at a business meeting or interview there is typically a seating order of some kind, whether it is planned in advance or has arisen spontaneously. The boss or decision-maker is not usually pushed into the corner, for one thing. But with online calls, other than having a designated host who may "control the dials," those status markers are largely absent. Furthermore, the person in control of the dials on the call often is a technical assistant, not the actual boss.

Many women have remarked on Twitter that they feel on more equal footing on a Zoom call. The (usually male) boss is not dominating the center of the room; he cannot so easily employ "me first" body language; it is harder to interrupt people; and the rotation of turns to speak is often more symmetric. So interviewers need to realize that they are not projecting leadership or charisma in the usual ways. Dress as a marker of status also plays a different role in online chats. Shirts, haircuts, and posture might matter more, but shoes, watches, gait, suits, and height all matter less. The notion of a commanding physical presence doesn't play a big role. Handshakes may be on the way out anyway, but you certainly can't do them through a Zoom call, so no one knows if yours is firm or weak. A lot of people used to coming across as high-status and charismatic in person will feel a bit lost through the screen. Witty repartee also can be hard to pull off over an internet call, and that too may diminish the stature of those individuals who are accustomed to using clever banter to command a room.

This all means you need to rethink how status relationships are projected in the online medium. Typically the online medium raises the influence and stature of people who can get to the point quickly. You should aim to do that anyway, but online that is all the more imperative. Many online professors report that for their longer scheduled sessions, they find it necessary to resort to Zoom breakout sessions to give the class some sense of control over their own education and thus to maintain the students' involvement and interest. Over the longer term, those methods will reward non-paranoid leaders who are okay with giving up some sense of control in the moment, and you will need to adjust your style more in that direction, if you have not already.[1]

People who need to feel that they are coming across at their best fare worse in the environment of online presentation, because they just can't do that well, and thus, they will become nervous, anxious, and feel inadequate. Those who are more oblivious to a sense of their own imperfections are more likely to have the upper hand. If you are easygoing and have a relatively secure sense of place in the world, you may end up coming across as higher status than the person who used to command the room through pushiness and signals of dominance.

It is striking that during the lockdowns traditional movie and television celebrities did not have access to their usual platforms. Many of them took to streaming personal content online, but as Spencer Kornhaber opined in *The Atlantic*, "celebrities have never been less entertaining." They came across as bored and inept rather than relaxed and genuine. Most of these celebrities are used to context-created deference or even worship, but at the other end of an iPhone-created video they are just another mugging face, except they are less likely to realize that. So when Gal Gadot, Natalie Portman, Jamie Dornan, Sia, Pedro Pascal, Zoë Kravitz, Sarah Silverman, Leslie Odom Jr., Jimmy Fallon, Will Ferrell, Norah Jones, and Cara Delevingne created clips of themselves singing John Lennon's "Imagine," this was embarrassing rather than fascinating.[2]

Don't be like these celebrities, no matter how much you are the boss face-to-face. Online interactions simply strip away a lot of your mystique, and you need to adjust accordingly.

One of the hardest mental adjustments for people to make is to realize how much their positive affect relies on their in-person projection of high social status. To give a simple example, you might not be as witty as you think! You will do better in the online call if you realize how much your in-person presence relies on a kind of phoniness, and allow your online charisma to be rebuilt on different grounds—those that are easier, more casual, more direct, and just plain charming (but in the modest rather than pushy sense of that word). So rather than treating that high status as something automatically conveyed by your suit and your place at the table, maybe now you, as an interviewer, will have to work harder for it. Treat that as a plus, and as a chance to learn something and to shine in a very personal and human way.

Another problem is this: if you are on "Zoom center stage" in the large box as the speaker, people have no choice but to look at you square on, unless they just aren't paying attention. That can be stressful for you, because everyone can notice all of your imperfections, whether a pimple on your face, your unusual speech patterns, or your head movements. You too can see those same imperfections, and perhaps you too are not sure where you should be looking, and so you are torn between looking away in an effort to forget about it and glancing periodically at your own weirdness in order to try to correct it. Unfortunately, the watching crowd knows something a little strange is going on. When speaking live, experienced lecturers use all kinds of misdirection, including hand motions, body movements, and charisma, to cover up their blemishes, but on Zoom that is much harder to do.

Some individuals try to use their customized Zoom backgrounds to convey their importance, but this isn't easy. Putting a skyscraper window view behind you is not good for the visual mechanics of the call—too much bright light—so maybe over time expensive works of art will come to play that role.

Overall, we've found that in the recent COVID-19 migration to the internet savannah, status symbols have changed from designer jackets to digital bitrate. High-powered investors and CEOs are spending thousands on studio-style cameras and lighting. Daniel has found that many of his Pioneers, on the other hand, are mimicking this style of status marking using clever software. Using green screens, voice-modifying software, and video filters, they are changing their appearance to make themselves look the part of an impressive founder, and doing it on a budget. This demonstrates not just impressive technical skills but also an interesting maturity. The fact that they care so much is a remarkable awareness of the perception of self by others, and none of this could have happened in a world of face-to-face interviews only. It is harder to send status signals online, but that in turn gives some people the chance to excel at that same task.

Tyler uses a David Burliuk sketch of books on a table for his Zoom background (Burliuk was a Ukrainian avant-garde artist from the early twentieth century), and if the camera tilts the right way you can see some classic Haitian art (Wilson Bigaud's *Night Market*). Tyler is signaling openness, including openness to different cultures, plus a sense of the mysterious, encouraging you to probe more deeply into what he is doing. Daniel is flanked by a bright yellow background, identical to the color of his website, reflecting the Pioneer brand. It radiates "tech" rather than "culture." There is not necessarily anything wrong with a candidate who has a mediocre background image, but still, it is one piece of information about that person's self-presentation to the outside world—namely, that you are more likely to succeed with this match if you are hiring for a "substance job" than for a "flair job."

Zoom calls can also provide collateral information about a person's home and family life. Maybe that isn't fair, but sometimes it is impossible to create a truly insulated environment for the online discussion. The phone can ring in the background, people may talk or yell, the dog might bark, and you may get a sense, however limited or vague, of the basic rhythms of family life in the house. And of course, you, as an interviewer, may be giving off comparable signals. Yes, sometimes you do have to get up to sign for a package from the UPS delivery person. The online chat breaks down the distinction between work space and home space; this is especially true if the parties are doing it during a pandemic, with everyone else at home, but it holds more generally too.

We view these as positive features of the online medium. We are not suggesting you take any kind of dogmatic stance as to what kind of home life is the right one to look for (should the dog's bark be shrill and yapping? Deep and guttural? Who knows?). Still, this blurring of home and work life introduces variation in the basic interview structure, and that is a good thing, a bit like observing how the candidate interacts with the workers at Starbucks. Welcome any possible easing of tensions, ambiguity, or strangeness offered by the interview setting. Lean into it. Treat it as a surprise topic to talk about, to get the candidate out of interview mode and into conversational mode. But don't start by prying into the person's home life. Lead with something about your own situation, and then see how it all unfolds. Sometimes the home environment offers more chances for serendipity than does an office interview room, so take advantage of that.

Along these lines, Tyler has found that teaching online, through Zoom, has given his students the feeling of "being invited into his home." His wife, Natasha, has walked over to the screen to wave to them; they see his sofa; and once or twice he has stood up to get a bottle of water from the refrigerator. Those are all small touches, but overall the feeling is a more egalitarian one. At least for his graduate students, that brings them further along the path of thinking of themselves as his peers—which they should aspire to be—rather than as drone-like students with homework due. Daniel, on his Zoom calls and seminars, typically is wearing a T-shirt. Silicon Valley was casual in the first place, but now it is easier than ever to bring the casual standards of the home into the workplace, as those two venues are increasingly one and the same.[3]

Many celebrities, when they began doing online interviews from home during lockdown, had bookshelves behind them, though we are not sure how much of this was design and how much was accident. Cate Blanchett, in her background, had *Postcapitalism*, by Paul Mason, and also the *Oxford English Dictionary*, both making her appear intellectual. In the background for Prince Charles was a book called *Stubbs*, by Basil Taylor, referring to the eighteenth-century English painter well-known for his portraits of horses. That volume would not suit Daniel or Tyler, but for Prince Charles it seems about right. One journalistic study of British members of Parliament found they were likely to cover up their bookcases and make their backgrounds bland and nondescript, perhaps out of fear that voters offended by visible book titles would be a bigger problem than any possible upside from showing off one's reading prowess. Nabokov's *Lolita* is a deeply subtle novel, but do you really want your constituents to see it in your home?[4]

While we enjoy the more egalitarian features of online interviews and interactions, we realize that new forms of status hierarchy are emerging in our own online interviews, and not just because of how the Pioneers program their software backgrounds. The more stripped-down the online environment, the more important the individual performance itself, in particular the answers to interview questions. These online interviews are a bit like online speed chess, where all that matters is the quality of the moves—in this case, it's the quality of the answers. If the fanciness of your shoes or cuff links matters less, the fluidity of your banter matters more. That may be a better signal of intellectual merit, but still, you as an interviewer need to realize you are receiving a very limited set of signals; you should not be too entranced by the smooth talkers, and you need to set your epistemic humility awareness on high.

Finally, Zoom and other online calls may penalize those individuals who are prone to suffer from "Zoom fatigue." As we've seen, when you are participating in a Zoom call or other online encounter, you don't have access to all of the social information you are accustomed to, such as many hand gestures and body movements. Instead, you are supposed to concentrate on the words being said, and indeed, you don't have too many other options (other than just being distracted and inattentive, of course). But many people thrive on interpreting social signals from body language and broader demeanor, and on mirroring those same signals back—if your interlocutor smiles, you smile too. The scientific evidence suggests that many of us—perhaps most of us—find it disorienting to be cut off from so many of the usual social signals and forced to focus on only a few markers of the communicative experience. So if the person you are talking to seems a little "out of it," don't be too quick to infer they are inattentive more generally. Zoom calls may penalize the extroverts among us to a disproportionate degree, and yet for some jobs those extroverts may be the people you are looking to hire. If you are trying to hire a "cold call" salesperson who will go around knocking on doors, put less weight on the Zoom call than if you are trying to hire a programmer.[5]

One of Daniel's suggestions to avoid Zoom fatigue is simply to shut off the video and just use the audio, like a phone call. Many times the video is misleading anyway, and phone calls can be more intimate than video calls. Furthermore, this decision may prevent you from getting sick of Zoom and other video calls altogether, assuming there will be cases when you need to use them whether you wish to or not. When it comes to talking heads, sometimes it is better just to say no.[6]

When We Avoid Face-to-Face Contact

In a Catholic church's confessional, the priest and the confessee are separated by a partition. There is no eye contact or chance of eye contact—unlike a Zoom call. Yet this setting seems to have useful features. Earlier in history, Catholic confession was performed in public; the "dark box" method did not come into use until the mid-sixteenth century. But the dark box method proved useful, and it spread through the church over the course of centuries. It seemed to make people more willing to confess.[7]

Arguably public confession is making a comeback in our "cancel culture," especially on social media, but it seems that making confession a public practice induces too much performativity and falseness rather than being uniquely suited to producing truth. That, again, suggests some reasons that less direct contact and less visibility might sometimes be better at eliciting truth.

The classical approach to psychotherapy also makes a point of deliberately avoiding a direct face-to-face interaction: the patient lies on a couch and does not look the therapist directly in the eye while speaking. To be clear, this is only one option for therapy—people who see therapists in person often do so face-to-face, and there is a good deal of therapy by Skype and Zoom these days—but many people still take the time, trouble, and expense to go to the office of a psychotherapist just so they can lie down and rather decidedly look the other way. It's yet another case of a time-honored practice where individuals are not pursuing the maximum degree of face-to-face contact, and we can learn from that.

One common element in the confessional and therapeutic settings is that a lack of eye-to-eye contact can be used to stimulate or ease confession, or at least an opening up. If the priest were staring the confessee right in the eye, it might be harder for the confessee to admit to having failed to fulfill one's family responsibilities. Furthermore, anonymity would be broken. Similarly, in psychotherapy, it might be easier for the patient to relate a childhood trauma when no one is offering a direct, visually available response ("Did he raise his eyebrow at that? Or sneer, or laugh?"). Eye contact can be a bond, but it can also be a threat, or a source of undue or distracting focus, and it makes it harder for many people to relax or open up. In the therapeutic setting, opinions differ on the effectiveness of the couch, but it may aid free association and the pacing of the session and make the overall environment less threatening.[8]

The lack of eye-to-eye contact also means that the mutual reassurance mode is probably weaker in an online call. There is less implicit pressure to be polite, or to smile, or to look for ac-knowledgment and approval by the other person. At least some-times, the removal of that conformity-inducing information can give us the opportunity to probe a little more deeply. And you can learn something about how the interviewee carries him- or herself when social trust is not entirely present or is not continu-ally being confirmed by the cues of direct social presence.

Some anecdotes from lockdown-inspired methods of online dating support this possibility that people may open up more in a more stripped-down environment. Consider twenty-seven-year-old Judy Kwon, a Brooklynite. She expressed an important sen-timent about the potential upside of online dating: "There are obviously a lot of drawbacks to this, but at least for me, this [sce-nario] has prompted more serious conversations. . . . I've been more vocal about how I feel, and I've asked him [the dating part-ner] to do the same, because we can't read each other the same way you would when you're getting to know someone in-person. It's made us more in touch with our feelings, for sure."[9]

It is both an advantage and disadvantage of the Zoom date that there are fewer ways of filling awkward pauses. You cannot easily pick up the pitcher of water on the restaurant table and pour to create a distraction or to fill time. So what do people—at least some people—do? They speak directly and start baring their souls. And this can lead two people to get to know each other more quickly and more deeply—at least if the date doesn't just collapse right away into boring awkwardness.[10]

When it comes to interviews, it may sound crazy to prefer less rather than more contact with the interviewee, but if you ever have enjoyed a "walking interview," where direct eye con-tact typically is minimal, you should not find these claims so strange. A walking interview can be more useful and more re-velatory than a face-to-face, across-the-table interview. There is somehow more room to explore tangential ideas, and a broader penumbra for topics and the sequencing of a discussion. Being side by side can create feelings of mutuality, safety, and even playfulness. Perhaps some conversants feel less "liable" for what they are saying, compared to a chat across a desk or small table.

Media interviewer Terry Gross, who has worked for National Public Radio, deliberately uses a distance technique that is not direct and face-to-face: "While guests sit in a remote studio, Gross sits in her 'little box' at WHYY in Philadelphia—a setup that provides a kind of faceless intimacy not unlike that of confession or psychoanalysis, where the patient and practitioner face away from each other, under the theory that the obscurity will allow thoughts and fantasies to flow more freely. Perhaps that is what lures her guests into such a revealing mode."[11]

In yet other settings, distance can provide a path toward openness. During the lockdown, researchers conducting telephone surveys have found that respondents have been more willing to pick up the phone and indeed to converse with the interviewer. Many respondents not only answered the survey questions but confided in the interviewer about their fears, their sadness, and how they were faring during the pandemic. Those conversations may have served as a safety valve of sorts, and it seems that many people found the faceless phone interviewer to be a sort of confidant. In one data set, a series of interviews that used to average ten minutes took fourteen minutes during the pandemic because the respondents were chattier than usual.[12]

With all that in mind, one possible strategy for online interviewing is to try asking a question or two that evokes a sense of confession. Don't make this a challenging or sharp question; rather, present it passively and openly, as if you are there to listen, not to judge. How about this?

- "We have all committed mistakes in the workplace, as have I. What is an example of a mistake you have committed but did not come to regret for a long time?"

Or try this one:

- "In the context of the workplace, what does the concept of deliberate sin really mean? And how does it differ from a mere mistake? Can you illustrate this from the experience of one of your co-workers?"

Note that the invocation of the co-worker makes the inquiry less threatening and is more likely to induce an honest response. If you wish to go direct, you might try:

- "When have you experienced great regret in the workplace and why? How much were you at fault in that interaction?"

In a face-to-face interview, the interviewee might feel too inhibited to serve up a useful answer. But online, if you feel you stand a chance of eliciting a "true confession," so to speak, these are worth a try. That said, if you receive a truly revealing answer, take it as information, not as a sign that the person is dysfunctional and falling apart. It is you who made the effort to draw out this information, and if the answer is more explicit than usual in some manner, remember that you sought it out. Adjust your expectations accordingly and try to see the positive in it. Such an answer is, in part, a reflection of your success as an interviewer, not necessarily a defect of the interviewee.

Note also that in some cases, especially those involving younger women and male interviewers, lack of direct eye contact may facilitate trust. Eye contact also can be a threat or a reminder of previous unpleasant situations, possibly involving harassment. This is yet another illustration of how the online medium simply is different rather than lacking or inferior in every regard.

Of course, if you are being interviewed, you may wish to protect against being too casual and open. Some Zoom daters have expressed that they feel a sense of comfort in the ritual of "a workout, a shower, and some date-worthy clothes" before going on an online date. Others have made a point to put on their best cologne or perfume and even to make their bed (just in case they get lucky?). Along similar lines, we think many individuals, to maintain proper levels of concentration, should dress and prepare as if it were a real face-to-face interview. So if you otherwise come across as not sufficiently disciplined, consider putting on your dress shoes for that Zoom call. But note: we do *not* recommend this for the more casual world of tech and venture capital interviews. Again, you wish to match your style of presentation to the worldview of your interviewers, and you should choose your mode of presentation accordingly.[13]

The Future of Online Communications

The sooner you realize that online interviews operate in an intrinsically different medium than face-to-face interactions, the better. You will know that your older standards for recognizing talent in the face-to-face interview need to be modified. Technological advances will not change that basic difference.

You should avoid the trap of thinking that the distance interviewing technology simply has to be "good enough." Maybe someday we will have a form of holographic virtual reality that approaches a perfect simulation of face-to-face interaction, but in the meantime, evolutions in online technologies are not simply better approximations of face-to-face interactions. Instead, they skew our attention in certain directions rather than others. Technologies do not improve along all dimensions at once (e.g., Viagra came before an Alzheimer's cure, so life extension for some people's body parts works better than for others), and future improvements we will see in online communications will have biased impacts on our perceptions. For instance, finer resolution on screens may boost information transmission without doing much for social presence. Yes, the new technology will be "better" in an objective sense. But if you don't realize that your assessments now may include more impressions based on the greater number of pixels and *not* more impressions based on social presence, you can be led astray. Again, it is a mistake to think that the purpose of distance communications is to approximate "being there."[14]

Alternatively, imagine that Oculus technologies develop very rapidly and that your virtual "Paris holiday" is almost as good as the real thing, except cheaper and more convenient. Your virtual-reality interview through Oculus still won't have the same emotional resonance as would a face-to-face interaction. If nothing else, your virtual interaction won't have the potential inconveniences of the face-to-face encounter. Your avatar likely is programmed never to stumble or spill the coffee, there is no question of being late for the appointment because of traffic, and the skill of reading a virtual three-dimensional room probably won't be exactly the same as negotiating the "real world." It is possible that in advanced virtual reality, everyone will seem just a bit too antiseptic. It is hard to give advice for a technology that is not yet mature, but when it does become mainstream, you will have to figure out how to compensate for those differences, no matter which side of the interview you are on. Just don't confuse that new technology with face-to-face reality.

To be futuristic again for a moment, imagine a future where online interviewing offers much *more* informational richness than face-to-face interviewing. You might imagine, for instance, that you can use AI to monitor the online interview and give you running commentary on how the person is doing, what kind of personality they have, and which questions you should ask next. Furthermore, it might be harder and more awkward to use such a technology during a face-to-face interview, if only because you could not so easily look down all the time to see what the AI device is telling you. It is also possible that, in the future, an on-line interaction offers better "personal presence" information than does a face-to-face interview. That may sound impossible virtually by definition, but keep in mind human heterogeneity. You have a particular experience of personal presence in an in-terview, but you don't know how others would have responded to the same interactions. It may be easier for machine intelli-gence to break down the online interview and report to you how the interviewee "performed" in terms of personal presence for typical others, not just for yourself. Again, we could find ourselves in the unusual situation of the face-to-face interview being the relatively more deficient mode of communication.

Yet even in this supposedly ideal situation, the AI-based in-terviews will introduce biases in your evaluations. In particular, such technologies would divert your attention toward what the AI can measure well and distract you from the noisier pieces of information. And if many institutions have access to the same AI technologies, as is likely to be the case, it may be precisely the idiosyncratic, noisy pieces of information that become the most important for you. Keep in mind that everyone is looking for talent, and you need to spot the talent that your competitors cannot. It is not obvious how much AI would help you in that quest if it was generally available, and in some regards it might make your task harder because it would make it easier for others to spot the same otherwise undervalued job candidates you're looking for.

Finally, keep in mind that face-to-face interactions can distract you from making the right interview decisions. Not all interview cues are the right ones. Over Zoom you have less of a sense of how the person dresses (shoes, anyone?), not much sense of how the person reacts to others entering the room, and no sense of how the person smells, among other missing pieces of information. We don't know which of those are valuable for making good hiring decisions (it is possible none of them are), and we may misinterpret cues in those areas even if in principle they might be properly informative. So again, don't go into online interactions with a defeatist attitude—in some cases such interviews may save you from being your own worst enemy. The online dialogue at least offers some chance of greater focus on the information that really matters.

Individuals will work pretty hard to obscure their true level of conscientiousness. In fact, they might be fooling the interviewer most of the time, because who wants to appear nonconscientious in an interview? Most interviewers consider a person's gait, microexpressions, and interactions with third parties when judging how trustworthy that person really is, whether those judgments are fair or not. And we don't know how accurate those signals really are. So if the online interview equalizes those signals across candidates somewhat, you may end up making a better decision. You may have to look more closely at what a person has done, and as you will see later, we are big fans of "demonstrated preference"—actual life activities and achievements—as the most reliable source of information about an individual.

The supposed information poverty of the online interview also may help some interviewers overcome potential biases against women and also some minority groups. We've already mentioned that the online world makes it harder for you to pick up on traditional cues of charisma and social presence, but for many jobs charisma and social presence can be misleading indicators. In particular, understandings of charisma vary across cultures. We have often found that individuals from non-Western cultures are what we perceive as "excessively" respectful when being interviewed (both online and otherwise), perhaps falling back on politeness because they are aware they don't have in-depth knowledge of the cultural world they are suddenly dealing with and are afraid of making mistakes (see Chapter 8, on gender and race). There is nothing wrong with politeness, to say the least, but it will be hard to judge the charisma of an individual who takes this approach. As a result, you, as an interviewer from a Western culture, may be tempted to conclude that such individuals are not very charismatic, but of course, that is a mistake—the person is simply afraid to display their charisma for you. The online interview, by making *everyone* less charismatic, may help counter your bias against these individuals. Once again, it is all about learning how to turn the online medium to your advantage.

4

WHAT IS INTELLIGENCE GOOD FOR?

Might it be that talk of intelligence tends to induce overly hier-archical thinking and ranking? After a long back-and-forth, we've concluded that intelligence usually is overrated, most of all by people who are smart. But research also suggests some very im-portant cases where intelligence really matters. We'd like to give you a guided tour as to when smarts really matter, and what is known and also what is not known about this question. As we've noted before, context rules when it comes to talent search.

We're going to start with the positive, because intelligence can help a person find new ideas and put the pieces together where others cannot, and extreme intelligence may be required to be credible when exhibiting the highest levels of leadership skills, especially when you are leading other very smart people. Let's now dig into the details of that.

Inventors, Leaders, and Entrepreneurs

Let's consider inventors in particular, because there are some very good data available and the results from them are noteworthy. These data are from Finland, and they cover the entire male workforce born between 1961 and 1984, matching their eventual professions with their measured IQs taken from their period of conscription (only men were conscripted during that period, and thus, women do not enter into this study). The researchers also have comprehensive information about those individuals throughout significant parts of their lives, including incomes and levels of education for them and their parents. As is often the case in the Nordic countries, the data are pretty comprehensive and considered to be reliable.[1]

The most striking results are for the job category of inventors. If you are looking for inventors, IQ is by far the most significant of all the measurable variables we have. Furthermore, at higher levels of measured IQ the probability of becoming an inventor rises all the more. The relevant IQ measure here, by the way, is a variant of the Ravens test, which focuses on visuospatial skills rather than verbal facility.

The relationship between IQ and the probability of becoming an inventor can be expressed in a number of different ways. For instance, being in either the 91st–95th percentile of measured IQ or the 96th–100th percentile increases the probability of being an inventor by about 2–3 percentage points. Alternatively, if we hold other factors constant, having all individuals in the highest IQ decile would, statistically speaking, involve a 183 percent rise in the number of inventors compared to the status quo.

It is noteworthy how much of the explained variation in the inventor profession is explained by IQ: a stunning 66 percent of that total (if you have statistical training, that is *not* the par- tial R-squared, as most of the choice of professions comes from unmeasured variables; instead, that 66 percent is how much of the available explanation, conditioned on measured variables, comes from IQ). That number is striking, in part, because it can be compared with other variables. For instance, the next most significant variable—parental education—accounts for only 1 percent of the variation in who becomes an inventor.[2]

The simplest way to put this is that most people do not be- come inventors, and who will become an inventor is very hard to predict no matter what. But still, of all the predictors we have in this data set, IQ performs by far the best.

You might be wondering how this all squares with our gen- eral view that IQ, or more generally, intelligence, is overrated as a source of professional achievement. Well, the same paper shows that IQ plays a much smaller role in determining who ends up in other notable professions. If we look at who in Fin- land becomes a doctor, of the explained variation IQ accounts for only 8 percent of the total. For a lawyer, the explained varia- tion by IQ is lower yet, namely about 5 percent. In other words, IQ is not, in general, very important, but to the extent mea- sured variables can explain the decision to become an inventor, IQ appears to be quite important, at least compared to other measured variables.

In that same data set, if you are considering what does explain who becomes a doctor or a lawyer, parental education (and not IQ) is the main explanatory variable, accounting for 39 and 52 percent of those career decisions, respectively. Furthermore, pa- rental income plays a larger role in pushing you into being a doctor or a lawyer than it does in being an inventor.

One lesson is that inventors are, on the whole, pretty smart, at least in Finland but probably elsewhere too. As for doctors and lawyers, it is very important to "come from a good family." Maybe that is the kind of socioeconomic background you really need to succeed at law and medicine, but another possible reading of the data is that entry into Finnish law and medicine is in some ways too exclusionary, and lots of smart potential candidates are being kept away merely because they do not have the right socioeconomic background and upbringing.

The Very, Very Top of the Market

We also believe that super-talented individuals, near the top of the achievement distribution, are in some fundamental ways like inventors. These individuals arrive at the top of their craft because they have pioneered new ways of doing things, whether it is Picasso and Braque creating cubism, Henry Ford realizing he should pay his workers $5 a day, or Sergey Brin and Larry Page realizing that the search problem could be cracked by sufficiently clever mathematics. These individuals need to see around corners that others cannot, and that's our best guess for where smarts will continue to be important.

One carefully done study considers the connection between IQ and lifetime wages at the very top of the IQ distribution, in this case in the top 0.5 percent. The data come from children initially chosen based on a survey in California schools in 1921–22, 856 men and 672 women, and the study traces how much those individuals earned over their lifetimes. In this study, one additional point of IQ correlates with earnings of about 5 percent higher, or in this data set about $184,100 more over the course of a lifetime. In other words, even within the category of people with very good test scores, being "smarter yet" correlates with a noticeable boost in pay. And here is the critical point: among this high-IQ group, that is a steeper pay/IQ gradient than we find for the population as a whole. That steeper gradient at the top is consistent with our view that intelligence probably matters most for the very high achievers.[3]

The claim that intelligence matters most at higher levels of achievement has been tested most extensively with a Swedish data set covering 12,570 workers and running from 1968 to 2007. The data for that population show that personality and conscientiousness matter most at the bottom of the distribution. For instance, in the bottom tenth of earners, non-cognitive skills—which include, for instance, features of personality—matter two and a half to four times more than do cognitive skills. However, for the population in general, a boost of one standard deviation in cognitive ability is associated with a larger wage gain than is a rise of one standard deviation in non-cognitive skills. (Standard deviation, by the way, is a statistical concept referring to spread; if a variable is "normally distributed" in a sample, about 68 percent of the individuals in that sample will be contained within a one-standard-deviation segment to each side of the mean or average value.) Furthermore, the relationship between cognitive ability and wages is convex, meaning that the higher we go in the wage distribution, the more potently cognitive ability predicts earnings. In other words, once again, the top of the distribution is where smarts really matter for performance.[4]

Yet even then we should not regard measured intelligence as any kind of guarantee of success, if only because most people with superior measured intelligence do not end up being extremely successful in their careers.

Arguably many top talents are well described by what is called the multiplicative model of success. In the multiplicative model, final success requires a fairly tight combination of several traits—variables expressing the strength of particular traits are in some manner multiplied together to achieve a powerful final effect. For instance, to be a top-tier classical music composer, you might need great work habits, musical genius, ability to play the piano, skill in orchestrating, persistence, and to have come from a major musical center in or near central Europe. If all of those traits come together, the result may be magic, as was the case with Mozart or Beethoven. But if you are missing just one of those traits, perhaps you fail altogether. Musical genius without great work habits, for instance, might mean you become a brilliant local improviser who never puts pen to paper to compose a major symphony.

Consider the words of Vladimir Akopian, the brilliant Armenian chess player who never worked very hard at the game and thus never rose to the top: "I believe there are many talented chess players. When I play, sometimes I see players who are very talented. And by talent, many players can be compared easily; it's not something special. But hard work is very important. And not only hard work but also a player's weakness in character or some psychological instability can make a difference. Chess is very complicated and all of this counts. Purely in terms of talent, I believe, not only me but many others even maybe surpass these top players. It's possible. But when you consider all things together—not only talent but the willingness to work hard, to sacrifice everything else, to be psychologically strong— not many have it in them to make it to the very top . . . there are many factors that need to be in place for a player to reach the world's elite." And outside of the very top of the game of chess, where the champions are indeed very smart, the evidence does not support a very strong link between chess achievement and intelligence.[5]

It is easy to think of other examples of the nonlinear importance of intelligence at the very top tiers of achievement. Being a top CEO, baseball pitcher, or Nobel Prize–winning scientist may require a combination of numerous traits, where again, the total is greater than the sum of its parts. We call this *the whole package*.

As a result, if you have a limited data set, you may make all sorts of choices based on variables you think ought to matter, such as extreme intelligence, but find you are getting nowhere. The people you are choosing need to have the whole package, again, especially at the higher levels of achievement. Even if some relatively well-designed statistical studies show that intelligence has a marginal value of zero, many top performers still may need to be very smart at what they do, otherwise they have no real chance of offering the whole package. In that sense, looking for extreme smarts is one necessary part of the talent search at these levels.

Underexplored Territory

The value of pursuing intelligence also is relatively high when you are the first one on the scene and there is no general competition to hire that same talent. That means intelligence is a better indicator of promise for the very young, for individuals from remote or economically underexplored areas, and for individuals being brought into networks for the very first time. In contrast, intelligence is a worse indicator of hire quality if you are considering a sixty-year-old individual with an established track record.

One implication is that if you think you are especially good at spotting intelligence and other desirable qualities, you should spend more time working with the young and trying to locate and develop young talent. Arguably, you also might want to devote more attention to foreign markets or relatively untapped cultures within the United States, which perhaps have not been combed over so extensively as, say, the American coastal cities and suburbs. Alternatively, if you have decided that trying to spot intelligence is a hopeless activity, at least for you, maybe go into a sector where a lot of older people are working and you can judge them by their experience and vitas, as indeed is most appropriate.

The import of underexplored territory is another reason intelligence and other features of talent can be relatively important to find at the very, very top of the market. If you consider how the Mark Zuckerbergs, Paul McCartneys, and LeBron Jameses—the absolute top performers—developed, you can do very well by looking for stars early in their careers. Peter Thiel was the first venture capitalist to support Mark Zuckerberg, and manager Brian Epstein found and cultivated the talent of the Beatles, in both cases with handsome returns.

In what might seem like a paradox, it can be hard to spot intelligence, drive, and other positive qualities at the very, very top. Why? Well, the very, very top of the market usually is underexplored territory, virtually by definition. The most talented people usually are doing something extraordinary and fairly new, and often they are so unbelievably talented that most of us just don't have the ability to appreciate their talents, at least not until their final achievements are on full display. If a young Gustav Mahler sat down in front of you and hummed one of his melodies, you probably wouldn't have the talent required to see his potential to become one of the greatest Romantic composers of all time.

In other words, the super-talented are best at spotting other super-talented individuals, and there aren't many of those super-talented talent spotters to go around. So if you are yourself a super-talented spotter of super-talented talent, you will find many instances of undervalued intelligence, undervalued positive work habits, undervalued drive, and so on. Those qualities will (correctly) appear to you undervalued because few other individuals will notice them. For example, circa 1961, who understood that the Beatles were going to shake up the world? (In fact, they were turned down by numerous record companies, and they offered their early American releases on the relatively obscure Vee-Jay label.)[6]

Do you know the story of John H. Hammond in music? He was the talent scout, enthusiast, and mentor who discovered and promoted Bob Dylan, Bruce Springsteen, Billie Holiday, Count Basie, Benny Goodman, Big Joe Turner, Pete Seeger, Aretha Franklin, George Benson, Leonard Cohen, and Stevie Ray Vaughan, among others. He also played a key role in reviving interest in Delta blues legend Robert Johnson. Now, that's a pretty impressive record, but if you read about Hammond, it is not obvious what his magic formula was or how anyone else might replicate it. He did spend a lot of time around music and musicians, he was independently wealthy from childhood, and he worked in a non-racist way in a racist time, which meant he was focused on spotting black performers that others were overlooking. Perhaps George Benson offered one clue to Hammond's success when he said, "John Hammond didn't necessarily care about how many records I could sell: his approach was more along the lines of 'look at what this talent can do, and I hope you enjoy him as much as I do.'" Still, at the end of the day, Hammond's history as a scout shows that most of the top talent is not spotted by the establishment right away, precisely because those creators are doing something new and original.[7]

When the multiplicative model holds for potential top performers, the notion of underexplored talent is especially relevant. Usually it is much harder to spot the whole package than to look for a person who is smart, or who plays the guitar well, or who has a 98-mph fastball. Those particular traits are *relatively* easy to spot or measure. Yet seeing the whole package requires a much deeper synthetic ability, a good deal of luck, and what we are calling entrepreneurial alertness—that is, the ability to spot and perceive talents that others do not see.

When Choosing a Whole Group of People Who Will Work Together

Talented people make each other better, often in dynamic, nonlinear fashion, and this holds for intelligence as a measure of talent as well. One of Tyler's colleagues at George Mason, Garett Jones, has written an entire book on this topic, called *Hive Mind: How Your Nation's IQ Matters So Much More than Your Own*, and in that book he stresses how intelligence can have a nonlinear positive effect. That is, smart people can feed off each other and make each other better, within companies and even within nations. If you put Bill Gates in the jungle alone, he might not do better than a less talented manager, but Bill Gates with a team of one hundred hand-picked helpers may enjoy a pronounced advantage.[8]

Or consider the intuition from another direction. Let's say you put one super-smart person into a dysfunctional company. That person probably cannot improve things very much on their own because bad cultures represent a series of dug-in bad practices, norms, and expectations, and such situations are very difficult to reform. Yet a company full of effective, cooperative people can make a big difference. In similar fashion, putting a good defender on a basketball team that doesn't play solid, attentive team defense probably doesn't help much. Someone is going to mess up their assignment and leave a shooter open, and a single good defender just can't cover all of the other team's shooters. Nonetheless, a basketball team full of first-rate defenders will demonstrate the power of team defense to great effect.

Silicon Valley has had much more success in writing software than any other comparable region, and that is because of its human (rather than natural) resources and how well those human resources cooperate with each other, which in this context is the smart thing to do. The productivity gap between Silicon Valley in software and, say, Chicago, Illinois, is much larger than the (relatively small) wage gap between higher-IQ and lower-IQ individuals. Silicon Valley has many very smart people working together trying to write software and also trying to teach each other how to do start-ups. Chicago does not have the same focus, and so Silicon Valley has many unicorns (start-ups that reach a valuation of $1 billion) and Chicago does not. That difference is a testament to the power of well-organized groups.

There is, furthermore, direct evidence that higher-intelligence people are better at cooperating. Researchers Eugenio Proto, Aldo Rustichini, and Andis Sofianos paid individuals to play varying games of cooperation for real money rewards. The researchers had data on the personality characteristics and IQs of the individuals playing the games, so it was possible to measure the strategies and successes of different types of people. The results were clear: high-IQ individuals in general cooperated more in these games, and IQ mattered the most in games where there were trade-offs between short-run goals and longer-run considerations. The researchers put it this way: in this situation, "intelligence matters substantially more in the long run than other factors and personality traits."[9]

You also need to get just the right kind of cooperation in place, and that means looking for complementarity across your smart and otherwise meritorious hires. There is a difference between individual intelligence and how an individual contributes to the productivity of a broader group. Stephen Curry fit into his Golden State Warriors team perfectly, as he was paired with other strong shooters who made it harder to guard Curry exclusively and to whom Curry could pass the ball; Curry probably would have been much less effective on a team of slower, bigger men.

For you as an employer or talent scout, what does all this mean, practically speaking? If you are hiring one person into a relatively mature institution, intelligence and other features of talent will matter much less, while ability to fit in will matter more. If you are creating a start-up, or otherwise building an institution from scratch, and hiring a whole team, various markers of talent—including intelligence and cooperativeness—will matter much more. Hiring a whole batch of very smart people has the potential to create strongly positive, dynamic, nonlinear benefits. Look more for markers of talent when you are hiring groups of people in a relatively short period of time.

So if you have a buddy in the start-up world (Tyler's friend here is Daniel, and Tyler wrote this particular paragraph) and he or she is working with very, very smart people . . . well, you don't have to feel jealous. Instead, you can go to bed at night knowing that something has gone right with our world.

The Case Against Smarts

That all said, smarts have truly significant limitations, and now let's look at those. The more you are talking about the population in general, the less intelligence is likely to matter for achievement and success.

Let's start by considering the views of one of the smartest people we have met: Marc Andreessen, who is a general partner and co-founder at Andreessen Horowitz and who invented the Web browser. As a venture capitalist, Marc helped fund companies such as Facebook, Twitter, Groupon, Lyft, Airbnb, and Stripe, among many others. If you have any doubt about Marc's smarts, imagine inventing the Web browser when such a thing never had been done before! But it's not just that. If you ask Marc about political philosophy, ancient Roman history, or how a Hollywood contract might work—virtually any topic—he will stream a torrent of brilliant observations that will just blow your mind.

Yet even Marc realizes that, in general terms, smarts are overrated. In 2007 he wrote an essay called "How to Hire the Best People You've Ever Worked With."[10] He argued that intelligence is overrated in making hires. Intelligence is context-dependent, and it matters most when a company already is favorably situated with respect to the market, Microsoft and Google being two examples of that phenomenon. No company has succeeded simply by putting out its shingle for intelligent individuals or by asking hires to solve difficult logic puzzles. While intelligence is, of course, a good thing, Marc argues that, all other factors equal, the more important qualities in a hire are drive, self-motivation, curiosity, and ethics. He also suggests that drive and curiosity coincide to a pretty high degree, especially in an era when the internet allows you, in your spare time, to keep up on your field for free.

We think Marc's points are well taken. Let's also consider some more systematic and data-driven reasons why maxing out on intelligence is not, in general, the right way to go.

Formal Measures of Intelligence Don't Predict Earnings Very Well

One way of judging talent is to look at how much a person eventually earns. It is not that the market always gets it right, but if a trait does not predict earnings at all, that trait probably is not so important for productivity.

One classic study of IQ and earnings, by economists Jeffrey S. Zax and Daniel I. Rees and based on data from Wisconsin, finds that, on average, one IQ point predicts less than a 1 percent increase in lifetime earnings. Overall, associating one IQ point with about a 1 percent increase in lifetime earnings is a slightly generous estimate of the correlation, as in some studies the point higher in IQ correlates only with a 0.5 percent increase in lifetime earnings. In sum, more IQ just doesn't convert into that much more money.[11]

Or for another result, a study co-authored by Nobel laureate in economics James Heckman found that moving from the 25th to 75th percentile for intelligence was correlated with a 10 to 16 percent boost in earnings. That 10 to 16 percent pay gap is a pretty modest difference in living standards (pre-tax, by the way!), and you would readily expect to find much bigger pay differences among those living on a typical American block, or between a starting salary and what an individual might earn after a year or two of raises in a typical job.[12]

Alternatively, you might consider a recent study on Canadian earnings. The math here is a little more complex, but the main result is that a one-standard-deviation increase in cognitive ability corresponds to an earnings boost of 13 to 16 percent. Again, that's a fairly large difference in smarts corresponding to only a modest difference in wages. In other words, we are looking at individuals who are pretty different but not extremely different in terms of intelligence, and finding they earn only a small amount more or less.[13]

Yet another approach is to look at top achievers and see how smart they are, at least as we typically measure that concept through intelligence tests. That is hard to do because the data are difficult to find, yet there is one study of Swedish CEOs, based on very good data, that does exactly this. The main results are that the median or "most typical" small-company CEO is above 66 percent of the Swedish population in cognitive ability, and the median large-company CEO is above 83 percent of the Swedish population in cognitive ability. In both cases those individuals are smarter than average, but they are not in the top 5 percent, much less the top 1 percent. So at least when it comes to CEOs, even very high achievers, at least as measured by their intelligence scores, are not as smart as you might think.[14]

There is also a sizable academic literature on intelligence and job performance. The most measured and thoughtful study is by Ken Richardson and Sarah H. Norgate and is titled "Does IQ Really Predict Job Performance?" IQ need not be the same thing as general intelligence, but the researchers' conclusions are pretty sobering: "In primary studies such correlations [between IQ and job performance] have generally left over 95% of the variance unexplained."[15]

So to put it another way, chasing high-IQ hires with few other considerations is not a good way to find talent. The general danger is that smart people—and maybe you are one of them—overrate the importance of smarts. Perhaps that is not a huge surprise.

Intelligence Is Often Priced into the Market

Another reason not to obsess over intelligence per se is that often it is priced into the market. Most people value some kind of smarts, so if you just go running after the people who are obviously smart, you may find you are paying full price for them. The obviously smart people are not always the obvious bargains.

Consider an analogy from finance. What if someone told you to "buy up the stock of companies full of really smart people"? That is not good advice. You can believe in the importance of smarts all you want, but quality companies also tend to have expensive share prices, and that will be true of these companies full of smart people too, at least insofar as those smarts really matter. Economists have known for a long time there are no extra gains to be had from investing by running after positive qualities but neglecting price. The key instead is to find undervalued companies, and that means companies with hidden virtues. The importance of hidden virtues holds for quality hires as well, whether the dimension in question is smarts or something else.

In some cases, a phenomenon known as "winner's curse" may mean that you end up overpaying when you get into bidding wars. If a number of companies are bidding for the same worker, the company most likely to win is the one that overvalues that worker and ends up paying too much. Even when the winner does not overbid relative to quality, the resulting gains from winning a bidding war may not be what you expect either.

How much you should chase after a particular talent marker depends on the nature of your business and the source of your profit. Let's say you have a powerful brand name, or a special location that your competitors cannot easily copy, and thus high returns. In that case, you do not need to profit from your particular hiring decisions; you just need workers who can keep the franchise up and running. It works perfectly fine to pay the going market rate for talented individuals—and that can include smarts—and you don't need to work hard to beat the market assessment. Your business has other virtues going for it, and you need to keep those virtues intact; going for the safe hires and paying full price for that talent is fine as a strategy.

Alternatively, your business model might be based on the superior picking of talent, as in the case of venture capital firms or sports teams. Then it is not good enough to pay the prevailing market price for ordinary measures of talent, and you need to think about going beyond readily available information to find the undiscovered gems. For instance, the three-time NBA champion Stephen Curry was picked no higher than seventh in the 2009 draft, right after the now-unknown Jonny Flynn, but Curry is headed for the Hall of Fame. At the time of the draft, Curry seemed too short, and when he arrived in the pros, he was not an obvious star and was injury-prone at first. So you can't just look at a person's underlying statistics and expect a revelation; you have to think carefully about how to select for the particular kinds of intelligence you really care about. It was not obvious in 2009, but Stephen Curry had not only an amazing athleticism but also the off-the-charts basketball intelligence to practice and master the deep three-point shot in a way that no one had before.

If you need to be talked down out of obsessing over intelligence and talked back into the importance of understanding context, look at many other jobs. How about U.S. president? To get even close to being president, you probably have to be pretty smart, at least along some dimensions, such as knowing how to appeal to enough of the public to get elected. But within that range of individuals, how much do smarts really matter for the job? Well, the data do not obviously support the view that the smarter presidents were the better presidents. Historians, for instance, typically have regarded Woodrow Wilson, Richard M. Nixon, and Jimmy Carter as three of the intellectually smartest presidents of the twentieth century. We don't intend to start political arguments here, but the records of these individuals are at best mixed by most reasonable standards. Wilson brought more racist and segregationist practices to government, he cartelized parts of the economy (temporarily), and his World War I legacy paved the way for World War II. Nixon had some significant achievements in foreign policy and with the Clean Air Act, but he was an inveterate liar and he was forced to resign, mired in scandal and disgrace; nonetheless, the level of intellect and literacy displayed in his books was remarkable. Jimmy Carter is one of the harder cases to debate, but many view him as a failed one-term president, weak in foreign affairs, who left America with a legacy of high inflation, high interest rates, and a troubled economy; maybe that wasn't his fault, but he is not an obvious example of a successful American president.

Partisans will disagree about which American presidents were successful, but Franklin Delano Roosevelt and Ronald Reagan are two common picks (obviously the choice depends on the party and ideology of the person being asked). Neither was intellectual in the traditional sense, and while each certainly had plenty of shrewdness, they are not typically considered the smartest of U.S. presidents either, at least not as might be measured by standardized testing.

We're not saying we should elect presidents with no consideration of their intelligence levels. Rather, we're pointing out that once we restrict our attention to people who have any chance at all of winning the presidency, other factors besides intelligence are very often more important.

You might look at the National Association of Colleges and Employers 2020 job outlook survey, where you will find more emphasis on intelligence, which is not surprising since the focus is on college graduates (a minority of Americans). The number one desired quality in hires is "problem-solving skills," which seems pretty clearly directly linked to intelligence. Still, next are "ability to work in a team" and "strong work ethic," and overall, seven of the top ten entries do not refer to intelligence. In this survey, intelligence clearly matters; it simply does not dominate in relevance.[16]

Okay, so that is our take on smarts. What about personality?

5

WHAT IS PERSONALITY GOOD FOR?
PART ONE: THE BASIC TRAITS

Elon Musk is not your ordinary guy. He has built and founded or co-founded multiple billion-dollar companies, including Pay-Pal, SpaceX, and Tesla. He has a plan to give the entire world internet access with Starlink, and he provided the initial capital for SolarCity, a successful solar venture. He founded The Boring Company to build tunnels. He has gone to space and back. He is also a co-founder of Neuralink and OpenAI. At times he is the richest man in the world. He also smoked pot on Joe Rogan's show (endangering his security clearance), tweeted what appeared to be obscenities at the Securities and Exchange Commission, and through shrewd publicity moves and tweets he took Dogecoin from a joke to (for a while) a highly valued crypto asset. You can't quite say "he does whatever he wants," but he probably comes closer to that designation than any other major player in the business world today. He also seems to have an extreme tolerance for risk.

Of course, most of the time you are not looking for the next

Elon Musk, which is fortunate, because quite possibly there is no next Elon Musk. Nonetheless, he demonstrates the importance of personality in extending one's reach and influence beyond what even a formidable intellect like his would have generated.

Which features of personality really matter in a given context, and which among them do people often overlook or fail to appreciate? What false assumptions do people hold about personality? This chapter will give our perspective on standard personality psychology and some of the most commonly discussed traits, whereas the next, more speculative, chapter will consider some more exotic and less well-tested personality concepts.

We'll start by dissecting the so-called Five Factor personality model, often used by Silicon Valley venture capital firms in evaluating talent. We'll then look at some of the buzzwords breathlessly cited in the media in describing traits necessary for workers of the future, who, we are told, have to be open, bold, and daring, or whatever else is the catchword of the day. Often those claims are correct to some degree, but *only within a particular context*. So one of the essential skills in thinking about personality is to be able to take a claim about personality and job and realize how that claim is context-dependent rather than universal.

We would put our view of the Five Factor model this way: if you've never heard of it or worked with it, it can teach you something, but at the same time, most of the practitioners who use or cite it tend to significantly overrate its effectiveness and overlook its limitations. To get this chapter written, Daniel and Tyler had to talk each other out of an extreme emphasis on the Five Factor model. In truth, both of us have ended up de-emphasizing the theory. Daniel benefited from having a sister who is a psychologist and understands the limits of predictive personality research. Tyler benefited from being an economist and knowing that economics is often more art than science, and that it typically fails to find universal predictive laws, including in the area of personality. After two years of debating the Five Factor model, this is what we ended up with.

Five Factor Personality Theory

Five Factor theory aims to boil down human personalities to their simplest and most intuitively understandable explanatory components. The dominant form of this theory, which is sometimes used to categorize potential hires, presents five major categories for understanding personality: neuroticism, extraversion, openness, agreeableness, and conscientiousness. Those five factors are complex, and subject to much debate, but here are some shorthand definitions:

Neuroticism
A general tendency to experience negative emotions and negative affect, including fear, sadness, embarrassment, anger, guilt, and disgust.

Extraversion
High extraversion will be manifest in terms of an outgoing personality, friendliness and sociability, talkativeness, and a proactive desire to engage with other individuals.

Openness to Experience
This trait involves open-mindedness, a willingness to explore new and diverse ideas, an experimental bent, curiosity, and an active imagination looking to conceive of additional possibilities.

Agreeableness
High agreeableness means a desire to get along with others, to help them, to be sympathetic with them, and to cooperate.

An individual low in agreeableness is more likely to be competitive and also contrarian.

Conscientiousness

High-conscientiousness individuals have high self-control, are very responsible, have a strong sense of duty, and usually are good at planning and organizing, due to their reliability.

Commonly, the very top venture capitalists, when seeking a hitherto undiscovered founder, will look for high disagreeableness and also high openness. The disagreeableness will motivate the individual to charge full steam ahead with a new idea, even when others are not convinced. The openness will make that person more of an innovator and more willing to accept feedback when needed.

To be clear, you should put aside knee-jerk judgments about which of these personality features might be "good" or "bad." Neuroticism may sound bad to you, and in some circumstances it is—but not unconditionally. If you are looking to hire a crusader on behalf of a social justice cause, someone who will notice injustices and then complain about them, neuroticism might be a desirable trait. Many of history's most important social movements were led by people who might count as highly neurotic in terms of Five Factor theory. We don't have formal information on how to classify, say, Joan of Arc, John Calvin, or Gandhi in terms of their personalities, but it does seem they were commonly regarded as pests or as prickly individuals. Again, context matters. Similarly, too much openness can suggest a lack of ability to distinguish between useful efforts and those that are not useful, agreeableness can suggest a lack of depth, and extraversion at the extreme can quickly become annoying . . . or not. You may need to *end up* with a judgment as to whether a particular set of qualities is desirable for a particular job, but you will handicap yourself intellectually if you *start* with a preordained take on whether these personality qualities are good or bad.

Furthermore, note that Five Factor theory de-emphasizes questions of motivation. Maybe you know people who are very conscientious when doing what they wish to do, but are otherwise pretty slack and unreliable. In fact, maybe that is *you*. (Or us? Tyler is highly motivated to seek out Indian classical music concerts, but not to clean up his office. Daniel is keen to run marathons, but less interested in waiting in line to buy concert tickets.) So again, Five Factor theory is just a starting point, and you will need to refer back to context. One of the most important questions about an individual is how that person's behavior varies across different contexts, and if anything, Five Factor theory discourages you from looking too closely into that matter.

What Is Five Factor Theory Good For?

As for how well Five Factor personality theory predicts earnings, one commonly accepted answer is that if you take fairly accurate readings of an individual's five personality factors, you can predict about 30 percent of the variation in earnings across individuals. In one of the highest-quality and best-known papers in this literature, the Big Five personality traits, taken together, predicted about 32 percent of the variation in career success as measured in terms of income.[1]

To make that statistical concept clear, if one variable fully explains another (for example, height measured in inches predicts height measured in centimeters *very* well), that variable would have 100 percent predictive power. Similarly, if one variable has nothing to do with another, it would have zero predictive power and thus explain none of the variation in the second variable (an example is that one flip of a fair coin does not predict the next flip at all). So predicting 32 percent of the variation in earnings is between those two performances, but it is not close to 100 percent.

Another of the sounder papers in this area considers data from the Netherlands and uses a different combination of five personality factors: extraversion, agreeableness, conscientiousness, emotional stability, and autonomy. That work is able to explain about 15 percent of the variation in earnings, so the 32 percent estimate is probably an upper bound, at least for the time being.[2]

One way to test these correlates between personality and earnings is to see if personality has a comparable impact on other measures of achievement—for instance, eminence in science. In one study of scientists, personality variables explained up to 20 percent of the variance in achievement, after adjusting for scientific potential and intelligence. That's not proof of how well personality variables predict wages, but it does show a broadly consistent picture regarding how much personality correlates with human success in mastering and climbing external hierarchies, whether those hierarchies concern pay or scientific recognition.[3]

Considering Five Factor theory as a whole, is explaining 15 to 32 percent of the variation in observed earnings a lot or a little? Does that make Five Factor theory strong or weak? Furthermore, remember that you are looking to fill a specific job, not just hiring a generic person for a generic job. For a specific job, personality could explain earnings by either more or less. Overall, you should not obsess over Five Factor theory, even though it is marginally useful.

For some further relevant results, you might consider a recent research paper based on Canadian wage data. Of the five factors,

only conscientiousness and neuroticism are statistically significant for predicting wages. A one-standard-deviation increase
in conscientiousness is associated with a 7.2 percent wage
boost, and a one-standard-deviation increase in neuroticism is
associated with 3.6 percent lower wages (again, standard deviation is a measure of statistical variance; refer back to Chapter
4 or see Google for an explanation). In our view, those results
hardly show an overwhelming performance for the personality
variables. We are back again to talent selection being an art at
least as much as a science.[4]

As for the reliability of this work: the studies on personality traits and life outcomes do replicate to a reasonable degree
(that is, redoing the studies yields roughly the same answers—
something that is unfortunately not always the case with academic
research). A study by psychologist Christopher J. Soto, of Colby
College, found that "87% of the replication attempts were statistically significant in the expected direction." Furthermore, the
results about personality and earnings discussed throughout this
chapter have been replicated in laboratory experiments where
people play games for cash prizes. In that setting, neuroticism is
associated with lower earnings and conscientiousness with higher
earnings—both outcomes that are consistent with the results
from labor market data. The main difference in results is that in
an experimental setting, openness is no longer correlated with
earnings.[5]

One nice feature of this topic is that you don't have to obsess
too much as to whether correlation implies causality. Let's say
that everyone who showed up for an interview wearing pointed
shoes was a highly productive candidate. You can just hire them!
You don't need to worry about whether pointed shoes cause productivity, productivity induces people to put on pointed shoes,
or other variables that have an effect on the relationship (per-

haps smart parents both send their kids to good schools *and* buy them pointed shoes). For our purposes, the causal story, or lack thereof, very often is not of first-order importance. Our main enterprise is *prediction* of talent, and in that sense we can learn something from correlations without always understanding the underlying causal processes.

Another problem is that personality traits are difficult to measure. One sorry truth about personality psychology is just how much the key variables usually are measured simply by asking people about themselves. A variable such as conscientiousness, for instance, actually is referring to how conscientious a person claims to be when asked on a questionnaire. In that sense, a great deal of personality psychology is built on relatively thin foundations. Very often there is no better way to proceed, as the researchers will tell you, but this gives additional reason to take the results of personality psychology with a grain of salt.

Furthermore, even well-trained interviewers cannot always divine personality traits from interviews. So however much you might be skeptical of the methods used in personality psychology, you yourself may not be outperforming those same flawed methods. In one study, there was a modest correlation between interviewer assessments and self-assessments of the candidates (0.28), though the interviewers could not evaluate the candidates as well as their close friends could—again, measuring both against the person's self-assessment. Interestingly, the two traits hardest for the interviewers to assess were conscientiousness and emotional stability, most likely because candidates actively manage those impressions during the interview process itself. Faking behavior in interviews is frequent and usually undetected.[6]

In particular, just about everyone knows they ought to be trying to fake conscientiousness, so that is one reason to be wary of your interview impressions. Unless you devote serious time to interviewing references, often you don't have a good sense of conscientiousness in advance; it's something you learn about after the hire is made. For this reason, we view "looking for conscientiousness" as overrated in the hiring process, even when conscientiousness is important for the job. Or when conscientiousness truly does matter, make sure you interview the person's references as well, a topic we cover in more detail later.

By the way, before we move on, you might be wondering why we should bother with all these personality categories and how they're measured. Can't we go right to the human genome instead and scientifically determine from it what a person "is really like"? Well, some researchers have been trying to do just that, and to date, they have been unsuccessful. One recent study concluded: "The attempts to identify specific genetic variants underlying the heritable variation in entrepreneurship have until now been unsuccessful." Someday that may change, but for the foreseeable future, genetic shortcuts are not available to us, and that makes the art of talent selection all the more important.[7]

Particular Personality Traits and Their Importance

Personality, such as the traits specified by Five Factor theory, probably matters most when you consider founders and entrepreneurs, individuals tasked with creating an enterprise and seeing it through to some level of maturity. The stakes are higher in the first place, and the high rates of start-up failure suggest that not everybody is good at these jobs. Those individuals must show initiative and daring, and they must wish to impose their will on the world in some way. At the same time, they will be called upon to perform many different duties and take on many different roles, often with no advance warning. They must be flexible and resourceful at a very deep level, open in some critical ways, yet stubborn and unyielding too, with high levels of discipline when needed.

Perhaps the most underrated challenge of being a founder comes from having "hung their name on the door." Unlike an employee, the founder often derives their sense of personal self-worth from the success of their venture. Failures and setbacks hit particularly hard when there's nobody else to blame. Great founders productively gain knowledge and momentum from their experiences, even the failures, and that requires a great degree of energy, curiosity, and power. Those are some pretty complex personality characteristics—they are not always easy to spot, and they can be very hard to find in the first place. Sam Altman, the former head of the venture capital firm Y Combinator, offers his own take on the idiosyncrasies of founders:[8]

> I look for founders who are scrappy and formidable at the same time (a rarer combination than it sounds); mission-oriented, obsessed with their companies, relentless, and determined; extremely smart (necessary but certainly not sufficient); decisive, fast-moving, and willful; courageous, high-conviction, and willing to be misunderstood; strong communicators and infectious evangelists; and capable of becoming tough and ambitious.
>
> Some of these characteristics seem to be easier to change than others; for example, I have noticed that people can become much tougher and more ambitious rapidly, but people tend to be either slow movers or fast movers and that seems harder to change. Being a fast mover is a big thing; a somewhat trivial example is that I have almost never made money investing in founders who do not respond quickly to important emails.
>
> Also, it sounds obvious, but the successful founders I've funded believe they are eventually certain to be successful.

Of course, we must look beyond founders, and then we may see that a single dimension of personality is much more important than the others in certain contexts. If you are hiring a cashier, the conscientiousness of that person probably is more important than their curiosity or openness to new ideas. (In fact, the person who is very open to new ideas might be bored more quickly by that job and thus be a worse candidate.) You don't need a complete personality profile if you're hiring a cashier, but you do need to know if they will show up and do the job properly with a good attitude. On the other hand, elite fighter pilots may need a certain amount of daring and bravado. Tom Wolfe, in his study of such pilots, *The Right Stuff*, cited this view: "Hell, we wouldn't give you a nickel for a pilot who hasn't done some crazy rat-racing [informal drag races] like that. It's all part of the right stuff." You want those individuals to show up for battle in perfect shape, but in some regards they will deviate significantly from the classical understanding of conscientiousness.[9]

Perhaps the best and most accurate study we have for personality psychology and earnings focuses on the very top of the IQ distribution, but the data and methods are good, so let's take another look at a study we already mentioned in the intelligence chapter. Miriam Gensowski, at the University of Copenhagen, revisited a data set chosen from California students in grades 1–8 in 1921–22, covering students from the top 0.5 percent of the IQ distribution (then scores of 140 or higher, covering 856 men and 672 women). The students also were rated on their personality traits, along lines similar to those of Five Factor theory, such as openness to experience, conscientiousness, extraversion, agreeableness, and neuroticism. Yes, 1921–22 was a long time ago, but that means we have very good data on final career outcomes, running through 1991 (it also means we focus on men, because labor markets for women have changed so much in terms of opportunity and discrimination).[10]

One prominent result in this data set was that conscientiousness really mattered for earnings. The men who measured as one standard deviation higher on conscientiousness on average earned $567,000 more over their careers, which measures as 16.7 percent higher average lifetime earnings (though again, we cannot be sure this is a causal relationship).

Extraversion also is correlated with higher earnings. Those men who were higher in extraversion by one standard deviation earned, over their careers, $491,100 more. Furthermore, the earnings premium from extraversion was the highest for the most highly educated of the men.

As for agreeableness, it turns out that the more agreeable men in this data pool earned significantly less. Being one standard deviation higher on agreeableness is correlated with a reduction in lifetime earnings of about 8 percent, or $267,600. While that result is confirmed only for high-IQ individuals in California for a particular span of the twentieth century, it is broadly consistent with the results of other studies, some of which have been cited here already. These people might just not be aggressive enough in pushing their own case forward, instead preferring to go with the flow.

Furthermore, a systematic study of venture capital pitches yielded some broadly similar results about agreeableness. The study looked at 1,139 venture capital pitches from 2010 to 2019, using machine-learning techniques to categorize the styles of the pitches. The main result was that venture capitalists like to hear very positive, optimistic pitches, but the people making those pitches underperform when it comes to actual results. So don't be too swayed by agreeableness, because very often it doesn't deliver on its promises. The disagreeable founders, who will tell you that you have it all wrong and that the world is badly screwed up and on the wrong track, may end up doing better.[11]

These data show another interesting feature: when personality matters (in terms of correlates) and when it does not. Personality traits correlate more strongly with income beginning when workers are in their early thirties, and the correlations peak in strength between the ages of forty and sixty, after which the correlations dwindle considerably. We are not sure how to interpret those results, but one speculation is that it takes a while for your most distinctive personality traits to fully blossom (or fester?), and also that there is an eventual evening-out of personality with extreme maturity.

Since Gensowski's study focuses only on high-IQ individuals, it is worth considering some other results to see if they are broadly consistent. For instance, one well-known study of Finnish identical twins finds that the more extroverted or the more conscientious of a pair of twins tends to earn more—roughly about 8 percent more for an increase of one standard deviation in those personality traits. Furthermore, the more neurotic of the two twins tends to earn less. Neuroticism harms earnings in part because the more neurotic individuals seem to have a tougher time staying with the same job long enough to acquire seniority and climb the ladder. A one-standard-deviation difference in the neuroticism score tends to lower expected earnings by about 8 percent.[12]

Those results are broadly consistent with the literature as a whole. It is a common result, for instance, that high conscientiousness predicts career success, as do low neuroticism, low agreeableness, and high extraversion. But again, keep in mind that context matters when it comes to most hiring decisions. It is unlikely, for instance, that low agreeableness is a positive for all jobs, and perhaps it is not a positive for most jobs.[13]

The research on personality has produced some incomplete

results regarding which personality factors are most useful for which particular kinds of jobs. These correlations have not, in general, been confirmed through reliable replication, but they are interesting as partial results or speculations. In one study, for instance, the researchers looked at West Point cadets and found that grade point average predicts early promotion better than cognitive ability does. This holds over a sixteen-year time horizon.[14]

The researchers sum up some additional results as follows:[15]

> For professionals, only Conscientiousness scales appear to be predictive of overall job performance. Similarly, for sales jobs, only Conscientiousness and its facets of achievement, dependability, and order predict overall performance well. For skilled and semi-skilled jobs, in addition to Conscientiousness, Emotional Stability appears to predict performance. For police and law enforcement jobs, Conscientiousness, Emotional Stability, and Agreeableness are useful personal characteristics. In customer service jobs, all the Big Five dimensions predict overall job performance. Finally, for managers, the Extraversion facets dominance and energy, and the Conscientiousness facets achievement and dependability, are predictive. Thus, different sets of personality variables are useful in predicting job performance for different occupational groups.

There is yet another specific result that is easy to believe: that charisma is important for CEOs but not for CFOs, with COOs falling in as an intermediate case between the two. Yet another paper compared GitHub contributors with tennis players, using linguistic analysis. (GitHub is an institution, now part of Microsoft, that allows individuals to post a kind of resume of their programming achievements). It turns out that GitHub contributors are high in openness and low on conscientiousness, agreeableness, and extraversion, while the successful tennis players were the exact opposite for each trait. One look at the literature on emergency personnel and high-reliability occupations (e.g., airline pilot, military) recommends high extraversion, high conscientiousness, and low neuroticism for those jobs.[16]

As for what predicts success in science, as measured by publications and citations (and distinct from earnings), scientists as a whole are conscientious, achievement-oriented, emotionally stable, and low in neuroticism compared to the general population. None of that comes as a huge surprise. Interestingly, eminent scientists are more likely to be dominant, arrogant, hostile, and self-confident compared to scientists as a whole. They are also more flexible in thought and behavior than scientists of lesser laurels. That is consistent with our more general view (presented in more detail shortly) that conscientiousness may be more important for tasks of lesser import and less important for leadership positions.[17]

Caveat emptor, of course, but still, those are starting points for your own pondering and talent search. Finally, before moving on, we would like to stress one very basic point about the importance of good ethics and honesty. We can go back to Marc Andreessen, who offers one of the best and least contingent good pieces of hiring advice you can find:

Ethics are hard to test *for*.

But watch for *any* whiff of less than stellar ethics in any candidate's background or references.
    And avoid, avoid, avoid.

Unethical people are unethical by nature, and the odds of a metaphorical jailhouse conversion are quite low.

This advice is so universal because bad ethics in a workplace can spread like cancer. Your ethical people will be repulsed by the behavior of the bad-ethics hire. And the bad-ethics people you have around—probably you have hired some—will find reason to behave worse and worse. There is little upside to hiring an unethical person, and the more talented that person is, the more trouble he or she may end up bringing (with an incompetent unethical person, perhaps the discontent will spread less far).

One study of the matter considered 58,542 workers and found that about one in twenty workers eventually is terminated for being a "toxic worker." Toxicity is defined in terms of behaviors such as sexual harassment, workplace violence, falsifying documents, fraud, and other "egregious" instances of misbehavior on the job. Unfortunately, toxic workers encourage others to be toxic as well. In part because of the contagion effect, it seems that the costs of having a single toxic worker are greater than the benefits of replacing an average worker with a superstar worker. Of course, talent search isn't just about finding the stars; it is also about avoiding the lemons.[18]

The main scenario in which hiring an unethical person makes sense is when you yourself have a fundamentally unethical business model. But then we don't really wish to give you advice at all.

In Which Contexts Is Conscientiousness Overrated?

Conscientiousness is, of the five factors, the single best predictor of overall job performance.[19] Nonetheless, there are some reasons you should be suspicious of conscientiousness as an end-all and be-all for job search.

First, as we discussed in the chapter on intelligence, non-cognitive skills tend to matter more for lower earners. In essence, it seems that conscientiousness is correlated with people being employed, which is good, but it doesn't do so much to boost their prospects of rising into the higher echelons of earnings. As we've noted, in the bottom tenth of earners, non-cognitive skills matter two and a half to four times more than do cognitive skills, but for the population in general (based on data from Sweden), a boost of one standard deviation in cognitive ability is associated with a larger wage gain than is a one-standard-deviation rise in non-cognitive skills. At higher levels of earnings, the relationship between cognitive ability and wages becomes increasingly significant.[20]

Second, conscientiousness can end up distributed in the wrong places, or at least in places where you as an employer may not want it, just as we earlier mentioned with the issue of motivation. A new hire may be very conscientious with respect to assembling his manga collection, or attending every local electronica concert, or swimming for two hours every day. The novelist Vikram Seth has said that he ended up writing his masterpiece, *A Suitable Boy*, because he did not have enough conscientiousness to finish his economics Ph.D. at Stanford. But that points out the need to ask the question "Conscientiousness *for what?*" He did finish a very long novel (and subsequent works) and work very hard on its quality, and the book went on to be a bestseller and also a literary classic. As Seth said: "Obsession keeps me going." He eventually developed the *right* obsession and piled hard work on top of that.[21]

It is a sorry truth that work responsibilities and family responsibilities may conflict. Arguably many performers at the very top neglect their families or are somewhat estranged from them. As a boss or talent selector, what exactly are you looking for? We can't presume to offer up the correct ethical judgment here, but conscientiousness does not always operate in your commercial favor, and it does not always boost extreme talent at the very top levels of performance.

Another possible downside is that some conscientious people stick to the job because they enjoy the familiar work process for its own sake. That keeps them on track and has some upside, but some of them end up piling on work for its own sake and taking delight in the satisfaction of process per se. Tasks end up taking more time rather than less, even though you observe the person working diligently the whole time. In the longer run, your organization can become less dynamic and more bureaucratic, in part because the people are doing exactly as they have been told.

The concept of "externalizing behavior"—that is, directing emotions and motivations outward—is linked to aggression and hyperactivity, and it is very often a bad thing. Nonetheless, for many individuals, especially for many men, such externalizing behavior predicts higher earnings, and you can think of this point as related to the virtues of disagreeableness. For these men, the externalizing behavior predicts both lower educational attainment and higher earnings; in other words, don't always look for superior performance in school. John Lennon was a talented writer as well as a brilliant musician, and effective as a marketer and media celebrity, but also, in his youth, he was an aggressive, drunken brawler. It is no accident that after the Beatles split up he wrote the song "How Do You Sleep?" eviscerating his former bandmate and collaborator Paul McCartney. And yet Lennon was one of the most successful musical stars of the twentieth century.[22]

The search for a rebellious, disagreeable outsider is common in venture firms too. Marc Andreessen of Andreessen Horowitz looks for similar traits, though with an outsider flair of his own. Andreessen's utensil is a little bit more dopaminergic. A famous night owl, he is someone who speaks quickly, eats quickly, and attempts to tug on the strings of reality faster than the universe will permit. He is equal parts cheery and angry at the same time, embodying contradictions in a manner that seems common among the top talent in venture capital. Note that Marc is paired with Ben Horowitz in the firm Andreessen Horowitz. Whereas Marc is bubbly and exuberant, Ben comes across as quieter, more establishment, and more corporate in his orientation. The mix works, in part because they trust each other so intensely, and they can read each other's signals in a millisecond. The normal, conscientious person is not exactly their typical pick for success; instead, they are looking for people who are true outliers.[23]

Note also that the connection between conscientiousness and cooperation seems to be low or maybe zero in some data sets, as we discussed in Chapter 4. If in a team endeavor conscientiousness does not feed into cooperation, it may be of less value than you thought. The conscientious worker still might show up on time and perform some basic duties, but the upside of the resulting teamwork will be limited. One reason conscientiousness might perform so poorly in predicting cooperation is that conscientiousness has numerous facets, and one of those facets is a kind of *cautiousness*. In some settings, cautiousness may induce individuals to cooperate less rather than more, for fear that others will not cooperate in turn, or perhaps because the cooperative act is a deviation from a set, known program. Many real-world instantiations of cooperation require some proactive behavior and indeed boldness, and the conscientious person is not always the bold one.

Here is a useful comparison to shake up your thinking about conscientiousness. Are you familiar with the hardworking nation of South Korea, which rose from poverty to wealth in less than two generations? Yet if you rank workers, nation by nation, according to their reported conscientiousness, South Korea—surprisingly, to many people—comes in second to last. Nonetheless, if you rank nations by work hours, South Korea comes in first. What does that mean? Are the metrics worthless? Or maybe South Koreans work hard because of money and social pressures and not because of innate characteristics? More generally, if you look at the rank-ordering table of all measured nations, there is no positive correlation between conscientiousness and hours worked; in fact, there is a (statistically insignificant) negative correlation. Again, that may mean conscientiousness is not as useful as you might have thought. Perhaps you want some workers who are not so conscientious but who respond readily to incentives and will end up doing what you tell them to. If the non-conscientious can mimic the behavior of the conscientious, at least under the right circumstances, perhaps conscientiousness is not always the best variable to look for. It may even embody a certain lack of flexibility.[24]

To push your skepticism further, another recent study found no connection between conscientiousness and the practice of mask-wearing during the coronavirus pandemic in Spain. Maybe there is something wrong with these studies, but an alternative possibility is that the research concept of conscientiousness has been so finely honed that it is replicable across time and across different methods of evaluation, but in the process it has become somewhat disconnected from the commonsense understanding of that term.[25]

Sometimes leaders of organizations can have too much rather than too little conscientiousness. We are not saying that all of these leaders need to be crooks, but leadership skills often involve a mix of creativity and daring and ability to reimagine the risky future, and those are not necessarily the traits found in the people who punch the time clock promptly every day. Elon Musk would have gotten in less trouble had he not smoked a joint on the live video stream of Joe Rogan's podcast, but a more sedate Elon Musk probably would not have built SpaceX and Tesla with the same fervor. Sometimes the leaders are the ones who need to decide when the rules can be broken, or at least bent. Consistent with that view, meta-studies suggest that conscientiousness is less important as a predictor of job success for more complex tasks and for higher-level positions. We wonder if conscientiousness is somewhat overrated for leaders and creators, and perhaps a degree of neuroticism is somewhat underrated as a correlate with job performance. It is a recurring theme of this book that what predicts well for the median worker is not always what predicts well for the top performers and the stars.[26]

Finally and perhaps most importantly, as a potential employer, you are not necessarily wanting to predict an individual's wage per se, for reasons we explained in the previous chapter. Let's say, for instance, that being conscientious explains a good deal of the wage in your particular sector, and that you know this for sure. But it is still the case that you, as an employer, don't necessarily want to hire high-wage individuals per se; rather, you wish to hire *undervalued* individuals. And there is not much serious research in Five Factor theory to help you identify those individuals, in part because it is hard to measure an individual's true net contribution to profits, that being relative to the wage you must pay. Most of all, the idea of hiring conscientious or hardworking individuals is hardly a novel one, so if there are any qualities that are reflected in the going market wage for an individual, you would expect conscientiousness and being a hard worker to be among them. Conscientiousness, in essence, is too easily and uniformly valued in the marketplace.

The Import of Stamina

We find it useful to contrast the concepts of conscientiousness, grit, and what we call *stamina*. We see stamina as one of the great underrated concepts for talent search, especially when you are looking for top performers and leaders and major achievers.

On stamina, economist Robin Hanson wrote: "It wasn't until my mid-30s that I finally got to see some very successful people up close for long enough to notice a strong pattern: the most successful have a *lot* more energy and stamina than do others. . . . I think this helps explain many cases of 'why didn't this brilliant young prodigy succeed?' Often they didn't have the stamina, or the will, to apply it. I've known many such people."[27]

Robin also points out that many high-status professions, such as medicine, law, and academia, put younger performers through some pretty brutal stamina tests in the early years of their career. In essence, they are testing to see who has the requisite stamina for subsequent achievement. (You might feel those tests are wasteful in some way, but still, those tests seem to survive in some very competitive settings.) Successful politicians are another group who seem to exhibit very high stamina levels—many of them seem to never tire of shaking hands, meeting new people, and promoting their candidacies. So if we meet an individual who exhibits stamina, we immediately upgrade the chance of that person having a major impact, and that the individual will be able to invest in compound returns to learning and improvement over time.

Bob Dylan is a good example of a famous individual who has incredible stamina. He has studied folk and blues music obsessively since he was a teenager, and he has put out dozens of albums over a period now stretching almost sixty years, mastering both folk guitar and lyrics, and experimenting with a variety of styles ranging from folk to rock to pop to gospel to blues and American popular standards. He has starred or played in several movies, worked as a DJ for satellite radio (picking excellent material), written a compelling memoir, won a Nobel Prize for literature, published eight books of drawings and paintings and had exhibits in major art galleries, and it seems he has been on tour constantly for decades (the "Never Ending Tour"), in the 1990s and 2000s often playing a hundred or more dates a year. He continues to give concerts (at least pre-COVID), even though he is eighty years old as of late 2021. You may or may not love his work, but there is a guy who's got stamina, and he has made a major impact on both music and the broader world.

Or consider John le Carré, the spy thriller author. *Washington Post* reporter John Leen spent two weeks with him in Miami, investigating the local crime scene with le Carré's assistance. At the end of that temporary partnership he wrote: "I was astonished by his energy, his drive, his ability to go out there every day and trundle through the hours of interviews, lunches, dinners. I was a little more than half his age and I was exhausted. He never appeared tired, never was less than sharp and penetrating. He already had half a dozen No. 1 bestsellers and more money than he could ever spend. Why did he want or need another one? What kept him out there, what was the engine that drove it all?"[28]

Sometimes the literature speaks of "grit," but we find "stamina" to be a more accurate term. Grit is sometimes defined as "passion and perseverance for long-term goals of personal significance," but that involves two dimensions, the passion and the perseverance. Furthermore, it turns out that grit is strongly correlated with conscientiousness. The one feature of grit that still seems to matter statistically, after adjusting for conscientiousness, is perseverance of effort, not passion. That result is close to what we are calling stamina, and so the stamina concept seems to transcend conscientiousness and to be the more relevant portion of grit. Ideally, what you want is a kind of conscientiousness directed at the kind of focused practice and thus compound learning that will boost intelligence on the job.[29]

Even for what are supposedly "unskilled" jobs (not a term we would in general endorse) stamina really can matter. Consider Dworsky, a sales guy from another company at Daniel's pre-pandemic San Francisco office. During the lockdown, a colleague asked Dworsky to take care of a plant; he responded by watering all sixty plants in the office every morning. In secret. It was just the sort of thing he felt compelled to do, for reasons that had to do with his intrinsic motivation. The people at Pioneer call this "Dworsky strength" because the default musculature is so strong, you do a lot without realizing it is a lot. In this case, all of those plants ended up being watered. No matter what the level of the hire, look for Dworsky strength.

Because stamina can matter a good deal, and because stamina can be so hard to read in a short interaction, this is yet another reason to interview a person's references. Remember our saying "Personality is revealed on weekends"? Well, a person's references often have a pretty good idea of what that individual is up to on weekends, or weekdays for that matter. A judgment of stamina in particular may require observation over longer periods of time, and so your skills as an interviewer need to be multifaceted and directed toward the references as well.

6

WHAT IS PERSONALITY GOOD FOR? PART TWO: SOME MORE EXOTIC CONCEPTS

Five Factor personality theory offers a general guide for starting to think about personality—and it is also a set of checks and balances, in case your intuition gets too carried away with your own pet theory of what really matters. But there is yet another use of personality psychology: namely, as a way of developing a common language so that you and your team can discuss and evaluate claims about personality. We suggest using Five Factor theory in this manner. When hiring or otherwise looking for talent, doing interviews, or meeting prospective partners, ask your team how individual candidates fare in terms of those categories. That will give you one very quick take on what the person is good at or not, and it will give you a framework for comparing one candidate to another and for matching candidates to the qualities required for particular jobs. Five Factor theory is thus an *entry point* for talking and thinking about people rather than a comprehensive theory of how much people will earn or a clear formula for assessing their creative value.

Most of all, Five Factor theory is useful because it is a "sticky" language, one that your co-workers can readily adopt, share, and eventually innovate upon. The five categories make intuitive sense to most people, and they are captured in memorable words and phrases. Simply having such a common language in the hiring or talent search process is most of the value in the concept.

Many researchers have criticized or tried to revise the Five Factor model. For instance, it has been argued that there is a sixth and culturally specific factor that is of relevance to East Asia and especially China: a tradition factor. Furthermore, there are numerous variants on the theory, some including as many as sixteen basic personality factors; of course, the more factors you add to your basic theory, the more different cases you can cover and the more explanatory power you can generate.[1]

But our goal here is simpler—namely, to create the proper framework for discourse among your team and come up with the factors that might matter *for you*. Even if a sixteen-factor model "predicts better" or is more useful in some research settings, it is probably not possible for your team to remember all sixteen factors (repeat after me, as a kind of tongue-twister, preferably without pause or consulting your notes: abstractedness, apprehension, dominance, emotional stability, liveliness, openness to change, perfectionism, privateness, reasoning, rule-consciousness, self-reliance, sensitivity, social boldness, tension, vigilance, and warmth). They will not become a common mode of discourse, and such a personality theory will, to those who work with you, seem like more of a cognitive burden than anything else. And besides: Why sixteen? Why not seventeen, eighteen, or more? Why not a separate list for every culture and region?

That all said, having the common language from Five Factor theory for personality discussions will help your team come up with new concepts that maybe aren't of general use but are relevant for the sector or institution you work in. If you are engaged in programming work, for instance, you might look for more specific forms of introversion that predict an individual's ability to lock him- or herself in a cave for a few days to meet a programming deadline—let's call that "Morlockism," after a character in H. G. Wells's novel *The Time Machine*. You may get a sense of a candidate's Morlockism from a well-done screen and interview, but we doubt it is going to have explanatory power in a broad-based earnings regression, and it will not force us to create a sixth major factor for theory. Yet for some employers, the concept is important.

To return back to the general point, personality theory—in its various guises—is a tool for mobilizing and communicating the dispersed knowledge to be found among your hiring network. So if you are going to modify Five Factor theory, or add to it, think more in terms of a useful language for your team rather than trying to reflect, replicate, or anticipate the latest academic results.[2]

If you are looking for a parallel from academic economics, consider economist Israel Kirzner's analysis of entrepreneurship, as outlined in his 1973 book *Competition and Entrepreneurship*. Kirzner stressed entrepreneurial "alertness" as a key variable behind good economic decisions, and here we have in mind alertness to the talent of others. For Kirzner, alertness is a kind of insight that cannot be reduced to mere hard work or deliberative search or formal rules but rather reflects a special ability of perception. But where does this alertness come from? You need to have some potential categories at hand, even if you end up rejecting those categories as universal explainers. Talent alertness derives from having a broad variety of conceptual matrices, empirical results, and regularities at your disposal. The broader and better your toolbox, the more likely the "aha!" moment is to strike you when you are looking for talent.

In the previous chapter we already mentioned stamina as a useful category for analysis. Here are a few more personality categories we have found to be of use or of interest for improving hiring discourse, within the context of what we are trying to accomplish in our various projects.

Compound Returns to Self-Improvement

Consistent with the import of stamina, as discussed in the previous chapter, look to see if a person shows signs of improvement each time you meet with them. Does the person have an obsession with continual self-improvement? Let's turn again to the words of venture capitalist Sam Altman:

> It's easiest if you get to meet people in person, several times. If you meet someone three times in three months, and notice detectable improvement each time, pay attention to that. The rate of improvement is often more important than the current absolute ability (in particular, younger founders can sometimes improve extremely quickly).[3]

The power of compound returns is important for human talent, just as it is for your stock portfolio. If a person improves, say, only 1 percent a year in terms of productivity, it will take about seventy years for that person's productivity to double. Probably you can't wait that long, and maybe a mere doubling isn't so impressive anyway. For that person, what you see is what you get. But say a person can improve by 35 percent a year. That is difficult for many people, but it is hardly utopian, especially for those who are young and/or intellectually flexible in the right ways. Those people will double in productivity every two years. And if their productivity is doubling every two years, after only eight years they are sixteen times more effective. That is how compound returns work. At first the power of the effect seems relatively small, but with the passage of time compound returns are highly significant.[4]

You might think that other evaluators already understand the power of compound returns to self-improvement, but there is good evidence that most individuals do not think very effectively in terms of exponential processes. If one economy grows at a slightly higher rate than another, say even a single percentage point, after a few decades the more rapidly growing economy is *much* wealthier. Early in the pandemic, many people, including policymakers, neglected the danger posed by the novel coronavirus because they were not good at thinking in exponential terms. The number of infections was growing rapidly, perhaps doubling as quickly as every five to seven days. When that is the case, "things seem fine right now" just doesn't cut it as a public health evaluation. The reality is that we wasted time in our preparations, not realizing just how quickly and powerfully this exponential process was going to come upon us.

One of your most significant skills as a talent evaluator is to develop a sense of when people are moving along a compound returns curve or not. So much of personality theory focuses on observing levels or absolute degrees of personality traits. You should instead focus on whether the person is experiencing positive rates of change for dynamism, intellect, maturity, ambition, stamina, and other relevant features.

If you are hiring a writer, look for signs that the person is writing literally every day. If you are hiring an executive, try to discern what they are doing *all the time* to improve their abilities at networking, decision making, and knowledge of the sectors they work in. In general, how open is a person to absorbing new ideas? Receiving critical feedback? Building small, resilient groups of peers who will motivate, inform, and mentor the candidate, expecting similar services in return? Again, don't just think in terms of levels of current ability, because over time, rates of change very often prove to be more important. Think in terms of trajectories. When it comes to a job or fellowship candidate, think about the person's developmental curve and whether the candidate is truly committed to consistent, perpetual self-improvement, as you might expect from a top athlete or musician.

As mentioned in the introduction, one question that Tyler likes to ask people is "What is it you do to practice that is analogous to how a pianist practices scales?" Tyler likes to think of many jobs in a way that a professional musician or athlete would find natural. By asking this question, you learn what the person is doing to achieve ongoing improvement, and again, as noted earlier, you might learn some tricks yourself. You also learn how the person *thinks* about continual self-improvement, above and beyond whatever particular practices they engage in. If a person doesn't seem to think much about self-improvement, they still might be a good hire, but then you had better be pretty content with their currently demonstrated level of expertise.

In response to this question, a few good answers might be: "I give practice talks to my friends to hone my speaking abilities," "I practice on obscure programming problems with no practical applications just to keep my skills fresh," or "I am building up my knowledge in a very small corner of science just to figure out what it means to learn something really well and thoroughly." A bad answer is simply "I don't know."

Here are some other categories we find useful for thinking about potential hires and affiliations.

Sturdiness

Sturdiness is the quality of getting work done every day, with extreme regularity and without long streaks of non-achievement. Sturdiness seems to be especially valuable in people working on longer-term projects. There is also evidence that sturdiness helps people make it through military training and also helps with jobs that involve high-stress management.[5]

You will note that sturdy people, in this sense of the word, often do not need much of what we have called Morlockism. Being perpetually early on deadlines is one of their distinguishing characteristics, and that is because they are working on the project from the very beginning.

If you are a writer, sturdiness is a very powerful virtue, even if you do not always feel you are being extremely productive. Imagine, for instance, that you are working on a book and you get one page done every day, but you do this every single day. That would give you 365 pages a year, which is longer than most books; furthermore, it is a pace that hardly any non-pulp author can match. If you ask Daniel to tell you about Tyler's productivity, sturdiness will play a prominent role in his account. After settling in at a hotel after a long day of travel, Tyler can be consistently found happily typing away on anything from a news column to a blog post or new book. (While for most people such feats of fecundity are commonly achieved with the help of caffeine, Tyler consumes no coffee or tea. The engine is within.)

Generativeness

Some people will call it ambition, some will call it extraversion, but there's a certain vitality to individuals that can be striking.

They talk quickly, move quickly, and in general seem to be enthralled with life. They run all possible combinations of ideas through their heads, if only to better understand the possibilities. Along these lines, they tend to be high in openness as a personality trait. We call this quality "generativeness."

If you hang around people like this, you are likely to come up with new ideas from your interactions. It is common, for instance, that a generative person talks about ideas that later blossom into companies, or perhaps policy proposals, or useful predictions about the future.

Being generative is a quality that is relatively high-status among the more intellectual segments of the Bay Area tech world. Balaji Srinivasan, the tech entrepreneur and crypto advocate, is a classic example of a person who is high in generativeness. He tweets his thoughts just about every single day on a wide variety of topics, ranging from media to crypto to the pandemic. A lot of it is speculative or maybe even wrong, but when he has a hit it is truly important. It is no accident that his predictions in January 2020 about the coronavirus crisis were so prescient: he foresaw that it would wreck society as we know it, kill many people, boost work from home, and lead to all of us wearing masks. That prescience arose because he was running all of the available information through his mind and exploring all of the different possibilities rather than adhering to fixed dogmas from the past. Will Balaji prove to be right about crypto? We do not share his degree of enthusiasm, but if you wish to hear the different scenarios for how crypto might evolve, Balaji is one of your go-to sources.

Generative people are valuable whether or not you agree with them, and they are often most valuable in the areas where you do not agree because there they will see possibilities that you will not.

Insecure Overachievement

Insecure overachievement, as we call it, is the (somewhat neurotic) quality of never quite feeling comfortable with your output, despite knowing at a deep level that it *is* good. The quality often comes with critical self-talk and a high level of aspiration. Since these individuals are never happy with themselves, despite high levels of achievement, they can be problematic team members. They can be very useful in motivating and disciplining those who need a further push, but often they push too hard and offer too few rewards for good performance — ever watch the ESPN special *The Last Dance* about Michael Jordan?

Insecure achievement often comes from family background, especially if the parents push the kids very hard, and sometimes it is associated with immigrant family backgrounds. One study of the psychosocial features of elite and super-elite Olympic athletes found they "came from families who strongly valued a culture of striving and achieving, while experiencing moderate sibling rivalry."[6]

Pessimistic Perfectionism

We've met plenty of smart people who, unfortunately, fall into the category of pessimistic perfectionists. Such individuals typically believe that their work is never good enough, and that their careers are either likely to fail or not meet a high enough standard. You can spot them when you see someone who is smart but never quite ready to put their work forward. They don't have the ongoing drive and impetus of insecure overachievers. Instead, it is common for individuals in this group to develop excuses and to sabotage their careers in advance, all so they don't have to keep on encountering feelings of ongoing failure. Somewhat counterintuitively, they fail preemptively, in order to get it over with and so they can feel they are in control along the way. For them, it is truly hard to push that "send" or "publish" button or whatever the equivalent may be.

Perhaps there are ways you can take advantage of the smarts of these individuals. Often they tend to be perceptive about human relationships (part of their problem may be an absence of self-deception; after all, most people are not world-class, but they may be more motivated if they overestimate their own prospects by a bit). But make sure you are not relying on them to be either the initiators or the finishers. Sometimes they can work well in teams where they contribute but don't feel so responsible for the final outputs or sign-off decisions.

Happiness (or Fun-ness)

Happiness is, in our opinion, an underrated quality to look for in people, at least when it comes to predicting their success. Always having a smile and a sense of amusement can be a powerful quality, ensuring that the person is almost always invited to participate in another endeavor. They're fun to be around. If you are a baseball fan, you may know that Chicago Cubs Hall of Famer Ernie Banks was renowned for saying "Let's play two!" — referring to his fondness for doubleheaders (two consecutive games in the same day). Commentator Scott Simon put it as follows: "It was a phrase he used to remind himself and other players that whatever their complaints, they got to play a game for a living, and hear the cheers of strangers. It was a reminder to all of us to cherish life and the chance to have work that gives enjoyment to others."[7]

Happiness or fun-ness is often an input into generativeness, because the people who play around with all of those new ideas typically find it entertaining to do so. But there is an entirely different class of person, not ideas-oriented by nature, who simply wants to get up in the morning and start tackling problems with gusto. They may well be steady, but there is a quality of "burst-ingness" to them as well, an effusion of positive sensibility and can-do attitude, infectious to so many of those who surround them.

Clutteredness

There is a particular kind of smart, often intellectual person who knows a lot and also works hard. But these people cannot express their ideas in clear, simple fashion. When you ask them questions, they will respond by piling new information on top of the old rather than by clarifying their initial point. Cluttered individuals have some real virtues, and they do often know a lot, as evidenced by the thickness of the clutter. But often it is not clear exactly how these individuals with cluttered minds can be deployed with highly positive productivity. Their words and writings are cluttered because their minds and thoughts are cluttered too.

By no means should you dismiss these individuals as potential contributors. But it is almost always a mistake to place them in positions that require clarity of thought and communication.

Vagueness and Precision

Distinct from the cluttered mind is the vague thinker. The cluttered person imposes too much baroque order on the relevant concepts and sees too many distinctions without ordering them clearly. In contrast, some minds are satisfied thinking in mushy concepts and unspecific terms and not really drawing any conceptual distinctions at all. The joy of discussion is so strong they forget to mirror the experience of the counterparty, leaving them confused as to what the discussion is even about. Vague thinkers are like the director of a film that was just too long—"What scene are we in?" And yet there is always more they are willing to say. Perhaps some of it is insightful, but it can be hard to edit and mobilize.

In contrast, many of those in the opposite camp are unsatisfied with vague, never-ending narratives and instead want laser-precise thoughts. Usually slightly more introverted, such people often aim more at conveying information than at creating camaraderie, and perhaps they may be a bit unwilling to explain the relevant points fully. To go back to the movie director analogy, people like this are constantly asking themselves if the film they're directing is entertaining to the audience of listeners. They take pride in speed and brevity. They're high in the "gettothepointplease" quotient, wonderfully exacting in their explications of relevant points though sometimes too terse for the comfort of all of their co-workers.

It may be worth asking yourself which bucket your candidate is in—and which bucket do you want them to be in? A vague thinker might be better as a salesperson, while a strategist might do better to be more analytical.

Precocity

When it comes to scientists, the evidence suggests that age of first publication correlates with the person's later productivity and prestige. Furthermore, Tyler believes that the age of first refereed journal *submission*—never mind publication—is predictive of later success as well. In most sports and in chess, precocity is pretty much required for success at high levels.[8]

As we will see in Chapter 8, precocity is a less reliable indicator of talent for women than it is for men. Furthermore, we don't think it is a good metric for all professions; for instance, great novelists and moral philosophers are not always wunderkinds. Older programmers can be saner and safer than younger programmers, which for many jobs (not all!) is an advantage. Precocity may predict well for areas that rely on fluid intelligence rather than synthetic or accumulated knowledge, and for areas where an early start and a long time trajectory is important for success. In any case, for the area you are hiring in, do ask how much precocity is required, or not.

Adhesiveness

The trait of adhesiveness, which overlaps with the concept of a "team player," is increasingly important as production grows more complex and roles become more specialized. Who can understand which kinds of efforts are needed for the team as a whole, then step up and supply them? Sometimes the phrase "glue guy" is used in sports, though this obviously includes "glue gals" and others. Social intelligence is at a premium, above and beyond whatever import you might assign to intelligence more generally. Team players tend to have a natural understanding of who is doing their job, who is slacking, who the leaders are in intra-firm groups, who is stepping out of line with aggressive behavior, and so on. Furthermore, they act on those intuitions to try to set things right. In one sense, we've been talking about team skills all along—for instance, with our treatment of ethics and also conscientiousness. Nonetheless, this ability to perceive group problems and to use social intelligence to step in to fix them is a distinct virtue. One recent study found that team skills add as much to productivity as does the overall intelligence of the group.[9]

One relatively straightforward way to find out about team skills is to ask about them: "Can you give us an instance where you perceived a team problem at work and stepped in to fix it? What exactly was your remedy?" Some people are capable of lying their way into an acceptable answer, but in reality a lot of the more clueless people (even if they are productive in other ways) just can't tell this kind of story because they don't think in socially adept terms. When testing for team players, see if the person has the skills to dissect and articulate a social problem in an institution and suggest its solution.

Other Traits

The value of the traits discussed in this chapter will vary according to the particular context of your industry and the position for which you are hiring. The most powerful advice we can give you is to work with your team to develop its own personality framework. Together, you should be able to come up with a common understanding of what matters in your context (as long as you're willing to question your assumptions) and a common language for discussing it with precision.

Which other traits can you think of?

One trait we would draw your attention to as especially important is *the ability to perceive, understand, and climb complex hierarchies*. This is another way of saying that a person is keen to understand and master what it takes to reach the top.

Tyler, for instance, is struck by many of the chess players he met as a teen. Many of them were smart, indeed brilliant, and they also had the ability to work on their own. Of course, they understood the idea of winning and losing, and winning and losing rating points, but it was hard for many of them to look outside the chess hierarchy and see that they weren't really headed anywhere fruitful. They saw only what was right before their faces. Chess gave them short-term positive feedback and a set of chess friends, and so they continued to pursue it locally, but too often they ended up at age forty-three with no real job, no health insurance benefits, and a future of steady decline. In contrast, Ken Rogoff was a great chess player but at some point left the game to become a Harvard professor and world-class economist—for much higher rewards, of course.

Or consider the world of early bloggers, inhabited by quite a few very smart and hardworking people. Some of them are still sitting in sweatpants in their parents' basement and writing some intriguing posts. But Ezra Klein saw that the sector was evolving, and so he helped found the website Vox, aspiring to a higher station by creating a start-up and later moving to *The New York Times*. Henry Farrell, of the blog *Crooked Timber*, helped found the blog *The Monkey Cage*, which continues to be published by *The Washington Post* and exercises great influence. Megan McArdle worked her way into being a columnist for *The Daily Beast*, Bloomberg, and then *The Washington Post*. Those are among the individuals who understood the hierarchies before them and developed strategies for climbing toward the top. Were they smarter than their bloggy competitors? Maybe. But what really set them apart was their ability to figure out new ways to climb the totem pole of achievement and to move from a narrower to a broader vision of what that totem pole really is.

When it comes to the start-up world, Daniel sees too many young people who are content to go to one conference after another, receiving positive feedback because they are bright and articulate and seem to have promise. They also may play around on Twitter, building a profile and garnishing likes and retweets. But which useful hierarchy are they actually climbing? The best prospects are more focused on their actual projects and the building of their companies. If they meet a famous founder, they are more likely to ask "How did you find and hire your first five employees?" and less likely to inquire about their attitudes toward meditation or Yuval Harari.

It is very easy for individuals to overshoot and focus on goals that are too small, such as the mechanics of how to keep the books or how to arrange the office. In academia, an assistant professor might spend time on cleaning up the data set (which is appropriate) but neglect to motivate the research by tying it into broader questions of actual import. Those are very different skills, and too often people will stick with the tasks they feel comfortable with. If someone is good at identifying, tackling, and climbing hierarchies, it is a sign they know how to allocate their efforts and that they don't let their insecurities blind themselves to the larger picture. It shows they are willing to take on the most relevant challenges, and if they are not good at those challenges initially, they will find the right help or invest in the proper self-education.

At the same time, other individuals choose goals that are too large and too indistinct, or which do not have useful intermediate outputs, test points, and checkpoints along the way. How would you feel about a job candidate who boldly announced "I am not interested in anything less than the elimination of all disease"? Even at the World Health Organization (*especially* at the World Health Organization), that is not a very practical attitude. Again, focusing on the "too large," like focusing on the "too small," is a sign that insecurities, blinders, and lack of perspective will prevent the person from climbing the relevant ladders of success.

Knowing how to perceive and climb the right hierarchies is one of the most stringent but also most universal tests available. It requires emotional self-regulation, perceptiveness, ambition, vision, proper sequencing, and enough order in one's activities to actually get somewhere. Whenever you see signs that a candidate has this skill, look much more closely. If anecdotes suggest cluelessness about hierarchies, give that person a significant downgrade, at least for all jobs requiring ongoing initiative and learning over time.[10]

Yet another underdiscussed personality feature is what re-searchers call "demand avoidance" (in some cases called "pathological demand avoidance," though in our view that's too value-laden a term). In its more practical (rather than clinical) sense, the term refers to people who have a hard time knuckling under to bosses. They perceive some workplace hierarchies *all too well* and suffer under them. Too many workplace requests become seen as impositions, and often unjust impositions as well. Such a view is by no means implausible, since most workplaces do place some unreasonable or at least inefficient demands on their workers, sometimes to an extreme. Many bosses and super-visors are indeed jerks, or worse. The problem, however, is that resentments can build because people with demand avoidance are not always sufficiently emotionally detached from the dep-redations of the modern workplace. They are not good at just "sucking it up" and getting on with the job. Their extreme per-ceptiveness can mean that many of their criticisms are justified, but that just makes their existential predicament all the harder.

On the bright side, demand avoidance sometimes spurs in-dividuals to start their own companies. If you don't like taking orders, well, you can be the boss—if you have the right stuff for an independent undertaking. Still, most people do not end up as the boss, not even within their divisions. Beware of potential ap-plicants who have demand avoidance. They can be very smart, very articulate, and super-sensitive, and for all those reasons they can make a great impression. Individuals with demand avoidance can be super-productive *if they find the right setting*, but those settings can be very specific. Many of them work as academics, or also as founders, and then there are many others who still go around cursing the boss and moving from one job to the next. Beware of this one, because it can trip you up rather easily, es-pecially if you have some demand avoidance yourself (as the boss!), and thus, you might relate to these individuals quite well. Just keep in mind that if you are the boss, they cannot be the boss as well.

One final trait we find important is something we call "selective agreeableness." Of the major concepts in Five Factor theory, as they typically are stated, agreeableness is the one we find the most problematic. If you will recall, the definition we gave earlier was: "High agreeableness means a desire to get along with others, to help them, to be sympathetic with them, and to cooperate. An individual low in agreeableness is more likely to be competitive and also contrarian." Many highly successful individuals have had a very strong disagreeable streak, such as Steve Jobs, who would berate team members because the designed product was not yet beautiful enough. Still, when we think about career success, whether at high or low levels, it is not obvious to us that a one-dimensional spectrum of agreeableness versus disagreeableness is the appropriate construct. If we consider highly successful individuals, it seems they are very good at being *selectively* disagreeable when it most matters to be so. At the same time, they also may be wonderful diplomats and co-operators when circumstances dictate.

Returning to the Apple founder, consider this apt description from Jobs biographer Brent Schlender: "Steve also knew how to get what he wanted, and he negotiated with both carrot and stick."[11] Jobs wasn't disagreeable per se; rather, he was extremely goal-oriented. A virtuoso of emotional scales, Jobs was always playing the right melody to accomplish his goal, whether through agreeable charm or disagreeable rancor. And it worked, as Daniel observed during the time he spent working at Apple early in his career, after Apple had purchased one of his companies.

So an alternative, more complicated, but also more sophisticated question is to ask, "Can this person be selectively agreeable

and then also disagreeable when called for?" That quality probably is harder to test for, but this question is the better one to ask.
When it comes to team leadership, there is a lot to be said for
independent-thinking contrarians who are tough but also fine
diplomats when that is called for.

Conceptual Frameworks at One's Disposal

Finally, another trait to look for is how many different conceptual frameworks an individual has at his or her disposal. We
could have put this discussion in the intelligence chapter, but
we believe there is something about this trait that makes it distinct from intelligence. Some people are simply keen to develop as many different perspectives as possible, for some mix
of both practical and temperamental reasons. This is a kind
of curiosity, but it goes beyond mere curiosity of the sort that
leads you to turn over unturned stones. This curiosity is about
models, frameworks, cultural understandings, disciplines, and
methods of thought, the kinds of traits that made John Stuart
Mill such a great thinker and writer. A more recent example
is Patrick Collison, CEO and co-founder of Stripe (and also
an active writer). His content can draw from economics, science, history, Irish culture, tech, and many other areas and
influences.

Is the person trying to figure out how engineers approach problems? What distinguishes the mental frameworks of programmers? How economists think? How the viewpoints of managers
and employees might differ? That's a person who's interested in
multiple conceptual frameworks. And you can extend this point
well beyond the professions. How about someone who asks,
"What is the Mormon conception of God, and how does it influence Mormon ideas about the world?" Or "Why are some

American and Canadian perspectives so very different?" You needn't expect individuals to be factual experts on these particular questions (though that would not be bad); rather, do they have enough conceptual versatility that they can understand what it means to have an understanding of such things? Could they acquire a substantive understanding of such questions if they had the time and will to do so?

That is one good way of thinking about a person's versatility in the workplace as well as with customers and other employees, including with you. Tyler sometimes refers to "cracking cultural codes"—how good is the person at opening up and understanding new and different cultural and intellectual frameworks? Does the person invest time and effort in trying to do so? Does the person even know what it means to do so?

One advantage of this skill, to the extent you seek to cultivate it in yourself, is that you can do it while traveling and on vacation—indeed, it may be best improved in this manner. If you are in a different part of the world, or even a different part of your country or state, how quickly can you figure out what is going on? What exactly changes when you cross from Virginia into West Virginia? What exactly makes Haifa feel different from the other cities in Israel? Are the people at a Balinese cockfight really enjoying themselves? Those questions may not sound like talent search questions, but increasingly they are. To the extent you can train yourself to deconstruct cultural codes in general, you will be better at spotting different kinds of talent and, in the longer run, better at managing it too.

This point also bears on the growing importance of race and racism in workplace relations. Does the person have the conceptual frameworks to make some start on questions such as "What is it like to grow up black in an all-white neighborhood?" or "What are the potential pressures of a racially mixed marriage?"

or "Which are the subtle, less often discussed problems of racism in academia or the tech sector?" As workforces grow ever more multicultural, those kinds of understandings will be more important in your job candidates and your affiliates. Again, you are not just asking whether the person understands those particular questions, but whether they have the capacity to acquire a superior understanding of questions in general. That, again, gets back to the question of how they manage different conceptual frameworks.

The productivity of conceptual frameworks is a neglected point. Silicon Valley has been successful for many reasons, but one reason is how many people there have mastered the framework of thinking that the future can truly be very different indeed. These people bring together their different visions to work the workable elements of common ground, which then get turned into companies.

Pattern Matching

Many of the traits we've discussed in this chapter and the previous one allow you to *actively* assess talent during interviews or a study of a person's career or vita. There's another form of thinking that's more *passive*: pattern matching, an approach especially popular with Daniel. As we meet people and observe their speech, hand gestures, words, and style, we are reminded of other people who display a similar affect, and so we predict the candidate might have similar traits to the person they remind us of. This can lead to both positive and negative consequences, and much has been written about attempting to suppress this particular trait of the human psyche during interviews. We think pattern matching is relatively unavoidable, and research has shown that training about unconscious bias has little to no effect on it. A different approach is to lean into this skill: pattern-match, but do it effectively.

The challenge is with a novice interviewer who struggles to match against a limited bank of experiences. If this is your first job and tenth interview, you're just not going to have a lot to compare to. This problem dwindles with experience, especially if you work with a wide variety of individuals from different backgrounds.

Until then, there's an experimental way you might bootstrap your data bank: television, and in particular, movies and TV shows about corporate environments. This helps for two reasons. First, your mind will have more anchor points to associate individuals with. You will have "seen" more people. Second, you might use these as shared references with your team if you all watch the same content. "He's very Jim Halpert from *The Office*" instantly conveys a specific simple likeability, while "She's very Elizabeth McCord from *Madam Secretary*" communicates an orderly leadership ability, and "He reminds me of President Palmer from *24*" is a rich way of exuding gravitas. Shows like *The West Wing* and *Madam Secretary* might be more useful here than *Spider-Man*: you want stories that are about organizations (although *Spider-Man* might be more useful if you are looking for the next hot artist or hit musician). Tyler is sometimes tempted to perform such matching exercises with professional chess players, although that tendency is virtually useless when trying to compare notes with other people.

We suggest matching strategies as an enhancement, not a foundation. Fictional characters are designed for entertainment, not accuracy, and often have significantly exaggerated traits compared to anyone in real life. We aren't suggesting you become an associative robot that maps candidates to TV shows; rather, you can use media as a form of cognitive enrichment. It is a way to extend your thinking about different types of people, in particular those that you don't ordinarily get exposed to. You might have a real edge as a talent spotter if you're the only person in town who can identify underrated talent others pass on because you're fueled by inspiring protagonists who are of a different gender, race, or personality type.

Know Your Place in the Pecking Order

Finally, when interpreting the data you have on potential hires, keep in mind where *you* stand in the pecking order. If you are at the very top of your sector, the selection process is very different than if you are in the middle or, for that matter, closer to the bottom. In particular, if you are not at the very top of your sector, an apparent positive can be a negative, and vice versa, all because of selection effects.

Let's say, for instance, that you are Apple or Google looking to hire programmers or management talent. You will be able to choose from some truly top candidates, and in your interviews you should be looking for that kind of quality. You don't need to be so preoccupied with the question "Why does this person want to come *here*?" Yes, you should ask yourself that question, because not everyone is a natural fit for your company, but there will be plenty of reasons top people will want to work at Apple and Google. You don't need a big, complicated theory to explain why that might be the case — rather, you could start with the fact that many incoming and fairly junior hires at these companies start at salaries of about $300,000 or more, with interesting projects to work on right away and further opportunities for significant advancement.

It is different if you are from the middle or bottom tiers of your sector. In that case, not everyone will want to work with you, and perhaps most people won't want to work with you, as they will be hoping for something better, whether realistically or not. If you are in this position, as many of us are, you need to think especially carefully about *what is wrong* with the people you are trying to hire. (Sometimes this is called the Groucho Marx effect, as Groucho once stated that he wouldn't want to belong to any club that would have him as a member.) Some of them will look great, and they also will do very well in the interview and by other metrics you use. But in that case, you need to start getting nervous. If they want to work with you, maybe there is something wrong with them you haven't seen yet. Why aren't they already working somewhere much better? Why are they talking to you at all? Maybe they are totally lacking in self-confidence, or their personalities will turn out to be poison, or they plan on leaving after a year and they are just using you in the meantime. We have noticed there is an entire class of highly credentialed, fairly talented individuals who spend their whole lives hopping from one job to another, restless, never happy, and never able to put down any roots. They are good enough to keep on getting hired, but still, most of the time you should avoid them.

To be sure, confronting these possibilities is a little uncomfortable, because it raises the question of what is wrong with you too, and most people don't like to face that question too directly. Still, if a candidate looks too good to be true, maybe he or she *is* too good to be true. You then need to figure out why that candidate wants to work with you and not with your industry's equivalent of Apple or Google. And that means being self-aware about your own weaknesses as an institution, having an understanding of who is "gettable" for you and who isn't, and knowing why there are sometimes positive exceptions to that.

As you assess candidates, you need to figure out what is "wrong" with the particular candidate who might accept your offer, and until you do so, your mind should not rest easy. Why would *that* person want to work here? Maybe his or her spouse has a job offer nearby, but another possibility is that the candidate simply isn't that competitive but still can thrive in a warm, welcoming environment. Your partial mediocrity makes this environment possible, and the candidate is smart enough to see this. Embrace that mediocrity (while still trying to overcome it along other margins) and hire this person, comfortable in the knowledge that they're not a pure lemon and might in fact turn out to be a pretty good match for you.

Again, the Groucho Marx effect means that unless you are at the very top, you shouldn't obsess over particular metrics of achievement, even if those metrics sound very good or very convincing in the abstract. Who could possibly be against intelligence? Isn't a charming personality a good thing? Yet if you run to find intelligence or charm as hard as you can, especially if you are not Google or Apple or Harvard, you may find it backfiring on you, and you will "pay for it" with other, hidden defects in the candidates you manage to recruit. The further down you are on the hierarchy of where people want to work in your sector, the more you need to think about making a fitting match and the less you should worry about the virtuous qualities of the candidate in the abstract.

In these cases—which are numerous and arguably the norm—often you will be relieved and sometimes even overjoyed when you begin to see the flaws in the candidate under question: "Ah, so *that's* why they might want to work here." It's hard to keep that perspective in mind, because most people have a self-image of being entirely meritocratic and of favoring quality above all else. That is the appropriate self-image; you just need to keep in mind that good can be bad, and bad can be good, so to speak. When it comes to hiring, most of all you need a good match, not some supposed vision of candidate perfection. So skill in spotting flaws in other people can lead to very positive matching outcomes, and that is another reason the dialectical perspective of seeing both the good and bad sides of talent is highly useful.

Another problem with self-honesty comes when deciding which qualities you really need in an employee. Organizations love to tell themselves how bold and innovative they are, but this description applies only to a minority of institutions at any given time. Nonetheless, when it comes to hiring, there is a lot of search for innovative pathbreakers as a kind of managerial self-deception. Be honest about what you really need. Is it perhaps possible that your company is one whose next employee should be more steadfast and reliable than innovative? Might your institution have more of a "loyalty culture" than you like to admit? Keep your mind open to the possibility that your institutional self-description is not entirely accurate. Again, the big enemy can be you. You need to avoid satisfying your sense of self-importance at the expense of seeing through a more appropriate and ultimately higher-quality outcome.

7

DISABILITY AND TALENT

Climate activist Greta Thunberg has been one of the biggest stories of the last few years. Sixteen at the time of her ascent, she had been diagnosed with autism, a condition often regarded as a disability. On her Twitter profile she describes herself as being Asperger's, a closely related condition (and in the American Psychiatric Association's *Diagnostic and Statistical Manual of Mental Disorders, Fifth Edition*, Asperger's has been rolled into the more general diagnosis of autism).

In 2019, Greta posted on her Twitter account a year-old photo of herself, sitting alone with a sign outside of the Swedish Parliament. In the photo, no one was paying attention, and she had a dejected look on her face. Yet within a year she became one of the best-known and most influential global celebrities, with 2.7 million Twitter followers and rising. She led a Global Climate Strike of over four million people in the fall of 2019, and she has been on the short list for the Nobel Peace Prize. She also was named *Time* magazine's 2019 Person of the Year.

Even if you do not agree with everything she says or does, Greta Thunberg has been wildly successful in drawing attention to climate change. The story of how she did it reveals important lessons about how people with "disabilities" can be startlingly effective not because they "overcame" their disability but *because* of it. Many autistic people are considered to be especially blunt in their manner of expression, to be very interested or even obsessively interested in social justice, to be potentially single-minded in their avocations, and to have a strong dislike of hypocrisy. It is those very qualities that have helped magnify Greta's appeal and drive much of her success.[1]

Greta also has an immediately recognizable speaking voice, which may be connected to the unusual prosody heard in the voices of many autistics. There isn't any other well-known orator who comes across as Greta does. She gets to the point quickly, and her delivery is memorable. And it seems that is exactly what the climate change issue needed to become focal and emotionally salient to a larger audience.

There is yet another reason autism may be correlated with Greta's success. Since many autistics have been socially marginalized or treated poorly, they may feel they have little to lose, and that can impel them to take more chances with their ideas and with their careers. They are some of the least likely people to be caught up in "establishment" or conformist modes of thinking. Furthermore, autism implies some different and unique modes of cognition, as we will see shortly.

Greta described herself as follows: "I see the world a bit different, from another perspective. . . . It's very common that people on the autism spectrum have a special interest. . . . I can do the same thing for hours."[2]

Peter Thiel also has suggested in numerous public talks that "being Aspergery" may be useful for insulating oneself from many social trends and thus for maintaining originality in one's thinking. In Peter's basic model of human behavior, influenced by his former Stanford professor René Girard, mimetic desire is strong—that is, human beings look to copy each other's behavior and also to display signs of status. (His knowledge of Girard's framework helped him see that Facebook would be a big success, since people would wish to signal their social rank and standing.) Yet if everyone is copying everyone else, who is left to be an original thinker? To the extent that autistic and Asperger's individuals remain outside of the usual loops of social pressure and mimetic desire, they may retain strong capacities for original, non-conformist thought. Indeed, they are sometimes *unable* to conform, and that may encourage their thoughts to move in new and different directions. Many of you will know that Elon Musk, when he hosted *Saturday Night Live* on television in 2021, "came out" as being Asperger's (or autistic, to use the now-preferred terminology).

You might think that Greta and Elon are just two examples, but they represent a broader trend—namely, that the world is mobilizing the talents of many more kinds of people than ever before. Greta is not only a woman and autistic, but at the time she came to public renown she was sixteen years old and was not living in a major media capital or political center. The question before us is pretty simple: Do you wish to be part of such trends for mobilizing the talents of strongly unique people, or are you going to let others eclipse you in the search for talent?

We're going to focus on cognitive disabilities (or supposed disabilities, in some cases) in this chapter, but much of what we have to say applies to individuals with physical disabilities or, for that matter, individuals with no apparent disabilities at all. Whether you are interested in the particular topics we will cover here or in others, please think of these as further examples of *how to look past the surfaces.*

Atypical Intelligences and Abilities

When it comes to talent search, we recommend having some understanding of various disabilities, why you might wish to hire individuals with these disabilities or promote their work, and why you might wish to hire them *because* of the disability. In fact, we are not entirely comfortable with the term "disability," as not every disability ends up being a disadvantage in every regard. One possible definition of disability might be "human differences in range and/or type of abilities, which are currently judged to impair essential aspects of functioning, regardless of actual outcomes or achievements."[3]

But please do not be offended or conclude that we are somehow trying to refute or deny your own personal experience with disabilities. Nor are we trying to diminish appreciation for those who have struggled with disabilities, whether their own or in their families. In our discussion we are not trying to give a complete picture of disabilities or consider all of their possible issues. Nor are we able to choose language that will accord with the wishes of every reader; for instance, some people prefer "person with autism" while others use "an autistic," with bitter disputes and no agreement in sight.

Instead, we are trying to show you the more positive cognitive sides of some well-known disabilities so as to improve your ability to find talent. That means we are going to emphasize the positive on the disability issues we are covering, because often that is the part of the picture that most people have the greatest trouble understanding. So please put the terminology and the politics aside, and focus on the substance of what you can learn about talent search.

To structure the discussion, let's begin by noting that disabilities can reflect or augment talent through at least three mechanisms:

1. Different focus and redirection of effort
2. Compensation and adaptation, or making up for an initial problem
3. "Superpowers," or ways in which people with disabilities also can have *superior* abilities

We'll consider each in turn.

Different Focus and Redirection of Effort

Consider dyslexia, which is defined in terms of difficulties in learning to read or interpret words, letters, and other symbols, yet without a loss in general intelligence. A small research literature suggests that individuals with dyslexia are more likely to become successful entrepreneurs. We are not convinced this relationship is causal, or that it is entirely robust. Still, there is a good chance this is true, and it is something to keep your eye on. As is the case in many contexts, it doesn't have to be a causal relationship to be a useful correlation for spotting potential entrepreneurial talent.

How might the potential entrepreneurial tendencies of dyslexics be an example of different focus and redirection of effort? Well, many dyslexic individuals cannot deal with each and every detail of a production process, in part because they have trouble reading all of the details or interpreting all of the relevant symbols with the required accuracy and speed. In response, they reallocate their efforts to the tasks they can perform successfully, including leadership roles. Sometimes that may be selecting talent and delegating authority, and so dyslexic individuals may learn to start their own enterprises and then delegate the tasks they are not good at. Again, this is a lesson in how apparent disabilities can be correlated with possible strengths on the job. Dyslexic individuals can face very real challenges reading, writing, and decoding information, but don't stereotype dyslexic individuals as inferior performers.

And maybe many of the rest of us have a kind of status quo bias, or risk aversion, that keeps us from being entrepreneurial, whereas perhaps more of the dyslexic individuals are pushed into entrepreneurship by their (partial) disability. They have less of a future from deciding to "stay put" and settle into a boring, repetitive job. Thus, they may strike out in other, new directions, and end up as higher earners and more likely to change the world. Perhaps it is our complacency and risk aversion that should be called a disability too.

Richard Branson, British billionaire and the founder of Virgin Group, explained how his own dyslexia helped him in his career: "[My dyslexia] helped me think big but keep our messages simple. The business world often gets caught up in facts and figures—and while the details and data are important, the ability to dream, conceptualise, and innovate is what sets the successful and the unsuccessful apart." In other words, an inability to focus on all of the details can, for some people, reallocate their attention toward a more important bigger picture.[4]

Branson also suggested that dyslexics will be well equipped to compete in the workplace of the future. That is very much a speculative opinion, but again, we are trying to open your mind to possibilities rather than to offer you a comprehensive account of dyslexia. If you understand why that claim *might* be true, it will be easier to spot the talents and virtues of others, including dyslexics. According to some estimates, there may be as many as 700 million dyslexics in the world. As a simple first step, you might consider thinking twice about individuals who appear to exhibit otherwise unreliable reading and spelling skills.[5]

This theme of redirecting effort is a general one. Just about any disability, by definition, implies that an individual is (at least initially) subpar at some set of skills. Many individuals respond to that initial deficiency by investing more in acquiring other, different skills. Disability is thus a potential marker for skill specialization, and skill specialization can be a very potent advantage, most of all in a world that is rapidly becoming more complex.

Compensation and Adaptation, or Making up for an Initial Problem

This second theme of compensation and adaptation is more counterintuitive than the point about redirection, yet it is an important theme when thinking about disability. Not only may individuals with disabilities be induced to excel in other areas unrelated to their disability, but *they may be induced to excel in the area of initial disability itself*. To see how that might be, let us consider an example.

A disability may sometimes turn a person's attention to the importance of a particular area. Darcey Steinke, writing in *The New York Times*, explained why her stutter in some ways turned out to be a blessing: "The central irony of my life remains that my stutter, which at times caused so much suffering, is also responsible for my obsession with language. Without it I would not have been driven to write, to create rhythmic sentences easier to speak and to read. A fascination with words thrust me into a vocation that has kept me aflame with a desire to communicate."[6]

Or consider the disability of aphantasia, the inability to visualize images in one's mind. That means you can't use your mind's eye to summon up visual images at will. Many individuals, possibly 2 percent of the population, have aphantasia but don't even know it, often because they don't have an intuitive sense of how other people *can* perform this function, and thus, they do not know what they are missing. You might think that aphantasia rules out an individual from working in visually oriented professions, as those individuals would seem to be at an extreme disadvantage. Yet that is not the case. For instance, it is reported that quite a few people working in computer graphics have aphantasia. One example would be Ed Catmull, former president of Pixar and Walt Disney Animation Studios; another would be Glen Keane, an Oscar winner who created Ariel from *The Little Mermaid*.[7]

We're not sure why such a connection might exist. Does the inability to see images in one's mind motivate a person to create such graphic images for a more public medium? Or are the mechanical techniques for making such images intrinsically more interesting for those with aphantasia? Perhaps the "marvel of visual image creation" is all the more splendid and enthralling for those with aphantasia. Or maybe they think more readily in terms of interesting narrative because their minds are not filled up with images. Or it could be that aphantasia is correlated with some other difference in the brain, and that difference brings some cognitive advantages. Whatever the reason might be, aphantasia might be a reason to hire someone for the task of visual image creation, not a reason to stay away.

The famous geneticist Craig Venter is considered to have

aphantasia (or to be aphantasiac). His main contribution has been to lead the first team to sequence the human genome and to first transfect a cell with a synthetic chromosome. Genetics is a field full of mappings and visual analogies, and the core facts about DNA are very often presented in visual form, such as intricate spirals. How is it that an aphantasiac might have ended up as the major leader in such a field? Might the aphantasiac have been induced to construct a compensating analytical framework, in lieu of the usual visual images, and perhaps that non-visual framework was highly conducive to further intellectual progress? Again, we don't know, but the point is that you should not use a superficial understanding of disability to dismiss the possibility that someone might be a top talent in an area closely related to their disability.

Another example would be blind lawyers. You might think they would struggle to read and digest the relevant laws and court documents. But there are many workarounds, one of them being text-recognition software that converts the written word to speech. Alternatively, many blind lawyers *might remember the law better*, knowing it is probably harder for them to look things up. There is, in fact, a National Association of Blind Lawyers with several hundred members, and the former lieutenant governor of Washington State, Cyrus Habib, is a blind lawyer. The point is not that every blind person can or should be a lawyer, only that what we perceive as weaknesses or disabilities can sometimes be beaten or transcended.

Let's take a look at one of the most common disabilities, attention deficit hyperactivity disorder (ADHD). The stereotypical picture of an ADHD individual is someone who can't pay attention to any single topic for very long and who flits from one thing to the next, perhaps flunking out of school or losing a job in the process. That might explain some facets of the ADHD experience, including a possible reliance on appropriate medication. We have noticed, in contrast, that a pretty high proportion of successful individuals seem to be ADHD in some manner, even though they usually have not been formally diagnosed. Rather than being distracted to the point of chaotic ineffectiveness, they have learned to redirect their cognitive impatience as a force that propels them through an enormous amount of work and learning.

For instance, accept for just a moment the oversimplified popular caricature of ADHD and assume it impels individuals to be switching their attention all the time. Well, being *impelled* to do anything is actually a great potential motivator. If need be, just set up your two projects next to each other, and keep on switching from one to the other, whenever your attention is distracted from the one you are working on at the moment. It is so often the workers who are not impelled to do much of anything at all who are the problem. Have you ever wondered how so many people can just sit there in the airport waiting for their flights, *doing nothing*? It astonishes us, and it is also a loss of productivity.

Or let's say you have ADHD and wish to read a long book. Is that impossible? Well, no. You might find a way to treat the next, forthcoming page as a "distraction" from the previous page, and that will keep you reading. When compensatory mechanisms are in place, an apparent disability doesn't have to be a disability but can become an advantage. The reality is that a lot of ADHD individuals seem to develop mechanisms that allow them to take in enormous amounts of information while staying motivated the whole way through, or perhaps being super-motivated.

It is also worth understanding how the ADHD individuals in your workplace, whether they are diagnosed or not, will have different skills and inclinations than your other workers. For instance, they may have a higher demand for novelty and constantly be looking for the stimulus of new problems to solve. Other workers may find such a "diet" to be disorienting, and instead prefer to apply known methods to known problems and feel in control the whole way through a large volume of work. We're not suggesting that any generalization will cover everyone, only that you should be aware of the heterogeneities in play here and understand human cognition as truly diverse.

Autistic individuals also provide numerous examples of how what might seem to be initial disabilities can be converted to strengths or at least partial strengths. By now it is well known that many autistic individuals are highly skilled at programming, mathematics, and other technical subjects; this has virtually become a cliché. There are whole companies, typically in the tech area, that specialize in hiring autistic people for jobs of this kind. That's great, but the next step is to broaden your understanding of how autism might fit into other roles too.[8]

For instance, autism therapist Tony Atwood has suggested, based on his professional experience, that autistics may be overrepresented in the acting profession, of all places. If some of their social instincts are less developed in the first place, they may have to learn the skill of acting throughout their entire lives from young ages. That might make them skilled at professional acting later on. Again, don't be captured by the cliché, but keep your mind open toward the various surprising possibilities in play.[9]

It is a common misconception that autistics lack social intelligence, and some definitions of autism make deficits in social intelligence core aspects of the condition. It is more insightful to think of autistics as having a high variance in social intelligence, noting that they are often not well in sync with social conventions. But that helps them to see many social foibles with special perspicacity or to understand situations in new and novel lights. For instance, the absurdity of rituals at cocktail parties or in higher education may be two of many areas where many autistics see through to the underlying reality more quickly. More generally, when autistics encounter social situations, very often they are absorbing *too much* social information and don't know how to order or process it, which may confuse them. Yes, that can be a practical problem, it is a disability, and it reflects some problems with the ordering principles behind autistic cognition. Still, the point remains that the autistics are processing huge amounts of social information—above-average amounts, sometimes extraordinary amounts. If autistics learn to order it properly, through study and practice, they can be extremely insightful about social situations, even if they do not grasp all of the ordinary angles that non-autistics are likely to understand rather more readily.[10]

Tyler attributes a lot of his own success to his hyperlexia—his ability from a very young age to read much faster than other people and to absorb that information very readily. Hyperlexia is often connected to autism and its information-gathering proclivities, although Tyler does not think of himself as having low social intelligence or disabilities in communication skills, the latter being part of the formal clinical definition of autism.[11]

Another common misconception about autism is that autistics are always introverts and thus ill-suited for jobs that require a lot of extraversion. That view confuses autism, which is largely a cognitive category, with notions of personality. In reality, many autistics are quite extroverted and very happy to be forward and outgoing in their dealings with others; some autistics may possibly be *too* extroverted when it comes to sharing or talking about their particular special interests. Other autistics do in fact *behave* in an introverted manner, in part because they feel discouraged by how they are treated in various social situations. But that doesn't mean they have the natural personality inclination to be an introvert. It is still unclear whether autistics, on average, are intrinsically more introverted, whether they simply act more introverted because they may understand some social situations poorly, or whether there is no correlation at all. In any case, don't leap to a hasty conclusion on this one. If you equate autistics with "introverted, nerdy guys," you are confusing different categories, and you will end up missing a lot of the talented autistics you might otherwise be trying to hire.[12]

Microsoft, for instance, found that "candidates with autism [often] don't get through the initial phone screen because they may have yes or no answers or they may not elaborate on other skills." In response to this dilemma, Microsoft adapted its hiring process to allow email to replace the phone call, gave individuals the chance to do a practice interview first, and gave individuals the option to code using their own laptops instead of having to do whiteboard work in front of other individuals. The company believes this allowed them to hire a greater number of talented autistic individuals.[13]

Also keep in mind that the generalizations about personality psychology are less likely to apply to autistics. For instance, it was already a weakness of personality psychology that categories such as "conscientiousness" might not be fully general but rather would depend on the degree of motivation in a particular area. This is likely all the more true for autistics, who typically have strongly "preferred interests" in specific topic areas. Do not, in general, expect to know when you are interviewing or reviewing autistics; nonetheless, especially when you are aware of it, look less for signs of conscientiousness in general and more for signs of conscientiousness (or not) in particular areas of relevance. For the interview process, bear in mind that autistics find "thinking in terms of stories" less automatic and perhaps less appealing as well, so if you try to engage them in the storytelling mode it may go poorly. Again, you can't hope to be diagnosing interview subjects as you are proceeding, but do keep in mind that human beings have a wide variety of means of organizing information in response to a question.

One good framework for understanding the role of compensation in disability comes from economics, and it is best outlined in a 1987 article by David Friedman, "Cold Houses in Warm Climates and Vice Versa: A Paradox of Rational Heating." The basic point of Friedman's article, although he does not express it as such, is that compensation for an initial disadvantage can lead to a higher level of skill or achievement. To cite Friedman's example, if you live in a cold climate, you might invest in a lot of home insulation and thereby end up warmer. Alternatively, if you grow up where the weather is usually sixty degrees, you might not have central heating at all, and thus, you can end up feeling pretty chilly at night.[14]

All this ties back to human disabilities. If you have a disability of some kind, you may need to work all the harder in that area and make a big adjustment. While that is a burden, and it will hinder or discourage many individuals, others will ultimately end up with superior performance. Just remember how Darcey Steinke's stutter made her more aware of words and thus a better writer, as discussed earlier.

Superpowers

The core truth is this: even if you think disabilities are disadvantages on net, many of them come with offsetting advantages in the overall package. And sometimes those advantages can be very impressive.

We draw the term "superpowers" from the story of cartoonist Dav Pilkey, a bestselling children's author who has sold millions of books, most of all from his Dog Man franchise. Pilkey is open about his dyslexia and ADHD, and often when he makes public appearances children with dyslexia and ADHD come to meet him and express their solidarity with signs. Pilkey once stated in an interview: "I don't call it Attention Deficit Hyperactivity Disorder. I call it Attention Deficit Hyperactivity Delightfulness. I want kids to know that there's nothing wrong with you. You just think differently, and that's a good thing. It's good to think differently. This world needs people who think differently; it's your superpower."[15]

Another part of the interview went like this:

Q: And you had to sit in the hall in elementary school?
A: So little was known about those conditions back in those days, and I think it was just seen as I was distracting everyone in the class with my silliness. I couldn't stay in my chair and keep my mouth shut. So the teachers from second to fifth grade just put me in the hall. It ended up being kind of a blessing for me, too, because it gave me time to draw and to create stories and comics. I guess I made lemonade out of it.

Cognitive advantages can benefit autistic individuals as well. Among the cognitive strengths of autistics, catalogued and replicated in the research literature, are the following:

- Strong skills in collecting information and ordering knowledge in preferred areas
- Strong skills in perceiving and collecting small bits of information in preferred areas, science being one obvious example here

- Strong skills in pattern recognition and noticing details in patterns
- Strong visual acuity and superior pitch perception
- Less likely to be fooled by optical illusions
- Less biased about sunk costs
- Less likely to be subject to framing illusions and endowment effects, as presented in the behavioral economics literature, so in this regard more likely to employ a rational approach to decisions
- Greater chance of savant skills, such as performing impressive operations with numbers, codes, and ciphers
- Hyperlexia, which commonly involves the ability to consume and retain vast amounts of reading material at high speed
- Strong sense of right and wrong and social justice; arguably autistics are more likely to place higher weight on the demands of impersonal justice than on the immediate claims of persons around them

The claim is not that all autistics have all of these abilities, but rather that autistics have strong skills in those areas at higher rates than do non-autistics. There is also good evidence that autistics have strong performance on Ravens IQ tests (the Ravens Progressive Matrices test measures fluid intelligence and the ability to pick up skills such as spatial visualizing, inferring rules, and engaging in high-level abstraction). The scores of the autistics were, on average, 30 percentile points higher on the Ravens test, and sometimes more than 70 percentile points higher, compared to Wechsler scales of intelligence, which place greater stress on linguistic and cultural forms of knowledge. A third of the tested autistic children scored at or higher than the 90th percentile for the Ravens test. More generally, other studies find that higher genetic risk for autism correlates with higher IQ.[16]

Most generally, autistics may have higher rates of de novo genetic mutations than do non-autistics. That means autism may be correlated with a large number of other, different conditions, due to the higher general propensity for mutations, even if those conditions are not themselves "part of the autism." That will make autistics "more unusual," and in ways that could either boost or harm productivity.[17]

In 2001–2002, Tyler played a critical role in hiring Vernon Smith and his experimental economics team to George Mason University; several years later Vernon won a Nobel Prize, and his colleagues also did impressive work, so that was obviously a very good hire. Vernon is well known as an "Asperger's autistic" and has written and spoken extensively on this, as he credits his extreme focus and work ethic to his autistic traits. For all of Vernon's virtues, which include an extreme good-naturedness, it was not the easiest recruiting process. Vernon has an auditory processing disorder (a trait correlated with autism), and so he did not always register verbal agreements made in the room. Someone in an intermediary role had to figure that out, and that person turned out to be Tyler. Furthermore, when Vernon was considering coming to George Mason, money was not his number one consideration; rather, it was the freedom to work on his own projects with an extreme degree of autonomy. The offer was structured accordingly, and Vernon accepted even though he and his team could have earned higher salaries at a number of other schools.[18]

Temple Grandin, one of the most famous and visible autistic individuals, has stressed her strengths in visual thinking and thinking in terms of images. She has written, "When I first started my career as a designer of cattle handling systems in the 1970s, I believed everybody thought in pictures the same way I did. Before I drew the plans for a steel and concrete structure, I saw the finished structure. But that's not how most plans are designed, I now know. Today, facilities and equipment I have designed are in almost all of the large beef processing plants. The visual thinkers, *similar to me*, have invented and created much of the really clever equipment used today such as intricate conveyor systems and ingenious packaging rigs." Grandin also has written extensively on autism, and not surprisingly, the work focuses on visual thinking as one possible autistic cognitive strength.[19]

Or consider José Valdes Rodriguez, ten years old when he was the subject of a newspaper article in 2019. Diagnosed with autism, he speaks four languages, has memorized the value of pi to two hundred places, and at the age of ten was taking precalculus math in Victoria, Canada. He aspires to be a professional astronomer. Will José Valdes be a good hire someday, maybe even relatively soon? Possibly so, but we don't yet know. Should you in any case give him a close look? Absolutely.[20]

We've only covered a few disabilities in this chapter, but you might be wondering about schizophrenics, or more broadly schizotypy, referring to a continuous spectrum of traits related to schizophrenia and psychosis. Might those individuals possibly have advantages, if only partial advantages, for some kinds of jobs?

The answer probably is yes. To be clear, we have found the literature on schizotypy and also on bipolar individuals difficult to interpret, in part because many of the papers seem to have low-quality data and also relatively few data points. Nonetheless, there are numerous accounts of how schizotypic individuals may suffer from local processing deficits (that is, they move too rapidly and too indiscriminately to global processing), working memory defects, an inability to maintain attention, disorganized behavior, hypo- and hyperexcitability, excessive speculative ideation, excess receptivity to information from the right hemisphere of the brain, delusions, and other problems. We do not contest this evidence or the very real human costs that may arise as a result.[21]

Nonetheless, we are struck by the large number of research papers that find a connection between schizotypy (and sometimes bipolar disorder) and artistic creativity. That indicates that schizotypy might boost particular kinds of insights.

Among the famous creative figures who have been labeled schizophrenic or possibly bipolar are Vincent van Gogh, Jack Kerouac, John Nash, Brian Wilson, Agnes Martin, Bud Powell, Camille Claudel, Edvard Munch, and Vaslav Nijinsky, among many others, to the point where this has become a cliché of art house cinema. Less anecdotally, some research papers suggest a more systematic positive relationship between artistic creativity and schizotypy. For instance, schizotypy is often associated with "the increased availability of distant or less common semantic associations," possibly connected with "a relative weakening of left hemisphere dominance and strengthening of availability of right hemisphere processing." Metrics for schizotypy correlate with metrics for creativity, including in relatives, and furthermore, polygenic risk scores for both schizophrenia and bipolar disorder appear to predict creativity. There is also genetic evidence showing that schizophrenia, bipolar disorder, and other mental health problems are correlated with other genetic factors associated with higher levels of education.[22]

Kanye West, one of the leading musical creators of our time, renowned for his generativity and versatility, is one recent artist who has come out as having a bipolar diagnosis. On one of his songs he rapped: "See, that's my third person. That's my bipolar shit. . . . [T]hat's my superpower, ain't no disability, I am a super-hero!"[23] As you might expect, this was controversial, as Kanye came under fire for glamorizing what can be a major problem for many individuals. It can be dangerous to view it as a super-power and not to exercise sufficient caution. Still, the notion that bipolar and schizophrenic tendencies are related to creativity in some positive way simply does not go away.[24]

There also seems to be a connection between schizophrenia and a sensitivity to at least some kinds of social information. If, for instance, the information coming from the right hemisphere is filtered in a less disciplined or stringent manner, individuals with schizotypy can be extremely perceptive, perhaps in some circumstances too perceptive. Such individuals are often able to pick up on otherwise unperceived social associations or subtle social cues, or to imagine possibilities that others cannot see. They have extreme openness along some dimensions, and they can embody the opposite of extreme literalness, which may account for some of the correlation with creativity. They take leaps of faith, often without justification. For that reason, individuals with schizotypy may have tendencies toward paranoia or believing in a lot of social facts that are not true or even close to true. There is also a tendency to overreact to the gaze of others and to infer intentionality when no intentionality is present. There is a high level of distractibility and a relatively loose association between the nature of stimuli and resulting thoughts and feelings, which, again, can bring hallucinations and delusions. There can be an exaggerated sense of self-consciousness and an excessive concern with one's position in the social order.[25]

That is a complicated set of traits, but the point is that many of these individuals may have superior creativity and also superior powers of discernment for some situations. They may be highly generative and a source of many new ideas. They also may have social insights and perceive social truths that others do not, even if their judgment is less than totally reliable, as reflected by the defects of many schizophrenics when it comes to "theory of mind." So if you would like some insight into a social situation or to hear a new creative option, consider asking a schizophrenic, or an individual with tendencies toward schizophrenia, for advice. After you are done asking the autistic, that is.[26]

You might object that schizophrenic individuals, or even those with schizotypy or perhaps bipolar disorder, will prove disruptive in the workplace. This is not the time or place to debate the effectiveness of medication and how much the negative characteristics of schizophrenia and bipolar disorder can be controlled. If nothing else, please recall that this is a book about talent search, not just a book about hiring. So if you meet a highly talented but potentially disruptive individual, schizophrenic or not, well, maybe you shouldn't hire that person into a full-time, on-site job. But consider some other possible roles, including telecommuting (with pay based on output), part-time consulting, buying their artworks or a share in their future income stream, or using the person as an advisor or a source of generative ideas.

Again, our goal here is not to present you with a definitive scientific understanding of schizophrenia, schizotypy, or bipolar disorder. Instead, we seek to open your mind to alternative possibilities for how you might spot talent in others, schizophrenic or not.

What Does This All Mean?

At the very least, please consider and internalize the general lesson that you should not let stereotypes dominate your thinking. Again, we are not saying the positive outcomes are the reality for all or even most individuals with disabilities, nor are we denying the very real possible hardships involved, even for successful individuals. We are saying that commonly labeled disabilities are complex phenomena, and they can have possible upsides, sometimes significant ones. You, as a searcher for talent, need to see as many sides of the picture as is possible and to spot the talent that other people are missing. Often that means understanding that apparent disabilities are by no means always disadvantages at the job.

In this chapter we have focused mostly on what might be called cognitive disabilities, but physical disabilities are relevant too. Many individuals have movement impairments, facial differences, or skin disorders; in your search for talent you are likely to encounter many other possible conditions. We will not list and consider them exhaustively. Rather, the general point is this: contemporary society still too often suffers from "lookism," which is expecting smart and "able" people to fit a very particular physical picture of how to move and act and sound. To whatever extent possible, try to liberate yourself from those biases. No matter how open-minded you may be in some regards, or no matter how much you may have overcome racism or sexism, you are still probably somewhat of a captive of lookism, which hardly ever receives media attention. Look past looks, so to speak.

As already mentioned, we do not find the word "disability" entirely appropriate. Very often disabilities are paired with corresponding *abilities*, but still "disability" is the word in general use. In our context, that of finding talent, the word "disability" still might be useful for its shock value. "Often you want to hire people with disabilities" is perhaps a more memorable catchphrase, especially for your team, than the probably more accurate "What are called disabilities often signal a complex mix of skills and deficiencies, and perhaps those are the overlooked individuals in labor markets." In any case, disability is a highly complex notion and by no means always negative on the whole, especially if your talent search is looking for the special cases and the outliers.

We don't expect you to be able to sort this all out, least of all on the spot. Just keep in mind that disability is a complex concept, the label probably is a bad one, and apparent disabilities can be correlated with some really good hires. Keep an open mind.

8

WHY TALENTED WOMEN AND MINORITIES ARE STILL UNDERVALUED

Clementine Jacoby has a most unusual background. She graduated from Stanford in 2015 and subsequently reported, "I left Stanford thinking that I would be a professional circus performer." Indeed, she had worked as a circus performer in Mexico and Brazil, specializing in aerial hoop. She spent her first year after college teaching acrobatics, not to Cirque du Soleil wannabes but rather in a Brazilian gang-diversion program, to encourage those individuals to put aside lives of crime.[1]

The experience left her with a profound understanding of the problems of crime and lawlessness, and it also taught her that rehabilitation was in fact possible. She then went to work for Google as a product manager for four years, working on Google Maps and Android, which gave her organizational experience and helped her meet and learn from a lot of tech talent.

But when 2018 rolled around, she found herself nagged by a feeling that she should be doing more to improve the world. She developed the idea for Recidiviz, a nonprofit designed to identify individuals in prison who might be eligible for early release without endangering the broader community. More generally, this was part of a bigger movement to bring data analysis to the U.S. criminal justice system. She applied to Tyler's Emergent Ventures program, asking for enough money so that she could quit her job and start the nonprofit. Tyler liked her pitch and within a few days sent a substantial sum of money her way, no further questions asked. Clementine did indeed quit her job and proceed with her plan.

Recidiviz really took off with the pandemic, when states wanted to release many prisoners in order to limit their COVID cases in penitentiaries. Many states consulted with Clementine and Recidiviz as to who could be released safely, and the result was that tens of thousands of prisoners were released and many lives saved. North Dakota, for instance, released 25 percent of its prison population in one month in an orderly manner. Recidiviz is now a highly successful nonprofit, and it has attracted many millions of dollars of additional funding.[2]

When Tyler thinks back to his video interview with Clementine, he was impressed by a few things. First, she had the vision of building Recidiviz with highly talented individuals only, rather than relying on a series of bureaucratized roles filled from the typical nonprofit pool of employees. Instead she drew upon her friends in the tech world. Second, she seemed determined and willing to do something "weird" (it seems less weird now that it has succeeded), even though it meant a big cut in pay and unclear future job prospects, or perhaps the lack of any future job trajectory whatsoever. She really believed in the project, and she was taking the plunge with no obvious parachute, usually a good sign.

At the same time, it's safe to say that Tyler and Clementine didn't entirely click during that first meeting. The call went just fine, but she wasn't playing the strategy of "the charmer." It was the facts and the facts alone, and that matched her vision for Recidiviz as a data-driven enterprise to advise policymakers. If she was going to pull that off, surely her pitch should be rational and data-driven as well, and it was.

Fortunately, Tyler had appropriate expectations for the conversation. Though Clementine didn't seem warm in a superficial sense, Tyler realized that she was doing her best to navigate the fairly limited range of behaviors allowed women in professional settings. We'll discuss this issue further in what follows, but often when a woman is interviewed by a man, there is less emotional space for her to inhabit in ways that would be considered both appropriate and impressive. With many interviewers, she would not be allowed to be too assertive, or for that matter "too smiley." Tyler felt she was, given these possible constraints, pitching herself and the plan just right. The substance of her case was thorough and impressive. And so the grant was made.

That is just one example, but we would like to teach you how to overcome a broader set of biases when it comes to gender and minorities. This is a chapter about how to overcome or at least limit your own biases. Out in the streets, you can be a social justice warrior all you want, but when it comes to talent selection and also the workplace, you may well be biased nonetheless. It is not possible to unpack each and every instance of particular bias ("What exactly is the right way to interview people from urban areas in Mozambique?"), so we will focus on some of the most general lessons. You can take that as a kind of superstructure for filling in particular pieces of learning depending on the issues you face in your own circumstances.

The first part of this chapter will consider biases related to women, who are a majority group in most societies. Later on, we will take those general approaches to bias and discuss how to be more perceptive and less biased when it comes to race, noting that most of this treatment will be set in an American context, rather than covering, say, bias against ethnic Chinese in Southeast Asia. Still, our goal is to uncover generalities rather than to detail each and every bias that might exist, so we hope the analysis will help you fight your own prejudices, or the prejudices of those you work with, no matter what your cultural setting.

And to be clear, we are writing this chapter as two white guys, if we may be perfectly blunt about that. We recognize that there is much about these topics we will never have an experiential understanding of, and that bias will remain in our treatment no matter what we do. We also are writing this chapter with the tone that we would use if we were speaking to people occupying positions of relative power in any situation and trying to educate them about *their* biases. We don't intend that as a prejudicial decision, but we think that approach will give this chapter the greatest impact and influence. If you, as a reader, need to make some adjustments, please try to do so, and in the meantime, please don't think we are intending to exclude you from this discussion. The whole point of this chapter is to help create the conditions for *broadening* the discussion.

Biases Against Women and How to Think About Them

Unfortunately, the arguments about the differences between men and women are usually frustrating and unproductive. Too often the core debate is about whether the differences between men and women are genetic and intrinsic or, alternatively, the result of socialization and thus perhaps malleable.

While we recognize those debates as important, we are deliberately leaving them aside as overdone and also as a distraction from our main mission. Rather than relitigating the James Damore memo (Damore was a Google employee who wrote about the intrinsic differences between men and women), we instead focus on a more practical question: How can we do a better job understanding women's initial presentations of themselves and then harnessing their talents in the workplace? And if you are a boss or talent selector, how can you do a better job hiring women while improving your workplace and easing whatever injustices might exist in broader society? The points in this chapter are intended for the interview process, the promotion process, how you communicate with your employees, and how you should understand the workplace roles and environment you are creating.

It is better for everyone — yourself included — if you side with an emancipatory perspective that improvement is possible and you can be an agent of positive change. This holds even if you harbor very strong conservative views about the intrinsic differences between the sexes.

Here is why even the most conservative gender theorist among us should adopt and, furthermore, embrace an emancipatory perspective. Even if men and women exhibit systematic differences from birth, there still will be unfair discrimination against individual women. There is still considerable variation within each gender, and intrinsic gender differences will make it easier to miss the standout performers who do not belong to the favored group. Take tennis, where we do know that men on average have stronger and faster serves, almost certainly for intrinsic biological reasons. In that setting, it would be easy to neglect the talented women players, or to forget that women's matches can be more interesting (longer, more complex rallies) and sometimes more popular with the crowd as well, all as evidenced by the world of women's tennis. Yet in this setting, statistical discrimination can feel justified, and that can make it more stable. Nonetheless, you, as an entrepreneur and talent spotter, will have opportunities to spot the possibilities in women's tennis, and also to spot the women who can beat most of the men, or perhaps the women who can innovate in tennis in ways the men do not. When it comes to gender, those opportunities may be all the greater precisely because many of the other talent spotters are wrapped up in the generalizations, even if those are correct generalizations on average. Indeed, it did take a long time for women's tennis to rise to its current popularity and status.

Or say it turned out that, in fact, women were on average worse at some other workplace activity. Still, likely many women would be better at that activity than most of the men, and you would gain from spotting and enabling those women. So even if you think "women are worse at [fill in the blank]," it is still a mistake to dismiss female talent. These may be instances when the returns on talent spotting are going to be high, because other people are too attached to their statistical discrimination.

Thus, there is a strong case for believing that *much* more can be done to elevate the prospects of women in society and in the workplace. That case does not require any particular view on whether the observed differences between men and women are biologically or socially determined.

Before we proceed, a few points.

First, we are going to focus on women, but we also will offer some remarks on dealing with individuals from other cultures — "cultures" being broadly defined in a way that may include cultures from within your own country.

Second, we are going to make the discussion deliberately dispassionate and for the most part drained of anecdote and moralizing. We are well aware there is a truly massive literature on women in the workplace, including numerous personal accounts of bias, discrimination, harassment, outrage, and more, with some of those accounts being *highly* personal. We consider these presentations important but feel we do not have much to add to them, and so we will not attempt to systematically present all relevant injustices. If it sounds like we don't "care enough," that is because we are trying to mobilize your analytic, talent-spotting side toward practical, beneficial ends, rather than playing to your emotions.

Our drier approach will focus on a few key results from data science and what they can teach us about finding and mobilizing talented women. That means taking the kinds of research studies already presented and asking what they might imply for women in the workplace. That also means most of the arguments presented here are ones you don't necessarily hear in the more popular discussions, and that is to ensure we are adding to the debate rather than just repeating what you already can find elsewhere.

Let's now look at a few of the central empirical results relevant to women and talent.

Differences in Personality, and Do Aggressive Women Get a Fair Shake?

First, note that women measure as having somewhat different personality profiles than do men. Women score higher than men on the traits of agreeableness, neuroticism, extraversion, and openness, with the largest differences coming on agreeableness and neuroticism. As always, we are using those terms in the formal sense specified in personality theory, and you should not assume either that agreeableness is intrinsically good or that neuroticism is intrinsically bad.[3]

In many cases, men and women have broadly similar scores

on the Big Five qualities but for different reasons, and thus, there are still underlying personality differences. Male openness and female openness are basically the same, but within that category men score much higher on self-assertion and women score much higher on being outgoing and friendly. Women are also more sensitive and socially flexible, and men are more likely to form larger competitive groups with relatively stable hierarchies. Men also have a higher variance of agreeableness, while women have a higher variance of extraversion. Just from personality differences as measured by scores, whether a person is male or female can be forecast with about 85 percent accuracy. That predictability is so high because the algorithms are looking at the entire constellation of personality traits, not just trait-by-trait differences between women and men.[4]

One striking feature of the research literature is that personality for women predicts earnings with more power than personality for men. That is a result from multiple papers, not just one; it seems to be robust, and it holds for Canadian data as well. For instance, in what is arguably the most systematic study of this question, by Ellen K. Nyhus and Empar Pons, personality matters *much* more for women in the workplace. (In technical language, in the unadjusted regressions, personality has an adjusted R-squared of 0.7 percent for men and 5.0 percent for women—a big difference.) For women, emotional stability measures as a greater factor determining wages, as does agreeableness, which in many studies affects wages negatively for women. That is, the agreeable women seem to earn less, for whatever reason. In the Canadian data, a one-standard-deviation increase in agreeableness for women is associated with a 7.4–8.7 percent income penalty, but there is no corresponding income penalty for men.[5]

Melissa Osborne Groves wrote her dissertation on gender and

earnings and found some striking results. Moving beyond Five Factor personality theory, she considers other factors that have predictive power for the earnings of women in the United States and the United Kingdom. For instance, she considers the factor of "externality," "the belief that outcomes are the result of fate or luck," and shows that a one-standard-deviation increase in a woman's externality score is associated with a more than 5 percent decrease in wages. This may mean that a sense of agency is good for productivity, but be careful that such an active temperament doesn't go too far in the wrong direction. A one-standard-deviation increase in the trait of "aggression" is associated with an 8 percent decrease in wages, while a one-standard-deviation increase in the trait of "withdrawal" correlates with a decrease in wages of more than 3 percent. Again, these and other coefficients in the paper show a stronger connection between personality and wages than what is typically found for male earners.[6]

It is striking to view the results on the personality trait of aggression as it relates to male and female earnings. For men, the trait of aggression correlates with higher earnings in high-status professions but correlates with lower earnings in lower-status professions. If you are a bowling alley attendant, you are not supposed to act like a temperamental founder, but a CEO can get away with this. Aggressive women, in contrast, have earnings penalties correlated with both high- and low-status professions.[7]

What should we make of the apparent fact that personality matters more for how much women earn? One obvious insight is that the talent search for women is more difficult or requires a subtler set of skills. For instance, effective, talented women seem to boast less and show less overt aggression, for fear of incurring workplace and broader reputational penalties. That arrangement is unfair, but still, it is a potential opportunity for you to find those individuals by other means—for instance, by asking a candidate and her references more explicitly about the candidate's skills and degree of dedication.

It's also likely true that some employers do not like all of the personality traits of women and/or fear that their workers or customers do not like those traits either. The employers then offer lower wages (or no job at all) to women who seem to possess the undesirable personality traits and higher wages and better posts to women who they think will be more popular. We call that "the nice girl hypothesis," presuming that employers might wish to hire "nice girls."

As an employer, you can take advantage of other people's prescriptive stereotypes. If a woman, or for that matter a man, has a personality trait that the marketplace finds not entirely desirable, a potential arbitrage opportunity, as well as a chance to undermine stereotypes, arises from hiring women with those traits. To be sure, some of the less-desired traits in question may actually hamper job performance. For instance, a male salesperson may be more persuasive in some contexts through his greater exercise of authority, even if unjustly so, due to the prejudices of his audiences. Still, in other cases where the market is less taken with the personality traits of women, they still can do just as effective a job. If you can view the matter more objectively than the rest of the market, you can make some relatively good hires.

There is yet another reason to give many supposedly "non–nice girls" an extra consideration. Even if the more aggressive women will alienate your customers or their co-workers, you don't have to let them alienate *you*. The market as a whole is penalizing the more aggressive women by measuring their impact on customers plus co-workers plus the boss or hiring authority (you). At the very least you can become more detached and eliminate that source of bias. It then remains the case that you should pay more attention to the talented women whose personalities do not always fit perfectly what the market currently favors.

There is pretty clear evidence, coming from a variety of quarters, that bosses dislike some personality traits in women for reasons unrelated to job performance, and some of that research gives clues to the possible mechanisms at work. We don't regard any of these pieces of research as bulletproof, but in combination they do seem to suggest some common patterns of differential treatment for women.

In one study, by economist Martin Abel, 2,700 people are hired to do transcribing work. Associated with the task is a fictitious manager who offers what is in essence fictitious feedback. In this setting, if the (fictitious) boss criticizes the worker, the worker's job satisfaction falls, and furthermore, the worker starts assigning less importance to the job task. Criticism from the boss isn't enjoyed, which is hardly big news. But here is the striking result: these effects are twice as large when the negative messages are perceived as coming from female bosses compared to male bosses. Since this is online communication, it cannot be that these (fictitious) bosses are behaving any differently. Rather, it seems that many people have a harder time being criticized by an entity they perceive to be a woman.[8]

The literature on female voices, and how female voices are perceived, provides further evidence that some kinds of reactions to women are often more negative than reactions to men. In general, deeper voices are perceived as more authoritative, and that makes it harder for women to exercise authority with the voices they usually have, at least not without appearing bossy or strident. Women have to work especially hard in this regard; for instance, Margaret Thatcher hired a speech coach to, among other things, dramatically lower the pitch of her voice. More generally, it is striking that the pitch of women's voices has dropped significantly over the course of the postwar era. Women's voices used to register a full octave higher than men's voices, but now they register only two-thirds of an octave higher on average. That suggests women are trying to fit into a more "managerial" set of social roles, but it is not always easy for them, in part due to voice bias.[9]

Finally, consider the evidence, cited earlier, that both neuroticism and agreeableness affect the wages of women negatively. This is consistent with the feminist critique that women are supposed to be tough but not too tough, firm but not obnoxious, like men but not too much like men, and that they are asked to walk an almost impossible middle line in the workplace (and perhaps when running for political office too). It is less consistent with the view that difficult women are simply troublesome to deal with, and troublesome employees are costly for the company. If that were the dominant effect, one might expect agreeable women to command a premium in the workplace, yet that is not the case. So again, be open to the view that the "difficult" women may be undervalued in the marketplace. That may mean women are forced into a somewhat narrower set of acceptable workplace roles, and you can do better by cultivating a broader conception of how they might fit in. Think a bit less in terms of "women taking care of problems in the workplace" and more in terms of "women as innovators."

Confidence Gaps?

Once you get past anecdotal observation, we find in the research literature several (interrelated) major gender differences that consistently survive replication challenges, including in papers authored or co-authored by women. These results also hold up on multiple methods, including real-world data from the field and also from lab experiments.[10] These differences are the following:

- Women behave in a more risk-averse manner than men do.
- Women are more averse to competition than men.
- Women suffer from a confidence gap relative to men.
- Women in some key regards "put themselves forward" less.

Let's start with the evidence that, perhaps in response to the labor market penalties suffered by aggressive women, women as a whole do not self-promote as aggressively as men do. One carefully done study recruited nine hundred workers on Amazon Mechanical Turk, both men and women. The men and women were given tasks with possible bonus payments. They also were asked to assess their own performance on the task. When the metric was "I performed well on the test," with a scale of 1 to 100, women reported an average of 46. The men on average reported an average of 61 on the same scale, even though the actual performance of the men was no better than that of the women. That is a remarkably large difference in self-assessment. Furthermore, note this gap persisted even when both the men and the women had perfect information about their actual performance on the task.[11]

Another recent study looks at written proposals submitted to the Gates Foundation and finds a different kind of evidence for women being more hesitant. It turns out that women and men have different communication styles: women are more likely to use narrow, highly specific words, and men are more likely to use broader, bigger-picture words. (Are the men "more conceptual" or "blowhards"? Depends!) And reviewers, it turns out, favor broad words, which are more commonly associated with more sweeping claims, and disfavor the use of too many narrow words. It is important to note that the research associated with the more narrowly worded proposals, once created, did just as well in the intellectual marketplace as the research associated with the broader, bolder claims; furthermore, ex ante applicant quality was also measured as equal. This seems a clear case of intellectual bias, one where the average style of the women had a harder time competing. So don't be too worried if the women you are interviewing aren't making such sweeping claims.

The net result is that "even in an anonymous review process, there is a robust negative relationship between female applicants and the scores assigned by reviewers." This discrepancy persists even after controlling for subject matter and other variables. Notably, however, it disappears when controlling for different rhetorical styles. This is consistent with the view that men often do not "read" very well the different rhetorical, intellectual, and, yes, perhaps personality styles sometimes used by women.[12]

Perhaps most significantly, much of the gender gap in wages seems to be mediated by the personality factor of self-confidence. In a large variety of workplace settings, women, on average, are less self-confident than men and exhibit less self-confidence in public settings. Yet labor markets often reward confidence, sometimes even excess confidence. Some of what appears to be discrimination against women is actually discrimination against lower-confidence individuals, with the burden falling on women disproportionately. Note that the wage gap between men and women is highest at the higher levels of achievement, consistent with this hypothesis about confidence really mattering for wages, as presumably high confidence is demanded more at the higher job positions.[13]

Finally, there is some evidence that this confidence gap comes from very early in our lives, from high school or perhaps earlier yet. In one paper, looking at school grades 7–12, young women exposed to "high-achieving boys" perform worse academically and show lower confidence and aspirations. In contrast, they are helped by exposure to high-achieving girls. The young men, in contrast, are not affected by their exposure to either high-achieving boys or high-achieving girls. That too suggests that female discouragement is possible and occurs too frequently.[14]

That said, confidence gaps to some extent are self-fulfilling prophecies. As younger women see that there are relatively few female role models in a particular area, that may lower their confidence all the more. A self-perpetuating cycle is set in motion, and that cycle can be hard for a society to break.

All of these results point to the notion of a *confidence gap* as one of the main differences between men and women in the workplace, especially for higher-level jobs.

What does that mean concretely for an employer or talent seeker? First, for some jobs, such as asset trading, a lower level of confidence may be an advantage rather than a drawback. The less bullish presumably will be less willing to trade so frequently and less willing to take outrageously risky positions with their portfolios. For many jobs, including in politics, diplomacy, and prudential supervision, epistemic humility is more important than risk-taking. There is evidence from economics, for instance, that the gender confidence gap comes mainly from male economists making proclamations about areas they don't know much about.[15]

Second, if you are thinking of hiring a woman who is genuinely self-confident, you may well be underestimating her abilities because you may not so readily perceive the strength and virtues of her confidence, given the gender stereotype of lower female confidence. So look extra hard for such candidates, because women who are more competitive and less risk-averse than their gender average might be neglected by the broader market. By appreciating the true and higher value of those female hires, you can gain from the world's statistical discrimination and in the process rectify an injustice. Furthermore, note that the confidence gap accounts for more of the gender wage gap at relatively high levels of achievement. So this point is especially important for top jobs and much less significant for, say, simple service jobs or lower-level managerial tasks.

Third, very often jobs frame risk-taking and competitiveness in manners shaped by the male leaders of a company, or perhaps those framings are a holdover from earlier practice and leadership. More concretely, that means that many tasks within an organization may be framed more competitively than they need to be, or there may be a "rhetoric of risk" surrounding activities and tasks that are not really all that risky. (Ever try reading one of those breathless magazine articles about how everything in business is so dynamically changing everything all at once? It's not actually true.)

In short, one way to mobilize female talent within your company is to remove cultural barriers to the advancement of women. One study, for instance, found that it was possible to induce more women to compete simply with nudges and changing the choice of architecture to make competing in a particular situation "opt out" rather than forcing people to "opt in." In this constructed experiment, women were induced to apply for more potential promotions and experienced no adverse consequences regarding either their performance or their reported well-being. That is hardly a definitive result about real-world institutions, but it does communicate the basic point that if you encounter a generalization that seems true to you, you've got a chance to do better and outperform the market, rather than accept a brief for fatalism.[16]

So far we've focused on women in typical workplaces, but a separate literature considers the role of women as inventors. The data on patenting also show that women could, if given better opportunities, contribute more to innovation than is currently the case. But this present shortfall also may have to do with the aforementioned confidence gap.

First, women patent less than do men. For instance, in the data from 1998 only 10.3 percent of U.S.–origin patents have one or more female inventors. European data from 2009 show that women are involved in 8.2 percent of patents, and in Austria and Germany the numbers are as low as 3.2 percent and 4.7 percent, respectively. You don't have to think that patents are such a wonderful measure of inventiveness to realize that these numbers nonetheless are reflecting very real differences in what men and women are up to.

The common response to this reality is to suggest that there is a serious "pipeline problem"—that not enough women from a young age are encouraged to be engineers or to hold other comparable positions in the innovation pipeline. There is some truth to this charge, but the numbers support it less than we would have expected.

If you look more closely at the gender gap in patenting, it has multiple causes, but here is the surprising fact: "Only 7% of the gender gap is accounted for by the lower share of women with any science or engineering degree, while 78% of the gap is explained by lower female patenting among holders of a science or engineering degree." (The remaining 15 percent of the gap comes from a lower rate of patenting among women who do not have a science or engineering degree.) The single biggest specific source of the patent gap is that women are underrepresented in patent-intensive fields of engineering such as electrical and mechanical engineering, and also underrepresented in development and design, which are the most patent-intensive job tasks. So practically speaking, to whatever extent the confidence gap might be closed, women might become more interested in entering the more patent-heavy fields.[17]

It seems highly unlikely to us that the distribution of talent across gender represents some kind of inviolate and immutable natural order. There is a feasible future where more women work in riskier, patent-intensive jobs, just as we have had ongoing shifts of women into many other professions. Furthermore, a better allocation of talent really could matter. According to the study just cited, if the gender imbalance could be fixed entirely, the rates of patenting and innovation would go up, and GDP per capita would rise by 2.7 percent. Attaining even a fraction of those gains would be a big deal in a $20 trillion economy. And they could be a big deal for a talent seeker.

Researchers also have studied women in the venture capital process. Here too the results point our attention toward some biases relevant to the confidence gap. One study, by Sabrina T. Howell and Ramana Nanda, found that exposure to venture capital judges following a VC competition increased the chance that male participants would go on to found a company. The chance that women in similar circumstances would go on to found a company was much smaller. A follow-up survey found that men attained this greater success in part because they were much more willing to proactively reach out to the VC judges compared to the women. That may indicate the men have greater confidence in their ideas—and also greater confidence in getting a fair hearing from the judges, fear of harassment being another factor in this equation.

More generally, confidence gaps will lead to network frictions—meaning that it is harder to build out a large, very effective, and very diverse set of contacts. The resulting weaker ties can harm entire groups and in turn create the conditions that make confidence gaps seem at least partially justified.[18]

It is important for employers—especially male employers—to understand where the gender confidence gap might come from, at least in part. Both anecdotal and statistical evidence indicate that women who negotiate for promotions are more likely to be seen as intimidating, bossy, or aggressive. It is harder for ambitious women to be seen as likable. Sometimes the problem is directly sexual in nature. A group of guys can hang out together at work, sometimes even engaging in rhetorical horseplay and some amount of sexual joking and innuendo. In more extreme (but not uncommon) cases, they may go out together and visit strip clubs, or maybe get drunk together. A woman just doesn't fit into those groups in the same way. Furthermore, a woman who fully engages in off-work socializing runs the risk of being propositioned, and in extreme cases she can be assaulted. There is also the risk of coming under suspicion from the spouses of coworkers. It is a more difficult social and networking environment for women to negotiate. Mentoring can be psychologically more complex across the sexes, and these days, in an environment of #MeToo, many men are reluctant to mentor younger women in a close or intense manner. In such a world, many women are not entirely certain how they fit into the workplace picture.[19]

One recent study of 1,139 venture capital pitches from 2010 to 2019 applied machine learning techniques to categorize pitches in terms of their styles, which in turn was correlated against how venture capitalists received those pitches. We've already discussed some of the broader results in Chapter 5, but the gender results are interesting as well. When women are pitching as part of single-gender teams, the women are judged more stringently on pitch quality than are the men. That is consistent with the view that women have to walk a thinner tightrope when presenting themselves to the outside world. But the really striking result was this: when women pitched on mixed-gender teams, the quality of the women's pitch didn't really matter at all. It seems the potential investors paid attention only to what the men said.[20]

Finally, given all of these constraints, talent spotters should pay greater heed to women coming from nontraditional backgrounds and also to women who are late bloomers. Precisely because women are in some ways different from men, and many talent-spotting mechanisms are more geared toward males, it is easier for super-talented women to go unselected. It is also possible that many women, in the earlier stages of their careers, had negative experiences with sexual harassment, or had children, and then made their "comebacks" much later in their careers. For those and other reasons, talented women might take longer to find their true avocations.

Consider N. K. Jemisin, a black female science fiction author who has sold millions of copies and won Hugo and Nebula Awards. When she started out, she believed that a career in fantasy writing was closed to her due to her identity. Instead she pursued a graduate degree in psychology and ended up working as a career counselor in a college in Springfield, Massachusetts. Still, she kept on writing, often anonymously online. When she was thirty, she hit a wall: she was in debt, she disliked Boston, where she then lived, and she disliked her boyfriend. Only after she committed herself to writing for a living did things begin to turn around.[21]

For a more unusual example, consider Sister Wendy (Wendy

Beckett), who in the 1990s wrote bestselling books on art history and hosted a BBC television documentary program. Almost single-handedly, she interested an entire generation in the Western art classics and was described by *The New York Times* as the "most famous art critic in the history of television." Her career background was as a nun, and she appeared on TV in full habit and with her signature buck teeth. She was born in South Africa in 1930, spent much of her earlier career living under a religious code of silence, and later devoted herself to solitude and prayer. She suffered from periodic bouts of ill health and spent years translating medieval Latin scripts. That hardly seems like an auspicious beginning for a television celebrity. Yet one day she was talking about artworks in a museum, a film crew asked to videotape her, the clip came to the attention of a BBC producer, and the rest, as they say, is history, with the core of her artistic career starting after the age of sixty. Needless to say, no one else on TV or in the field of art history had the aesthetic or historical perspectives of Sister Wendy.[22]

Judging the Intelligence of Men and Women

So far we have focused on personality across genders, because we know personality effects are real and there is less of a case that intelligence differs between men and women. Still, there are some interesting results about intelligence and gender, and they are of direct relevance to the hiring process. Perhaps most importantly, it seems easier for many bosses and talent scouts to pick out the smarter men than it is for them to pick out the smarter women.

In one study, people who looked at photographs of men and women were, on average, better able to spot the men who measured as smarter in tests than the women who did so. Some people "look smart," and even if that judgment is highly subjective, some of the time it is correct. The countenances of those men offer socially accessible cues about their intelligence, but the countenances of women do not, at least not on average. In other words, it is harder for people, including male bosses, to pick out the smart women just from their looks. That result is open to several interpretations, but one obvious possibility is that smart women fit into stereotypes less, and also that many people are more accustomed to learning how to spot intelligence in men rather than women, perhaps because smart women do not always have the same high social status as smart men.[23]

Another interesting result from the paper is that women are in general better at assessing the intelligence of both men and women. We are not sure why that might be, but it is one reason (among others) to ensure that enough women have feedback into your hiring process.

There are also people who look smart but aren't—watch out for those candidates. One study, for instance, suggested that people give higher intelligence ratings to those who are smiling and to those who are wearing glasses, even when those traits show no particular correlation with actual intelligence. Those results are based on strangers rating 1,122 Facebook images, where the individuals who supplied the images had been given IQ tests. It is possible you have those biases too, so consider how you might limit them. Maybe give the frowning candidate with contact lenses a closer look, but at the very least don't be too confident in your looks-based assessments of how smart other people really are. These particular results about glasses and smiling have not been established through repeated replication, but we agree with the general idea that our intuitions about and judgments of intelligence can be led astray, so don't get too cocky.[24]

Anecdotally, we have found that men have a harder time judging the intelligence of women because women often present themselves as more agreeable in an interview setting than men do. The agreeableness may be pleasant to interact with, but it obscures critical judgment and smooths over the transmission of "data" about the intelligence of the interviewee. Many men, in particular, will incorrectly downgrade the intelligence of an especially agreeable woman. They may find her likable or "pretty smart," but the men won't be sufficiently open to the idea that perhaps she is very smart indeed. This is one bias that men (and many women) should try to avoid.

In essence, male judgment often goes astray when women are (a) quite agreeable or (b) not very agreeable. That's a lot of cases! One of the virtues of Five Factor personality theory, for all its limitations, is simply that it gives you some categories to help you think through and overcome some of your possible biases.

If evaluations of women's intelligence are "smoothed out" in this manner, as it seems they are, women may end up being favored for many midlevel jobs, especially those requiring high conscientiousness, because the woman seems like a safer choice. At the same time, it will be harder for a woman to demonstrate that she deserves to be considered for much higher positions. There might not be any bias *on average*, but still, many evaluators will find it harder to perceive and identify the highest reaches of the female talent distribution in a given endeavor. That result can hold even if male (and many female) evaluators are not prejudiced *on average* against women in the workplace.

On net, many of the biases against women in the workplace can be thought of in terms of this idea of smoothing. When it comes to personality, it seems that observers smooth out *too little* when forming their impressions of women, and instead embrace the exaggerated impressions. The "difficult women" are considered more difficult than they really are, and the "good girls" are favored and viewed as meek and cooperative more than is actually the case. When it comes to intelligence, likely we see the opposite, excess smoothing: really smart women are undervalued and the not-so-smart women are overvalued, with too many impressions bunched near the mean. So as a single, simple recommendation, you might try smoothing out your personality impressions of women more and your intelligence impressions less.

It is interesting that Y Combinator, a leading venture capital firm, always has at least one woman as part of a three-partner interview panel. Historically, that position was established by Jessica Livingston, one of the original four founders of YC. Jessica's acumen is legendary within YC circles, as she has a powerfully accurate gut instinct for talent, and in particular for weeding out bad apples. Jessica has since stepped back somewhat, but the organization has realized that much of that special *je ne sais quoi* wasn't unique to her. Women partners seemed better than men at detecting deceit or disingenuous founders. The addition of a woman also changes the conversational dynamic of the screening quorum's post-interview discussion in subtle and profound ways. We are not sure *why* but find it interesting that one of the most successful and durable talent screeners in the world requires that women be part of the screening process.

Cracking Cultural Codes
and How to Limit Your Biases About Race

Finally, in terms of general principles, what should you do when interviewing or otherwise evaluating individuals from another country, culture, or religious or linguistic background? How do you pull out the noise from the signal? Let's consider those questions, but we will focus on race as the relevant application, most of all in an American setting, because that's what we know best.

Being black in the United States is an increasingly diverse experience, in part because of significant immigration from Africa and the Caribbean and Latin America. The Washington, D.C., area, where Tyler lives, is now by far the world's second-largest "Ethiopian city," to provide a simple example. If Tyler encounters a black person in the course of daily life, the chance that person is an East African is fairly high. The Bay Area, where Daniel lives, also has a relatively high representation of East Africans. And within African American communities more narrowly defined, histories and experiences differ greatly. For instance, Clarksburg, Mississippi, is a very different environment from Los Angeles, and both are different in turn from Boston. In 2020 many Americans were surprised to learn that Minneapolis has such a serious problem with racism, although if you know the history of the city, you'll be aware that racial inequities have been a major theme there for a long time. On top of all those diversities, black men and black women in America may face very different kinds of racial barriers.

Our first piece of advice—and we mean this for individuals of all races—is not to pretend that you understand race as an issue very well. Don't approach the problem, and the issue of bias, with some pet theory about how the world works with respect to race, because the diversity of racial issues, problems, and biases likely will defeat your schema. Mostly, as an outsider, you want to shed many of your preconceptions, whether explicit or implicit ones, and open yourself up to the talent possibilities in minority communities, particularly communities you may have no connection to personally.

The interview setting is one straightforward way to see the relevance of racial issues. To provide an example, both Daniel and Tyler have noticed that interviewees from many foreign countries and cultures are much more polite—and also more distanced and formal—than are white Americans and most other white Anglo-American interviewees (Canadians, British, Kiwis, and so on). American blacks are often similarly polite and formal. These groups of interviewees are sometimes not sure what cultural rules they are operating under, or what kind of impression they are making, and so they respond with risk-averse strategies of politeness and formality. That eases communication in some regards, but it also makes it harder to understand them and to judge their talent strengths and weaknesses.

Quite simply, individuals from different cultures are harder to read. Furthermore, a basic question arises: If these individuals are behaving more politely, is that because their culture places greater value on politeness, and so maybe on the actual job they will actually *be* more polite? Or is it merely a temporary exigency, designed to deal with the unfamiliar situation of being interviewed by a person from a different culture? Or maybe it is a *permanent* exigency, to deal with what will continue to be an unfamiliar situation on the job? Very often you do not know the answer.

To the extent there is a cultural gap between whites and blacks (or other groups) in an interview setting, it is a common strategic response—on both sides—to take fewer chances. To be less natural. To tell fewer jokes. To reveal less about one's personal life. And so on. It is thus harder to move into the highly productive conversational mode that we discussed in Chapter 2. The end result is that you—even if you have no prejudices in the narrow sense of that term—are less likely to see the true talent strengths of the people you are talking to.

You will note that this mirrors some of the problems faced by women, as we discussed earlier. Women often feel—correctly in many cases—that there are fewer personality roles they are allowed to comfortably fill in terms of asserting "bossiness," dominance, or other qualities. Nor are they necessarily allowed to show a comparable degree of emotional weakness. And so they often (rationally) respond by putting themselves out there less, role-playing more, being blander and superficially more pleasant or perhaps super-formal, or even trying to hide behind particular styles of makeup and dress. Those information-obscuring behaviors are a reaction to workplace bias, even if no single person in a particular workplace has strongly sexist opinions about women. The response to broader social pressures is to choose and invest in particular modes of self-presentation to the world, and those modes cannot be changed at the drop of a hat in all circumstances, even when such changes would be advantageous for all parties involved.

Returning to race, when President Obama ran for office and served, he had the sense (probably correctly) that his options for displaying angry behavior were far more limited than white candidates and presidents have experienced. He always had to sound reasonable and to act calmly, in a way that never constrained his predecessor, George W. Bush, or the assortment of other politicians who use ranting and raving and outrage as rhetorical tools. For a black leader in America, those strategies are much harder to pull off without alienating or even frightening a significant share of the electorate. And so Obama remained famously cool. It is no accident that America's first black president is a personality type to whom such a cool mode of presentation came fairly naturally anyway.

The idea that "all white people are racist" may be upsetting to some white people who make an earnest effort to oppose racism, but it is important to see the truth in it. It is not that all white people intend racist outcomes. But it is the case that in a society with some racism and with some very definite cultural differences, one group of people—the wealthier and more powerful majority—will systematically be unable to see a lot of the talents of the less wealthy minority, in this case blacks. That is an obstacle that many, many black talent candidates face, and which is very difficult for the majority group to understand and to emotionally internalize as being real.

In sum, even in the absence of outright prejudice, blacks and other minority groups can face very real obstacles in making their talents known.

So what then to do? We don't have cure-all answers, but we would like to present a few steps you can take to better improve your perceptions of the talents of people outside of your immediate, closely connected groups. These are not silver bullets, but at the very least, marginal improvements are possible.

How to Broaden Your Perspectives on Race and on Many Other Matters as Well

The first thing you can do is to understand this problem. Plant in your mind the thought that a significant subclass of potential workers goes around with many of their talents invisible or at least significantly harder to spot. You can and should believe that, no matter what your exact view on the degree of explicit prejudicial intent in the modern world. The number of people who believe and internalize that truth simply isn't high enough, and you should make a point of being on the proper side of this ledger.

Again, this point applies to people of all races. No matter what your background, a significant portion of the hiring pool probably comes from people of races and backgrounds different from yours. This will be all the more true as "work from a distance" spreads and American companies continue to hire the best talent from all over the world, even if those individuals do not immigrate to the United States.

The next step is to adjust your behavior accordingly. Look harder for talent, and learn to look better, including across racial (and other) divides. We're not saying this is always easy, but it is remarkable how many people still have not even arrived at the stage of having any consciousness of the underlying problem at all.

Toward these ends, one concrete step you can take is to put yourself in environments where other people do not perceive *your* talents very readily, not only to get a sense of what that is like, but also to make the idea emotionally more vivid to you. For example, if you go to Finland, don't assume that everyone there hates you, is pissed off at you, or doesn't want to speak with you. The prevailing norms there are for people to be more distant and taciturn. When Tyler visited Finland, he felt he was crude and loud much of the time, and he went out of his way to moderate his behavior so as not to stick out so much. Maybe the Finns could not spot his talents or his articulateness as a result. That is the kind of experience you are trying to have—to feel what it is like when the perception of your talents is blunted. In turn, you will have a better sense of the possibly hidden abilities of others, whether the barriers be those of race, culture, religion, gender, or whatever.

Trying to learn a foreign language—and getting far enough to actually communicate—will serve this same end, though it can be very costly. For a long time, you just won't sound that smart or that clever. Tyler found it instructive, in his twenties, to live in Germany. At the time, he spoke good but not perfect German. From his demeanor and dress, he clearly was not an

American serviceman, and furthermore, most servicemen don't learn much German. As a result, many Germans assumed that he was Turkish or someone from some other area that often sent migrants to Germany, like the Balkans. Once he heard an angry "Get out of here, you Turk!" (in German) in response to one of his queries. That is, again, the kind of feeling you wish to experience and grow to understand, though we do not recommend having to stay in such a world all the time (to be clear, most Germans were very nice to Tyler during his year living there).

Try to see what it feels like to be the one assessed by a very different culture and not always assessed so generously. See how helpless or clueless you can at times feel. Without summoning up whatever external markers of status and wealth you might possess, try to ask someone in a (very) foreign culture to do you a significant favor. Try to measure whether the responses you get to this sort of test are different from what you might do at home when asked by a comparable stranger. Then emotionally internalize those lessons and recall them next time you interview people from very different racial or cultural backgrounds. Also keep in mind (depending on your circumstances) that you might always have the option of stepping out of such situations and returning to a relatively privileged life, but maybe the person you are interviewing does not have a comparable liberty.

Part of Daniel's success at talent selection may spring from the dual backgrounds in his personal history. He was born and grew up in Israel, but his parents are American Jews, and Daniel has a closer connection to American culture than most Israelis typically would have. Still, he is an outsider. Living in America, he has the perspective of a Jewish person who grew up in Israel and who also had Arab and Christian friends. Living in Israel, however, he was at least partially American in outlook, due to his parents and cultural ties and his flawless English and accompanying American accent (you can notice that Daniel does not have the American accent or vernacular of any particular region—often a giveaway that someone grew up abroad). An Arab swimming instructor taught him much more than the backstroke: the real lesson from Mr. Amos was that the inspiration to excellence could be found with someone who had a very different outlook on life. There was also no single religious community where Daniel felt at home, and so his whole life he has been used to looking at things from the outside. And his native bilingualism reinforced the notion that there is always more than one way to express or frame a particular idea—a source of mental flexibility and a natural entry point into the notion of multiple perspectives.

Maybe you were not born into such an environment, but at the very least, you should consider traveling to countries that would count as unusual relative to your native culture, as that can help you unlock and better understand the wide range of cultural variations. So instead of taking your next vacation on the North Carolina shore, try India or Tanzania (conditions permitting). Don't think that you now "get India," however. You had only a short period of time there, you probably don't speak the major native languages, and India itself is amazingly diverse, with multiple major religions and language groups, just as Tanzania is. What you can see, however, is just how far cultural variation can extend. How much your earlier presuppositions were based on contingent facts rather than human universals. How easily and how frequently you can be surprised by your interactions with people from other cultures.

Visiting Africa in particular may be useful for understanding race in the United States. It is not that any African countries are "like" the United States with respect to race, but rather you can learn from the contrast. In most parts of Africa (parts of southern Africa excepted), people do not grow up feeling race as an issue in the same way that an American black person might, in part because everyone around them is black. Often African migrants report that they first "learn race" only when they come to the United States. To spend time in an environment where most people are black but race is not the same kind of issue as it is back home in America can be remarkably instructive. And if you are white or Asian or Latino, you will be the one who sticks out and who is frequently conscious of that—another instructive way to learn something about what it is like to feel different all of the time.

More generally, making such trips will mean you will be caught less unaware when you are assessing and interviewing people from other cultures. Working off these principles, do send your kids to study abroad, or to live for a while in another country, if at all possible and affordable. If nothing else, you are contributing to their long-run success as a manager and talent selector.

It usually doesn't suffice on its own, but reading books is another way to broaden your horizons. When it comes to reading on race issues, we do have some very specific pieces of advice (again, keep in mind this is written from the perspective of two white guys).

First, read autobiographies, as their first-person narrative gives you a direct pipeline into the thoughts, feelings, and talents of some people very different from you. American history is remarkable for having so many superb African American first-person narratives. You can start with Frederick Douglass, Booker T. Washington, Zora Neale Hurston, Malcolm X, and James Baldwin. It is better to start with works from the more distant past, as they are less likely to collide with your current political views, and thus, you can absorb the content with fewer distractions. Reading President Obama's autobiography, in contrast, *might* be useful and instructive, but your opinion of it possibly will be too caught up in whatever you thought of Obama as president. So deliberately seek out a bit of distance, and history enables you to do that.

If you would like another concrete suggestion that goes beyond reading, visit a black church at least once, arguably more times if you find the experience to be meaningful (again, assuming public health conditions allow). It is one accessible way to see a very open side of black America, and you will be welcomed heartily.

If you wish to get more intellectually daring, here is another step you can take. Read or listen to some of the more radical takes on race, whatever might be outside your comfort zone. Recognize that you don't have to agree with them. But try to spell out in your own mind why somebody might possibly believe and promote those claims. If necessary, write out, if only privately, what you think are the best arguments for those points of view. That is one good way of trying to put yourself in the minds of others. See if what you come up with is at all convincing—not in the sense that you have to agree with it, but whether you think you really have come up with the strongest possible version of those arguments. Would the people on the other side of the debate recognize this as a smart and good-faith attempt to represent their perspective? Keep on working at this until you sincerely believe you have done your best in building a plausible case for views you disagree with.

We are recommending this as a means to deal with racial issues, but the method is general. If you have trouble getting along with people of different political or religious views, or have trouble spotting their talents, try to talk or write out their views in what you consider to be the most persuasive form possible. If only for a very short period of time, you will feel yourself, at least intellectually, put into their shoes.

We don't pretend to have covered any more than a sliver of the relevant issues when it comes to race and culture. At the very least, know what you don't know. The next step is to realize there is a problem and that there also is something you can do about it by improving your talent selection abilities. We hope we have helped you to make a few steps in that direction.

9

THE SEARCH FOR TALENT IN BEAUTY, SPORTS, AND GAMING, OR HOW TO MAKE SCOUTS WORK FOR YOU

One lesson from the world of fashion supermodels is the importance of scouts and scouting. A key question in talent search is when you should rely on scouting and when not. For a better understanding of that question, let's start with an anecdote about a case where scouting works pretty well.

Alisson Chornak used to drive his pink SUV around southern Brazil, searching schoolyards and shopping malls to find women with just the right look for a lucrative modeling contract. He is now CEO of a talent-spotting agency, Tango Management, for "street scouting and placement."[1]

It is striking how many well-known women models were discovered by scouts; for the most part they did not graduate from modeling schools. Gisele Bündchen was at a mall in São Paulo when a scout named Zeca, who worked for Elite Model Management, came up to her and said, "Do you want to be a model?" He spotted that "something" in her. At first Gisele yelled for her mom, but she ended up accepting Zeca's offer. Christie

Brinkley was discovered by a photographer when she brought her sick dog to the vet in Paris. Kate Moss was discovered by a model scout while she was squabbling with her father at JFK airport. Claudia Schiffer was discovered at age seventeen dancing at a disco in Düsseldorf, Naomi Campbell was spotted by a scout, and Behati Prinsloo approached by a man in a Namibian grocery store, who referred her to a modeling agency.[2]

There are beautiful women (and men) all over the place, but even in a model-rich environment such as southern Brazil, it is impossible for any talent agency to visit every village and meet and scrutinize every young woman. Furthermore, the school system is not an obvious venue for finding fashion model talent, at least not in the same way they can find mathematical or engineering or musical talent. Beauty is not on the curriculum, and it is institutionally awkward for the schools to too explicitly single out some women as much more beautiful or more appropriate for the modeling profession, even if they might do the same for tennis or gymnastics. In an age especially sensitive to #MeToo, fairness, "lookism," and self-esteem problems, publicly rating women for their modeling talent is a highly fraught issue.

Therefore, to help find the appropriate talent, the modeling sector has multiple tiers of scouts. There are photographers who may approach women in the hope of getting a successful photo shoot or two and maybe developing a good long-term reputation as discoverers of talent. But in addition there are full-time and freelance scouts who try to find the right women and then sell their finds to a modeling agency or magazine. For one quick dose of how this sector works, try visiting modelscouts.com.[3]

It is worth thinking about why the scouting model works in this context. First, the relevant talent could come from many different parts of the world, and the number of women to be scouted is very large. It is hard to imagine a centralized process getting the job done. Second, many of the scouts plausibly have a decent sense of who might make a good model. Looks are hardly the only factor behind modeling success, but they are a kind of "first stop," and expecting the scouts to judge looks well from first impressions is more plausible than expecting the scouts to use first impressions to judge talent well for skill in, say, quantum mechanics. Third, especially in some of the poorer locales, such as in Brazil, a reasonable fraction of the women have some interest in pursuing a modeling career. The scouts are not wasting their time by approaching these women. Finally, a follow-up investigation to judge the modeling talent of the chosen women is not extremely costly. You can have them in for a photo shoot and see how popular they prove in the market without having to invest millions of dollars right away.

One feature of the scouting model is how well it induces scouts to look in all sorts of nooks and crannies for talent. It is now well established that remote parts of Brazil and Russia are scrutinized closely for potential modeling talent. As the more obvious venues (say Manhattan) become crowded with scouts, scouts have to find their promising prospects elsewhere. If you see a tall, beautiful woman on Fifth Avenue, she may already be a model, or more likely she decided against pursuing that line of work. Thus, there has been an increasing push for scouts to look for prospects in the American Midwest. In Missouri, "nine times out of 10, they've never thought about it before," noted one commentator.[4]

In general, the scouting model tends to be effective when talent search is about starting with a very large pool and needing to narrow it down to a much smaller number of plausible competitors. For the final major decisions, however, typically full-time experts are required. Modeling agencies hire full-time experienced evaluators, or those evaluators are the agency owners themselves. In broader commercial contexts, the general partners in a venture capital fund make the final decision as to whether a promising prospect has a viable, executable project.

There is yet another reason the scouting model is robust, including in the supermodel context. Whether we like it or not, the returns to scouting are higher when income inequality is higher. Let's say you are facing a trade-off: bringing in a proven veteran or scouting for fresh new talent. The higher the salary of the proven performers, the greater the incentive to go scout some new talent. Compare this to the so-called good old days. At that time, there were still better and worse performers, but salary scales were more compressed, if only because the norms within firms were more egalitarian than today. That meant the top performers were underpaid, and you could always raid somebody else's company or institution for a top (veteran) performer by paying them just a bit more. (In fact, that is part of the story of how those older pay scales came to an end.) These days, in contrast, the top talents are paid what they are worth, and so there is a much stronger incentive to find quality talent that has not yet been identified as such.

For similar reasons, a very rapid 24/7 news cycle, driven by social media, also increases the returns to scouting. Everyone is looking for "the next big thing" or the next celebrity, and you won't find that among the tried-and-true performers, no matter how talented they may be. In the world of music, the Paul McCartney tour makes a lot of money, as do the Rolling Stones, but most of those gains accrue to the performers themselves. The talent spotter who wants to make money would like to find the next Billie Eilish.

Scouting is also becoming more important because the options for self-education are rising. Vuvu Mpofu, a female opera singer from a lower-income background in South Africa, is another paradigm of this new era. Her family loved gospel and choral music, but she had never heard opera until she was fifteen years old, at which time she fell in love with a Mozart aria she heard at a school concert. Yet living in Port Elizabeth, South Africa, she had no access to opera teachers. Nonetheless, she found two opera DVDs—*La Traviata* and *The Magic Flute*—and learned how to mimic them, thereby developing an operatic vocal style on her own. Later she applied to the South African College of Music at Cape Town University and was accepted despite her lack of formal training. A vocal coach spotted her talent, and the rest is history. In 2019 she had a premiere at Glyndebourne in England, one of the most exclusive operatic venues in the world. She seems destined for a very successful career and perhaps global stardom.[5]

Mpofu's marvelous story illustrates how talent search is changing. With more people trying their hand at various avocations than ever before, that places more and more burden on talent search and allocation mechanisms. We need to be more open to the accomplishments of self-taught individuals without traditional training. At the same time, many aspects of Mpofu's story are traditional. She is from the East Cape, an area sometimes called the "vocal breadbasket" of South Africa, a country with a long and rich tradition of (non-operatic) vocal music. She rose to the top by performing well in competitions and by attracting the attention of coaches and mentors. Yet the added element was being self-taught through relatively new technologies, in this case DVDs. (We note that YouTube has since become a primary medium for self-training in many areas.)

In any case, talent searchers need to be more open to self-taught talents than ever before. In the area of gaming, just about everyone is a self-taught talent in some fashion or another—no one shows up to *World of Warcraft* with a master's degree in the subject or with letters of recommendation. That means a higher burden on talent search, as there are more plausible candidates to sample and evaluate. Fortunately, candidates now are able to send more signals, whether through competitions, online postings, game performances, social media displays, or other indicators of quality.

Never before has there been so much information to sift through. It is a far cry from the older days of apprenticeships in many fields. Consider some corners of Indian classical music, where very often the main performers were the sons of previous stars who were identified rather readily at a young age. Even today, principles of family transmission continue. In the NBA, Klay Thompson of Golden State Warriors fame is the son of Mychal Thompson, formerly a star for the Los Angeles Lakers. Stephen Curry, also of the Warriors, is the son of former all-star shooter Dell Curry (Stephen's brother Seth plays in the NBA as well). Today, LeBron James has a son, LeBron "Bronny" James Jr., who was a sensation in high school basketball. Are you surprised to learn that Bronny was being tracked by scouts ever since he was young? In late 2019, when he was fifteen years old, he had 3.7 million Instagram followers, and fifteen of his high school basketball team's games were shown on ESPN. One of his teammates was Zaire Wade, the son of the elder LeBron's former star Miami teammate, Dwyane Wade.[6]

Even when the talent transmission is not from mother to daughter or father to son, today's talent-finding mechanisms still seem too dependent on parents. Consider the early history of Taylor Swift. Her path to success relied a great deal on geographic location and also on parental income. At age eleven, she made a trip to Nashville (from Pennsylvania) and started writing songs and playing the guitar with greater seriousness. She also started singing at sporting events as a means of becoming better known: "When I was eleven years old, it occurred to me that the national anthem was the best way to get in front of a large group of people if you don't have a record deal." That was a nice start, but what next? Her family knew to move from Pennsylvania to a suburb of Nashville when she was thirteen, and that enabled Taylor to be near the major studios, both to learn more about music and to meet people in the music business. At age fourteen, Swift signed a publishing deal with Sony/ATV Music Publishing, at the time being the youngest person the company had ever signed. Not only were her parents smart and supportive, but they were able to move to Nashville because the family already had accumulated enough wealth through their careers in finance. Furthermore, in her junior and senior years of high school she was home-schooled, which gave her the time and flexibility to focus on her music. And so we wonder: What about all of the Taylor Swifts whose families did not have the means and desire to move them to Nashville and also to switch them to home schooling?[7]

Venture capital firms have found an opportunity in scouting for hidden entrepreneurs. Traditional venture capital has fairly centralized means of evaluation run by a small number of prestigious and highly paid general partners. But Sequoia has had a scouts program for over ten years, and the new venture capital firms Village Global and AngelList Spearhead rely on scouting models to find their talent. With Sequoia, there are many independent scouts who have the authority to write checks in the range of $25,000 to $50,000 for potential start-up founders. The scouts play their biggest role at the seed stage, when often smaller amounts of money are called for, while the general partners might be writing much larger checks ($10 million and up) for more advanced projects. You can think of those seed deals as part of the pipeline for the eventual larger investments, and some of the economic upside is shared with the identifying scouts. The scouts can be given part of the profit from the deal, or a general share in the broader fund, or be paid on a performance basis, depending on how well they invest the funds they are given. The scouts are paid much less than general partners would be, and most of them will not be anything close to full-time, which further economizes on expenses.

Ben Casnocha, one of the founders of Village Global, expressed his scouting philosophy as follows: "There's an explosion of software-driven, diverse entrepreneurship around the world and across almost every industry. We believe this explosion of opportunity requires a fundamentally different approach to sourcing, selecting, and supporting. We believe a wide sensor network (i.e., a network of dozens of scouts) is more likely to discover a talented founder on day zero."[8]

The Limitations of the Scouting Model

In most cases, the scouts take care of only the early parts of the talent-finding and cultivation process. A particular kind of look may be a prerequisite for being a supermodel, but much more is required (think back to the idea, from Chapter 4, of the multiplicative model for top talent). Very often supermodels have to be in the right kind of shape, maintain the right kind of skin tone, have to know how to "carry" clothes, have to be photogenic, have to understand how to pose and walk, have to be willing to spend money getting the right look for their teeth, have extreme discipline, and ideally should be good at working with photographers and directors, plus much more. One problem that scout Alisson Chornak had was that some of his prospects from rural Brazil could not stand life in the big city, in this case

São Paulo. Discovering a potential supermodel with the right look is only one step in a very difficult process.

Note that when it comes to these other steps for identifying prospective supermodels, the sector relies more on centralized talent evaluation and less on scouts. A centralized talent agency or modeling agency or magazine or some other institution will make its own determinations about the skills and work habits of the candidates under consideration, because looks are only one part of the equation. The supermodel sector thus illustrates the limitations of scouting as well as the upside.

Another problem is simply that the scouts need to be paid, one way or the other. Furthermore, scouts need to be recruited. (Do you use other scouts for that? Is it "scouts all the way down"?)

But beyond those obvious challenges, introducing scouts into the equation creates what economists call agency problems. One set of agency problems may result from the discretion that scouts inevitably will have. In the modeling sector, for instance, that discretion may manifest itself in terms of sexual harassment or just general unfair treatment of the scouted, given that many of the scouts may be biased, may be unfair, or may behave in a way that's insufficiently heedful of the general reputation of the broader enterprise. The background searcher for talent, in this case the modeling agency, is not directly liable for scout behavior, either legally or reputationally, but still, bad scout conduct can translate into reputational penalties for the company.

Other problems stem from too much caution and possibly too little discretion along the dimension of talent hiring. A lot of scouts will lead to bureaucratized procedures for evaluating the performance of those scouts, and an inevitable loss of dynamism. The scouts may care more about their personal reputations than about the success of the broader enterprise. In particular, the scouts may be risk-averse, afraid to recommend the truly weird or outside-the-box options for fear of looking silly and losing their jobs. The old saying was "No one was ever fired for buying IBM." The new saying is perhaps "No scout was ever fired for recommending the future Rhodes scholar." Nothing against Rhodes scholars, who have a distinguished record of accomplishment, but the world is going to find and recruit them in any case. That is probably not the direction you want your scout to be looking, as those individuals already are on their Rhodes scholar track, and probably they are not so keen to join your new and risky enterprise.

Investing in lots of scouts also can lead to overconfidence and overbidding for the individuals with the best scouting reports. Perhaps the best and most extensive study of bias in talent scouting has been done by Cade Massey, at the Yale School of Management, and Richard Thaler, a Nobel laureate in economics at the University of Chicago Business School. They studied National Football League draft picks and found that first-round draft picks are systematically overvalued relative to later picks in the draft. That is, teams thought they could discern talent far better than actually turned out to be the case once the true talents of those players were revealed. Furthermore, over time teams do not seem to learn their way out of these evaluations. In essence, the early-round picks, even though they end up having the most talent, are too expensive, and the players picked later in the draft are the bargains.[9]

To grasp the import of this result, keep in mind what a specialized area pro football is. The potential players in the pro draft typically have been tracked for years, often all the way from high school. Their previous performance can be measured by collegiate statistics, there is plenty of tape of them playing, and a large number of professional scouts are attending these games or watching them on TV or tape. They and their families and friends are available for extensive interviews and personality profiling. Furthermore, football teams invest millions of dollars into each player, not just for salary but also for facilities, medical assistance, and training. The stakes are high, and it is hard to think of many areas where there is so much information about the quality of new workers. Yet the teams still overpay for the early draft picks. Massey and Thaler interpret their results in terms of overconfidence, and probably that is a relevant factor, but these biases also likely reflect agency problems. Scouts talk up the very talented prospects in order to affiliate themselves with the later winners, which will make the scouts look good. In the process, the scouts are not thinking much about team profitability, and so the teams end up overpaying for those players.

It is a general problem how to get the scouts doing something other than looking good to their bosses. Recently Tyler has started using a very talented scout for his Emergent Ventures program, and he is trying to work out how to incentivize scouts to do something other than to try to copy his judgment. "Don't please *me!*" he has urged, but you can see the potential contradiction in that dictate.

The key to a good scouting program is incentives. Initially the Emergent Venture scouts were venture capitalists themselves, hunting for the best talent, incentivized to compound the money of the partners. This worked: from Google to Apple, rebellious outsiders were admitted into the system, and the gatekeepers were handsomely rewarded. But as scouting expands and becomes a more general concept, the incentives needn't always be financial. Rewarding with status can work too; for instance, some of Y Combinator's greatest hits (Airbnb, Dropbox) have come from referrals. Daniel's Pioneer firm maintains a leaderboard of its best referrers, and that is one of Pioneer's most frequently visited pages. In these models, most referrals are bad, but the exceptional candidates often are referrals.

This in turn brings us to the second incentive dynamic: skin in the game. Venture funds also run scout programs in which various founders are provided free money to invest. No downside, all upside. These programs often perform poorly, but occasionally a scout will spot an exceptional company, which the VC then doubles down on. This is unlike the proper venture world, where the partner of a fund has both economic and status interests at stake. The founder investing free money is not putting up either dollars or status, and the primary avocation of those founders is being a CEO, not a venture capitalist. Nonetheless, that may give them a certain freedom of imagination that enables them to spot some opportunities that others would not.

In essence, skinless scouting games boost variety at the expense of precision. You can engage a broader set of actors working on other things to send you their deal flow in exchange for value. This is a good idea if your filtering costs are low. Conversely, if deal costs are high, you might want to consider some element of risk. Either financial risk (a mix of personal capital with external) or status risk (demand that your scouts do scouting under their own name and as their primary job) may be used to impose additional discipline on the process.

Centralized Evaluation and Its Advantages as an Alternative to Scouting

In contrast to the supermodels, consider a very centralized mode of evaluation. Soviet chess was an example of a talent search method that sampled nearly all possible candidates as part of a common national system. Virtually every Soviet child went to school, all schools supported and taught chess, and chess was socially focal in Soviet society and offered relatively high returns to the best players, including the possibility of travel abroad. A significant number of parents played chess in the home and taught the game to their children at young ages. There were also active chess clubs just about everywhere, not just in the schools.

If you had the potential to be a top Soviet chess player, the chance you would be found by the dragnet was very high. It was hard to slip through the cracks, and talent search did not rely on finding an obscure candidate hidden away in a village somewhere. There was no scout going up to young kids at a Soviet shopping mall or discotheque and saying, "Hey, you look like you might be a good chess player!" Instead, through Soviet chess and scholastic institutions you would be identified and encouraged at a young age, and you would indeed have your chance to become a great chess player, even if you did not live in one of the major cities. Scrutiny and measurement were near-universal, and so potential talent had a chance to shine.

The result was that Soviet players dominated world chess from the 1940s through the 1990s, when the Soviet system (not only for chess) fell apart. Since that time, Russia has been "just another chess country," with only a modest advantage in the sector.

The Soviet talent search method, however, is not feasible in most sectors. For one thing, there just isn't that much top-down control in most parts of society these days, not even in the still partially communist China. Furthermore, talent search is more global, and the relevant tasks, skills, and outcomes are not as well defined in most sectors as they are in the world of chess. Sometimes you don't even know exactly what skills you are looking for in a candidate. And if you find a potential candidate, there is no obvious test of talent as easy as "Hey, let's play a chess game!" It is in this world that scouting takes on greater importance, and search takes priority over measurement within the talent pool.

Note, however, that at least some Soviet-style conditions may reemerge in the future in a greater number of sectors—not soon, but it is possible to imagine worlds where there are so much data on individuals, including genetic data, and at such a young age that measurement would once again dominate search. You wouldn't have to "look for" anybody, at least not if you could access the data in the system. To provide one extreme example, if everyone is tracked and recorded by facial surveillance, you can imagine a futuristic science fiction world where the AI picks out the top possible fashion supermodels and sends them a text message, scheduling the appropriate appointments with the modeling agencies. The point is not that this can or will happen soon; rather, you should keep an open mind as to how the balance between measurement and search is going to evolve. Right now the search dimension is relatively important, but some of the balance could swing the other way in the future. You shouldn't take the current configurations for granted.

We expect there will be more and more cases where talent is found "by the numbers," or by AI scouts. If you look at the Houston Astros, one of the most quantitatively advanced teams in professional baseball, they already have eliminated in-person advance scouting, instead preferring videotape and measurement using Statcast, a state-of-the-art tracking technology based on massive amounts of data.[10]

The future likely will make talent search more and more like the gaming environment, where potential candidates are invited to step up and be measured. If you think about the very best gamers in, say, *World of Warcraft*, there was no scout visiting local high schools trying to talk kids into giving the game a try, spotting them in the shopping mall ("your thumbs look strong and your skin has that basement pallor"), or measuring their

IQ, reaction speed, or game stamina. Rather, millions of people wanted to play the game in the first place, and the gaming process itself measures how good they are. There is, once again, a kind of Soviet-style centralization, but with the game itself and its data systems taking the place of the Soviet government and chess establishment.

Heidi Klum is one of the supermodels who is an exception to the scouting method of talent search. In contrast to many of her peers, she got her start by winning a modeling competition with thirty thousand competitors. In the future, this kind of path will be more likely, except information technology will play a larger role in the judging.[11]

Could it be that the very best *World of Warcraft* players are not picked up or spotted by current institutions? Maybe. But *World of Warcraft* is pretty well known, millions of people have tried it or comparable games, and it seems plausible that those who do not want to try or to pursue the endeavor don't in any case have the dedication to rise to the top tier of players. The odds are that the search for the best *World of Warcraft* players is more efficient than the search for supermodels. Furthermore, the emphasis on precise measurement means that your *World of Warcraft* score doesn't depend on sleeping with the talent scout, having an uncle in the modeling business, or, in the case of Soviet chess, censoring your political views so you would be allowed to travel abroad to play in the best tournaments. Current gaming is meritocratic in the sense that if you score more points you will win.

And these days, gaming isn't just something you do for fun. There are plenty of individuals who play online games for a living, cultivating a fan base and interacting with their followers. The game tournament is now "for real," and it has become an economic sector and a source of entertainment and event in its own right. More and more, in today's world of talent search, people have the chance to try.

One upshot here is that if you are doing talent search, you need to figure out whether the scouting model (search) or the gaming model (measurement) best applies to your endeavor. Most likely you will need some combination of both. Still, the market as a whole is not thinking very analytically about either scouts or games, so understanding this distinction is a source of potential competitive advantage to you.

Who Makes for a Good Scout?

Reliance on scouting raises the question of how to find the best scouts. There is plenty of literature on how to find and hire workers, as we have surveyed. But how about finding scouts? How much does intelligence matter, or conscientiousness? Or maybe neuroticism here is a big positive? Hard data are not available, and even anecdotal data are hard to come by. If you try to read books on baseball scouting, for instance, they are entertaining, but they do not seem to yield easy answers as to who makes for a good scout.

Nonetheless, we will offer the following (highly speculative) points for finding and evaluating good scouts. First, a good scout does not in general have the same qualities as a good performer overall. Good scouts typically are masters of networking rather than performance per se. Still, the quality scout still must have an excellent understanding of the topic area, but he or she does not need to have been a star. In fact, having been a star may interfere with the objectivity and judgment of the scout. Top stars too often have a kind of intolerance toward other, different kinds of talent, or they expect too much of prospects too quickly.

Second, a good scout should have some measure of charisma.

The scout isn't just searching for prospects; prospects are also searching for scouts. The personality of the scout has to stand out in some manner, and it has to attract the aspirational side of potential top performers. In this regard, think of talent search as a kind of two-way matching platform. Put yourself, at least temporarily, in the shoes of a prospect and ask what kind of scout might attract you. Scouting is competitive, and your scout is not the only one out there, least of all for a potential top prospect. In some ways, picking a scout is more like "picking a scout*ed*" than you might at first think. After all, where is the bargaining power in this market really going to lie—with the scout or with the potential future star?

Third, excellent scouts should be very good at communicating back to the home office, especially in larger, more bureaucratized organizations. It's not enough to find the next big thing; you need to convince others you have done so. Therefore look for writing and presentation skills—and, yes, once again, charisma—so that what the scout learns can be translated into action. In smaller organizations, if you are scouting for yourself, this factor is less likely to matter, and if you are a charismatic brooding loner you still might be pretty effective as a scout, at least provided your personality matches the level of scale you are operating at.[12]

Fourth, if you are using nontraditional means to look for talent, don't just load up on specialists in the old-style methods. The Houston Astros, for instance, used a McKinsey consultant and also a former blackjack dealer (he was a former engineer as well) to help them turn their baseball talent quest into a highly advanced quantitative pursuit. The old-school baseball scouts, as you might expect, thought it was all about intuition and personal contacts, and so they were not ideal choices to usher in these new methods of search, in spite of their expertise in the game and in player development. So keep an open mind about what kinds of backgrounds you might be looking for. Either a "quant" or a humanities specialist could turn out to be more valuable than someone with narrow sectoral expertise (again, subject to the condition that you are trying out new methods of talent search, and the skills of the scout must match the methods of search).[13]

It is an interesting question how much one should look for objectivity in a talent scout. As we mentioned in Chapter 1, we understand the talent search methods of Peter Thiel—one of the most successful talent finders of all time—as intimately linked to Peter's philosophical and indeed moral judgments of people. Peter is objective in the sense of seeking successful outcomes from the talent search process, but he is highly subjective in the sense of mobilizing his own emotions and judgments to energize and finely hone his sense of who is a potential talent and who is not. No matter what your point of view, Peter's worldview will be quite different from yours, and that is a big part of Peter's strength as a finder of talent—namely, that the way he imposes his will and judgment on the talent search process gives him access to energies and insights that most other people simply do not have.

Investing in Your Network— Perhaps the Biggest Lesson

One final point is this. For all the resources you put into scouting, interviewing, and trying to suss out the better candidates, there is no real substitute for having a good or great pool of candidates. That will depend on your soft networks, ones that you and your institutions have been cultivating for years (you hope). It depends on the people you know, the other institutions willing to recommend you, the image of your institution in the eyes of the informed public, your network of previous employees, the media coverage you have received, your social media presence, and possibly donors or board members, among other factors. Most of these possible candidates you will not know personally; maybe no one on your team will know them personally. Still, they know you, in some manner or another, and it may be possible to get them to come out of the woodwork and apply for a job or a fellowship. In other words, most talent search really isn't about driving a pink SUV around southern Brazil.

Biomedical venture capitalist Tony Kulesa, in his article on Tyler's Emergent Ventures project, explained the approach to networking very clearly:

> Tyler promotes the opportunity in such a way that the talent level of the application pool is extraordinarily high and the people who apply are uniquely *earnest*. . . . Tyler is famous for his eclectic and hyper-cerebral content, which he distributes through a curated set of media channels tailored to the talent he searches for. He co-writes the widely read economics blog *Marginal Revolution* (~1M monthly readers according to *SimilarWeb*), he has 186K twitter followers, he hosts the podcast "Conversations with Tyler," and appears on podcasts from Tim Ferriss, Eric Weinstein, and Shane Parrish.

Tony then cites Tyler (on Tim Ferriss's show) speaking as follows: "I try to stay a bit weird and obscure enough that mostly quite smart people are writing me. If I had too many not smart emails I would feel that I was doing something else wrong with what I'm writing. . . . The rate of good applications is reasonably high. Maybe I'm lowering it just by talking about the program."

Tony also wrote:

> Once Tyler discovers a social circle enriched for talent, he expands and many members are quickly funded. The goal seems to be to

hook an initial person, and then generate referrals. One can imagine Tyler's search strategy as fishing in a well-chosen set of pools, not yet overfished from the mainstream. And when he hooks one fish, sometimes he also discovers a whole school.[14]

Or consider the import of prior networking in the context of online interviews, the focus of Chapter 3. The best way to do an online interview is to have a formidable online reputation and presence in the first place, because that will attract the more desirable candidates. Furthermore, the more skeptical you are about the interviewing process, the greater the importance you should attach to pre-selection and filters in the first place. To the extent that the difficulties of online (or for that matter in-person) interviewing makes you doubt the quality of the knowledge you gather from interviews, it can have the useful effect of forcing you to invest more in the quality of your network in the first place.

If you believe that talent is the greatest asset of your institution, you also ought to believe that your soft network is one of the greatest assets of your institution. Because that is how you will attract your talent in the future; furthermore, those subsequent hires will help you retain your current talent by making your institution more successful and a more attractive and prestigious place to be.

When it comes to Pioneer, the soft network started with the generally high prestige of venture capitalists, the Bay Area, Daniel's background at Apple, and the backing of both Andreessen Horowitz and Stripe, prestigious firms in their own right. Word about Pioneer spread through podcasts done by Daniel, through Twitter, and through the affiliation of Pioneer with Stripe and Andreessen Horowitz. It was helpful that *The New York Times* published an article about Pioneer as the early tournaments were opening, and that article helped frame Pioneer as interesting and cutting-edge. A later article in *Wired* was more snide, but still it presented Pioneer as a difficult, gamified challenge that many young people were interested in. Pioneer affiliated with the ideas of global talent, gamification, open entry for the world, and a willingness to consider projects that were not just "same old, same old," such as Axon, a portable MRI machine, or a programming language for physics. Eventually, the network of Pioneer winners, near-winners, and wannabe winners became major spreaders of the word about Pioneer.

When it comes to Emergent Ventures, much of the soft network behind the applications came from readers of *Marginal Revolution*, Tyler's blog for the last eighteen years, and one with a relatively curious and intellectual tone. It is a magnet for people who might become public intellectuals in some manner. Many of the other applicants were people who knew someone who read *Marginal Revolution* and were told about Emergent Ventures. Other applicants had some familiarity with Tyler's podcast, or they were people who had worked at Mercatus (the home institution for Emergent Ventures) or had known someone who had worked at Mercatus. All of those factors were selecting for some kind of intelligence, intellectualism, curiosity, engagement with public issues, and strong conceptual ability. In due time, some Pioneer winners promoted Emergent Ventures (and vice versa), which further boosted the quality of applicants.

Most people, if you ask them, will agree on the importance of soft networks, but in terms of actual practice, such networks remain neglected. On any given day in your business or institution, there are fires to be put out. Acting to extend your informal networks feels like a nice thing to do, but rarely does it seem urgent or necessary. Furthermore, building up a soft network is not always so easy. Doing quality work, in some publicly observable manner, often does more to build up the soft network than waking up in the morning and proclaiming, "Hey, let's build out the soft network today!" It is often the case that institutions with very strong informal social networks ended up with them indirectly, as the result of projects they wanted to undertake anyway, rather than through the direct planning of an informal soft network.

One striking example of the power of soft networks is given by the career of Aretha Franklin, chosen by *Rolling Stone* magazine as the greatest American vocalist of all time. Obviously she was a black woman, and furthermore she was an unwed teen mother, twice. You might think it would be very hard to discover a talent with that background, and in some ways you would be right. Nonetheless, the black musical community in Detroit discovered Aretha early on, in part because her father was a very well-known preacher. Aretha was known for her singing by the time she was twelve years old, and she also dated an older Sam Cooke at that time. But known to whom is the key question here. If you were not in touch with the people who knew of Aretha's talent, you were not in touch with Aretha either. By eighteen, Aretha had a recording contract with Columbia Records, in part because musical scouts knew to tap the soft networks of Detroit and other major American cities for top talent. You are probably not going to find the Aretha Franklins of your world by standing on the street corner, so you need to be investing in those soft networks as much as you can.[15]

Here is a broader set of options for building out your soft networks.

Loyal, Preexisting Communities

Top schools explicitly cultivate cooperative networks across their alumni and also across current and former faculty and students.

That creates a preexisting community interested in, and aware of, the problems of Harvard, Stanford, Princeton, and so on. And if those schools are advertising to fill their jobs, or looking for those who might perform a task or favor, there is a very talented cooperative network already in place.

Some private companies invest in similar communities. There is, for instance, a network of McKinsey alumni. And people who have been through Y Combinator have the sense of having been through a common experience and sharing something from their backgrounds. These communities are drawn upon for hires, recommendations, and favors, and to some extent those individuals are pre-vetted and likely to be more cooperative or more talented than average.[16]

Talent Community of Experts

Some organizations explicitly organize a collection of experts and later draw on that community for help and advice, and perhaps also for hires. Professional and scientific associations would be examples, but so is the Gerson Lehman Group, which connects experts to businesspeople and intermediates their consulting. Think tanks and research centers often build up their own networks and later turn to those networks, either to hire from them or for help and hiring recommendations.

Building a Talent Community in Advance, Often from (Relatively) Undiscovered Individuals

We've already discussed this method in the context of Pioneer and Emergent Ventures. The Thiel Fellowship program is another example of this approach, as is On Deck (beondeck.com), which markets itself to entrepreneurs as the place to look when they wish to do their next big thing. Readers of a book can create such a community on the internet as well.

Build a Platform or Set of Tools That Attracts Talent

Twitter accounts, blogs, podcasts, YouTube channels, and online publications (Reddit, Hacker News, and many others) all build communities, filtering in some individuals and filtering out others. When messages or job ads are later broadcast on these channels, a highly selected set of individuals is reached, for better or worse. To the extent the initial audience is of high quality, this can be an effective means of raising the quality of applications. Both Pioneer and Emergent Ventures have used this approach.

Most likely, your set of filters should be part of an integrated strategy. Whom are your filters bringing through the door? And which strengths and drawbacks are those individuals likely to have? Your talent search and interviewing techniques never start from a totally blank slate; they should start from an understanding of where your institution stands in the broader scheme of things, and what are the main problems you face when trying to attract talent.

10

HOW TO CONVINCE TALENT
TO JOIN YOUR CAUSE

We have focused on finding talent, but in reality, finding talent is not completely separate from helping to *create* talent. "Being found" is a big part of what encourages individuals to take the next step toward achievement and excellence. You will do best at finding people and making the most of your discoveries if you understand how these two features are related. And that will make you better—reputationally and in practice—at attracting that talent to come and work for your cause or your organization.

It is well known that venture capital gives people money if they are starting a new company with promise, and also that venture capital gives them a business network and a lot of hands-on advice and training. It is less well known that the very act of being selected by a good venture capital firm raises people's confidence and aspirations and encourages their ambitions. Much of the value of venture capital comes from that latter effect—helping to create and improve talent rather than just finding it. Toward this end, many venture capital firms (and nonprofits) have an air of self-importance surrounding them, in part to radiate status, motivate their affiliates, and raise everyone's aspirations.

Raising the aspirations of other people is one of the most beneficial things you can do with your time. At critical moments, you can raise the aspirations of other people significantly, especially when they are relatively young, simply by suggesting they do something more important and ambitious than what they might have in mind. It costs you relatively little to do this, but the benefit to them, and to the broader world, can be enormous.

As George Eliot put it in *Daniel Deronda*: "It is one of the secrets in that change of mental poise which has been fitly named conversion, that to many among us neither heaven nor earth has any revelation till some personality touches theirs with a peculiar influence, subduing them into receptiveness."[1]

Once you understand the power of raising people's aspirations in this manner, you will realize that the value of talent search is that much higher. There is a large payoff to finding the right people to encourage.

So often potentially talented people just don't see that they could be doing something different and better than what they are currently engaged in. Barack Obama had no plans to run for president until he found himself surprised by the positive media reaction to a speech he delivered at the 2004 Democratic National Convention; only a few years later he won the presidential election.[2]

Don't underestimate how little people, including your employees and applicants, may think of themselves. There is an ongoing crisis of confidence in many human beings, even in the best of times, and that means high returns from nudging talent in the proper direction. If you are able to spot people who are having a confidence crisis and if you understand the nature of those crises, you're all the better placed to give them the right kind of positive nudge.

Sometimes employees may come to you with job offers or potential offers from other quarters. It is striking how some people will consider offers that are inferior or unsuited to their skills and work ethic. "I want to see you leave this institution for a better offer than that—and you will!" is sometimes the message you need to send them. That too is an instance of raising their aspirations. Don't assume that your best and most productive workers actually know what they are capable of, because very often they do not and need nudging in the right direction to realize their full potential.

When you raise the aspirations of an individual, in essence you are bending upward the curve of that person's achievement for the rest of his or her life. There is a powerful multiplier effect of compounding returns that can continue for many decades. Actually, the full net impact can be longer yet, if that individual in turn works to later raise the aspirations of others. If you are helping to create an individual who raises the aspirations of *many* others, the return on your initial aspiration-raising activity can be that much higher. It may even turn out that aspiration raising is a kind of eternally growing, never-ending source of plenty, giving us ongoing compound returns without end—a concept Tyler discussed in his earlier book *Stubborn Attachments*.

If you have any doubts about the power of environment and the framing of aspirations, consider just how much genius and achievement have been clustered in time and space throughout history. The statistician David Banks wrote a paper on this phenomenon called "The Problem of Excess Genius." Ancient Athens in its time had Plato, Socrates, Thucydides, Herodotus,

Sophocles, Euripides, Aristotle, Aeschylus, Sappho, Aristophanes, and many other notable figures. It wasn't "something in the water"; rather, Athens had the right ethos and cultural self-confidence, combined with institutional structures for learning, debating philosophy, and writing for the theater, all of which identified and mobilized this talent. That allowed those individuals to learn and draw inspiration from each other as well as to develop rivalries for excellence, friendly or otherwise.

The Florentine Renaissance produced a long string of first-rate artists, culminating in Leonardo and Michelangelo, even though Renaissance Florence had a population of only about sixty thousand plus the surrounding area. The Venetian Renaissance, another powerful cluster built on a limited base, is associated with Bellini, Titian, Tintoretto, Veronese, and others; since the end of the eighteenth century, however, Venetian art has produced little of note. In Germanic classical music, the era 1700–1900 brought the Bach family, Handel, Haydn, Mozart, Beethoven, Schumann, Brahms, Wagner, and many others, even though the Germany of that time had much lower population and wealth than the Germany of today. There is some genetic luck behind these outcomes (what if Beethoven's parents never had met?), but still, those eras did an amazing job of identifying and then inspiring the available talent at hand.

Closer to the present day, the Bay Area has been a major petri dish for attracting, cultivating, and mobilizing talent for tech, software, start-ups, and much more—think of the region's role in hippie culture, alternative and psychedelic cultures, and gay liberation.

The bottom line is that environment, ethos, and competitive rivalry really matter, and to the extent you can create the proper conditions in your local ecosystem, you can have a major impact on talent mobilization.

Methods for Raising Aspirations

The key theme here is to raise personal and career and creative trajectories—in other words, to boost the entire slope of possible future achievement. Those interventions offer by far the highest potential boost. You can think of them as you, on a modest scale, trying to create the next Florence, Venice, or Vienna.

There is an old saying (with many variants): "Give a man a fish, and feed him for a meal; teach him how to fish, and feed him for a lifetime." We think that is remarkably unambitious! The value of learning how to fish is not that high, as reflected by the only so-so wages earned by fisherfolk. Furthermore, knowing how to fish still doesn't, on its own, get you a job with the most successful and highest-paying fishing ventures.

We say instead: "Boost the rate of productivity growth in that person's fishing company." Or better yet: "Teach a person how to start a fishing company that will feed millions. Teach a person how to hire talented people to make a better fishing company." Those are increases in trajectory, and along the way they will teach many thousands of employees how to fish or how to contribute to the fishing process. Always look to take it one step higher and to teach other people how to do the same.

If you've ever found yourself saying that silly fishing maxim to yourself in your head or to others, purge it from your thoughts. Upgrade it. Imagine a future company that will replace fishing altogether, instead producing a superior foodstuff at lower prices that is also better for the environment. Teach a person how to replace fishing. *Now* we're getting somewhere.

So many interventions to benefit others provide them only with one-time benefits. We don't mean to discourage you from performing these acts of kindness, which are essential to interpersonal benevolence and also for the smooth functioning of civilization. But also realize their limitations. A one-off benefit for someone looks like this:

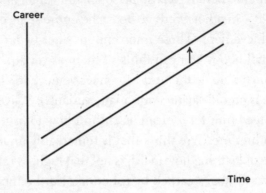

Raising the slope of their trajectory can look like this:

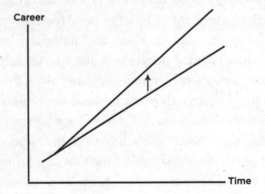

In the very short run, the benefits from those two activities may be virtually identical. But over time, the benefits of the steeper slope are much, much greater, and those benefits will include everyone who is learning from that person along the way.

You might wonder: If the benefits from a higher slope are so great, why isn't the higher, steeper slope chosen in the first place? Arguably this is one of the mysteries of human nature, but we think it springs from the nature of choice. When making decisions, people do not usually have a complete map of the options and their probabilities before them. In fact, many of the options can be difficult to imagine. For instance, a talented young person may not take seriously the notion that he or she someday could be a major CEO. That person has heard of CEOs, and maybe has not actively dismissed the possibility of being one. But if it's going to influence the young person's behavior, that possibility needs to be brought to mind as a live, vivid alternative. Once the alternative is properly, mentally real and alive in the person's mind, then perhaps it will raise ambition and in some cases lead to a trajectory that culminates in a CEO position. The default has been shifted for that option to move from unconsidered to being on the table, whether or not it ultimately happens.

Making those alternatives vivid is the role of the mentor, the talent scout, and the role model. Just as America's entertainment sector makes action or romance scenarios vivid, so must the mentor and talent scout perform a similar function. In this regard, the mentor is drawing upon expertise in the humanities, either explicitly or implicitly, even if he or she imagines the enterprise to be involved in tech, STEM, or something else rigorous and distinct. A key role here is for the mentor or talent scout to shape and present him- or herself so that he or she embodies an alternative and inspiring vision of what the mentee's life might be like.[3]

If you are going to raise the aspirations of others, they should view their affiliation with you as a matter of pride. They should feel selected in some manner. They should feel like they have gone through trials and tribulations to get to their current point. They should feel like members of some exclusive club where they can look around and feel good about their affiliations with the other club members.

The easiest way to create these feelings is to have them be true. Create institutions and designations that reward those you consider to be talented. This can be a venture capital firm, a named scholarship series, a prize, or many other things. Focus on the substance, but also understand that the substance is working in part because of the theater surrounding it. You will then do a better job of raising the aspirations of those you consider to be talented, and you will be a partial co-creator in their rise to the top.

One of the seminal cultural takes on mentorship is the 2014 movie *Whiplash*, about a drumming teacher who pushes his students as far as they can go. Daniel has been struck by how many of the people he has interviewed at Pioneer cite this film as an influence. Perhaps the film is appealing because it describes the pursuit of excellence and validation through hard work. Great people want to be great. They want to be pushed to become the best version of themselves. They're also equally uncertain, often searching for recognition as to where they stand in the world. The story of a young drummer clamoring for his teacher's approval resonates with them. No, we don't argue for throwing drumsticks at your charges, but still, your approval has to be seen as something worth earning.

You should also help your awardees see that what may appear to be distant is partly familiar (though not easy to reach). It is striking how much evidence has accumulated in the social sciences in recent years about the value of role models, especially for women and minority groups but also for virtually everyone. If you see "someone like you"—which can be defined in various ways—doing something, that something then has a greater chance of becoming a live, vivid alternative, and it is in turn more likely to be chosen.[4]

So you, as a talent scout, employer, mentor, friend, or role model, can have a staggering amount of influence. You can open doors for other people at relatively low cost (perhaps zero cost) to yourself just by making some options more vivid to them. You can do that through your writing, your YouTube presence, your friendship and mentoring, and just meeting people and being yourself. You embody *something*, and that something will stir some others into action.

Use those powers wisely!

This mentorship effect has been measured, by the way, and it seems to be powerful. In 2019 Tyler had a podcast interview with Abhijit Banerjee, co-winner of that year's Nobel Prize in economics. Banerjee and co-authors (including his wife and co-laureate, Esther Duflo) published a 2015 paper that showed very high returns to making cash transfers to the very poor *when those transfers were combined with coaching*. In a series of six countries (Ethiopia, Ghana, Honduras, India, Pakistan, and Peru), cash transfers with coaching yielded net returns of over 100 percent, sometimes ranging up to 433 percent—a remarkably successful aid program. Yet the same cash transfers without coaching had only a modest positive impact. When Tyler asked Banerjee why the coaching made such a difference, he explained that the recipients of these cash transfers had grown up expecting very little of themselves and had virtually no confidence. The main function of the coaching was not transmission of any particular kind of expertise but simply to show the recipients that another way of life, another destiny, was possible for them.[5]

Here is his explanation:

And for them, I think confidence is an enormous issue because they've never actually done anything in their life successfully. They've been living hand-to-mouth, usually begging from people, getting some help. What that does to your self-confidence, your sense of who you are—I think those things, we haven't even documented how brutal it is. People will treat you with a little bit of contempt. They might help you, but they treat you with a little bit of contempt as well.

This is the kind of people—at least the one that I was a big part of studying was the one in India and also one in Ghana. Especially the one in Bengal. These women—they were living in places where nobody should live. One said, "Oh, we get snakes all the time." Another one said, "I'm now vending knickknacks in the village," basically kind of cheap jewelry, that cheap stone jewelry or plastic jewelry.

"Before the people from this NGO showed me where the market was to buy wholesale, I had never taken a bus, so I had no idea how to go there. They had to literally put me on a bus, show me where to get off. And it took a couple of times because I had never taken a bus. I couldn't read, so if it's a number X bus number, I don't know what X is, so how would I know I'm getting on the right bus?"

All of these things are new. If you start from a place where you really never had a chance, I think it's useful to have some confidence building. You can do it too. There's nothing difficult about it. . . .

[The coaching is] also saying, "You can do it, and here are the steps." Turning things into a set of processes is important. Otherwise, it looks like an unlikely proposition that I can do it. I've never done it. I've never bought and sold things. In fact, I've never sold anything, and how do I do it?

It's a bit more than that. Turning things into process is important also, that here is how you get on a bus. You go there, you pay this much money, they give you something, you bring it back. One of the things they are doing is also turning it into a set of procedural steps, which is very different from saying, "Go do that."

Returning to the wealthier countries: Daniel in his online memoir gives another example of how to bend aspiration curves in an upward, steeper direction:

> Lastly, there was this pretty *remarkable paper*. Two researchers in the US reported that an extraordinarily cheap intervention ($6 per student) targeted at high-achieving, low-income students— basically, just *encouraging* them to apply to top-tier colleges—had a marked impact on their propensity to do so. (Students who simply saw their notice were, on average, admitted to colleges whose median SAT score was 53 *points higher* and that spent 34% more on their students.)[6]

Once again, help others dare to think in terms of higher career trajectories.

The Travel Grant

One of our core views is that potential top achievers should be exposed to the highest levels of talent in their area as early as possible. This is much of the value of having a very talented tutor or mentor, or going to a top university such as Harvard, Stanford, or MIT. It is not that the classes or instruction are so much better than elsewhere (often they are worse); rather, at those schools students have the chance to see what the very top minds in a field are like. (Those top minds are sometimes the other students, not just the faculty.) That includes taking in how they think, how they talk, how they evaluate problems, how they decide what to work on, and even getting a sense of what their work habits are like, especially if the students serve as a research assistant for them or perhaps write a paper with them. Students even get to see what their possible failings and blind spots might be, why they have succeeded nonetheless, and just how strong their strengths are.

That kind of experience is invaluable, and it's usually more important than mere book learning because book learning can be acquired on one's own. Receiving such exposure is one of the biggest arguments for going to a famous major research university rather than the instructionally superior smaller liberal arts colleges such as, say, Middlebury or Claremont. At those latter institutions, the professors are very smart and more dedicated to their students, but typically they are not world-class research talents.

Given those realities, one way to invest in talent is to find highly promising young individuals and expose them to a higher level of achievement than what they have seen to date. Send them somewhere, and if you can, arrange meetings for them. Not everyone can get to meet with Jeff Bezos and Bill Gates, but do the best you can. Show them a higher level of talent, achievement, and aspiration than they have experienced previously in their lives. If they have real ambition, that will be not merely a one-time gain but a more fundamental steepening of their entire trajectory of future achievement.

For many talented young people, the travel grant means a trip to Manhattan or the Bay Area, which host amazing clusters of talent. But for someone working in entertainment it could be Los Angeles; for the biomedical sciences it could be Cambridge, Massachusetts (or Cambridge, England); for culinary skills it could be Paris or Tokyo. Nonetheless, it is striking how few places make sense for most of the people who might be getting travel grants, since most places do not have clusters of world-class talent in any significant amount. In fact, we view the scarcity of appropriate travel destinations as one sign among many that the world is not doing a good job at discovering and mobilizing top-tier talent. Since most people never get their chance to see "the big time" in their preferred field or avocation, their full potential is never realized.

Better yet than a travel grant—but also more costly—is living in the preferred area of clustered talent for a year or more. Money aside, however, a lot of people aren't ready to take that step yet, and so the travel grant is one way of introducing them to the area where they properly ought to be.

Finally, a small percentage of travel grants should be directed away from geographic clusters of particular expertise. Some people are too embedded in a particular world or community, too stuck in its presuppositions and conformities, and they simply need to get away, perhaps to an isolated or highly idiosyncratic locale. We don't view this as the main case, but it is worth keeping in mind if you are wondering what kind of travel grant to give somebody who grew up on the Upper West Side of Manhattan. Six months in rural Ethiopia might be exactly the right prescription (keeping in mind a lot of rural Ethiopia still does not have reliable connections to the internet). And if the visitor comes to learn that many rural Ethiopians have amazing expertise in teff farming or in particular kinds of icon painting, so much the better.

Send Them to an Event (or Create an Event)

One advantage of an event is that it may expose the attendee to top achievers and performers and help make those trajectories vivid alternatives. In those regards the event is similar to a travel grant, except you are sending them to a location that is important only temporarily.

But event attendance may serve other purposes as well. An event may convince the attendee that a social or tech movement is real, or that it is benevolent, or that it is popular and desirable to belong to, or that it is not crazy. Events make that knowledge vivid in a way that reading about a movement does not: "Look, here are all the other people interested in nuclear fusion!"—or cryptocurrency, or venture capital. For exactly the same reason, events are risky, as they may scare some people off ("Hey, those people are crazy!"). Usually, though, the scared-off individuals were not going to make major contributions to that cause anyway, and so event attendance speeds up their possible reallocation to another cause or venture, one that might prove a better match. Or maybe those people really are crazy; if so, it's better to find that out sooner rather than later. Events are an accelerated test of cultural fit.

Creating your own event is costly in terms of time and money, but it can be an ideal way of raising the aspirations of those you consider talented. You get to control everything, from the invitees to the program to what they will eat for breakfast. Daniel has organized successful events for Pioneer winners, and Tyler has done the same for Emergent Ventures.

But here is the important thing to understand about organizing your own event: the group has to gel. You can raise their aspirations a bit, but the group itself creates most of its own dynamic and its own theater. The members of the group will raise each other's aspirations, at least if you have selected well and structured your event to give them enough interaction with each other. When the leader (you) and the peers are pushing in a common direction—the raising of aspirations—the effect can be very powerful indeed. But you will need to give them the freedom of letting them contribute to defining what the group is all about.

Write a Book? Read a Book?

Finally, to close our journey, we note that writing a book is yet another way to make talent and talent search vivid. Not everyone can go to a select event, or move to the Bay Area and hang out with venture capitalists, or run a venture capital firm. But most people can read a book. Even if you've been everywhere and met everyone, you want a book as a touchstone for what you have been thinking about—a kind of memento, even if you do not agree with all of the contents, to keep your mind fixed on the topic, and to help you discuss the topic with other people you know.

If nothing else, we have written this volume to make the idea of talent search more vivid to you. We are certain that many of the empirical results will change over time and be updated with new studies, new learning, and new information. But the vision that talent search is "a thing," that it is an art that can be learned and improved upon, and that it can be taught and communicated to others—that is the fundamental point of this presentation.

Go and do it! And please communicate back to us what you have learned.

ACKNOWLEDGMENTS

For useful comments and discussion and assistance, the authors wish to thank Adaobi Adibe, Sam Altman, Marc Andreessen, Christina Cacioppo, Agnes Callard, Bryan Caplan, Greg Caskey, Ben Casnocha, John Collison, Patrick Collison, Natasha Cowen, Michelle Dawson, Alice Evans, Richard Fink, Elad Gil, Auren Hoffman, Reid Hoffman, Robin Hanson, Ben Horowitz, Coleman Hughes, Garett Jones, Charles Koch, Sandor Lehoczky, Kadeem Noray, Shruti Rajagopalan, Daniel Rothschild, Hollis Robbins, Michael Rosenwald, Virgil Storr, Alex Tabarrok, Peter Thiel, Erik Torenberg, Peter Tosjl, and others we surely have forgotten. None of them is responsible for any of these contents.

APPENDIX: GOOD QUESTIONS

These are mostly pulled from the text, but we have added a few extras for your reading pleasure. Consult Chapters 2 and 3 for information on how and when to use them.

- "What do you think of the service here?"
- "Do you usually find rooms to be so noisy?"
- "Why do you want to work here?"
- "What are ten words your spouse or partner or friend would use to describe you?"
- "What's the most courageous thing you've done?"
- "If you joined and then in three to six months you were no longer here, why would that be?" (Ask the same question about five years as well, and see how the two answers differ.)
- "How did you prepare for this interview?"
- "What did you like to do as a child?"
- "Did you feel appreciated at your last job? What was the biggest way in which you did not feel appreciated?"
- "Who are our competitors?"

- "What are the open tabs on your browser right now?"
- "What have you achieved that is unusual for your peer group?"
- "What is one view held by the mainstream or as a consensus that you wholeheartedly agree with?"
- "Which of your beliefs are you least rational about?" (Or maybe better yet: "What views do you hold religiously, almost irrationally?")
- "Which of your beliefs are you most likely wrong about?"
- "How do you think this interview is going?"
- "How successful do you want to be?" (A variant is: "How ambitious are you?")
- "What would you be willing to trade to achieve your career goals?" Or "How do you think about the trade-offs that might be required to achieve your career goals?"
- "In the context of the workplace, what does the concept of 'sin' really mean? And how does it differ from a mere mistake? Can you illustrate this from the experience of one of your co-workers?"
- "In which ways might a Skype or Zoom call be more informative than a person-to-person interaction?"
- "In what ways are you not WYSIWYG [what you see is what you get]?"
- "Is this person so good that you would happily work for them?"
- "Can this person get you where you need to be way faster than any reasonable person could?"
- "When this person disagrees with you, do you think it will be as likely you are wrong as they are wrong?"
- "How would you rate yourself on a scale of 1–10 on X? . . . And why is that rating the right number for you?"
- Something about revealed preferences in their past lifetime.

NOTES

1. Why Talent Matters

1. Here is Daniel's autobiographical Medium essay: "Introducing Pioneer," August 10, 2018, https://medium.com/pioneerdotapp/introducing-pioneer-e18769d2e4d0. Otherwise, this section about Daniel was written by Tyler alone.

2. See "What Will You Do to Stay Weird?," *Marginal Revolution* (blog), December 24, 2019, https://marginalrevolution.com/marginalrevolution/2019/12/what-will-you-do-to-stay-weird.html#comments.

3. See Peter Cappelli, "Your Approach to Hiring Is All Wrong," *Harvard Business Review*, May–June 2019, and Sarah Todd, "CEOs Everywhere Are Stressed About Talent Retention—and Ignoring Obvious Solutions for It," Quartz, January 15, 2020.

4. See Eric Berger, *Liftoff: Elon Musk and the Desperate Early Days That Launched SpaceX* (New York: William Morrow, 2021), 20.

5. While writing this book, we have seen that negative or near-negative yields on safe government bonds are common around the world, covering trillions of dollars in assets. What does that mean operationally? The demand for loans and capital is not so strong as to push interest rates into positive territory, or in other words, capital is not so scarce. What is scarce for successful enterprise is talent.

6. On these points, see Chang-Tai Hsieh, Erik Hurst, Charles I. Jones, and Peter J. Klenow, "The Allocation of Talent and U.S. Economic Growth," *Econometrica* 87, no. 5 (September 2019): 1439–1474.

7. See David Autor, Claudia Goldin, and Lawrence F. Katz, "Extending the Race Between Education and Technology," National Bureau of Economic Research working paper 26705, January 2020.

8. See Laura Pappano, "The Master's as the New Bachelor's," *The New York Times*, July 22, 2011; "37 Percent of May 2016 Employment in Occupations Typically Requiring Postsecondary Education," Bureau of Labor Statistics, June 28, 2017, https://www.bls.gov/opub/ted/2017/37-percent-of-may-2016-employment-in -occupations-typically-requiring-postsecondary-education.htm.

9. We will not cover the new artificial intelligence programs for talent search, as are used by companies such as HireVue and Pymetrics. It is too early to feed all of the CVs and demographic data and interview tapes into an AI black box and come up with useful answers. There is even talk of measuring brain waves, other real-time biometric data, and social media profiles, but again we are skeptical, at least for the time being. Right now such programs will not remove the need to exercise human judgment, and so that judgment will be the focus of this book. On measuring brain waves and other more speculative options, see Hilke Schellmann, "How Job Interviews Will Transform in the Next Decade," *The Wall Street Journal*, January 7, 2020.

2. How to Interview and Ask Questions

1. See Mohammed Khwaja and Aleksandar Matic, "Personality Is Revealed During Weekends: Towards Data Minimisation for Smartphone Based Personality Classification," working paper, July 29, 2019, https://arxiv.org/abs/1907.11498.

2. See Brooke N. Macnamara and Megha Maitra, "The Role of Deliberate Practice in Expert Performance: Revisiting Ericsson, Krampe & Tesch-Römer," *Royal Society Open Science* 6, no. 8 (August 21, 2019): 190327, http://dx.doi.org/10.1098 /rsos.190327.

3. See Tyler Cowen, "Sam Altman on Loving Community, Hating Coworking, and the Hunt for Talent," *Conversations with Tyler* (podcast), February 27, 2019, https:// medium.com/conversations-with-tyler/tyler-cowen-sam-altman-ai-tech-business -58f530417522.

4. On the macro and organizational issues, one very good recent book is Colin Bryar and Bill Carr, *Working Backwards: Insights, Stories, and Secrets from Inside Amazon* (New York: St. Martin's Press, 2021).

5. For one typical anti-interview piece, see Sarah Laskow, "Want the Best Person for the Job? Don't Interview," *The Boston Globe*, November 24, 2013. Or see Jason Dana, "The Utter Uselessness of Job Interviews," *The New York Times*, April 8, 2017, a poorly titled piece that refers primarily to a single specific study. For a meta-analysis regarding the value of structured interviews, see Allen I. Huffcutt and Winfred Arthur Jr., "Hunter and Hunter (1984) Revisited: Interview Validity for Entry-Level Jobs," *Journal of Applied Psychology* 79, no. 2 (1994): 184–190. See also Therese Macan, "The Employment Interview: A Review of Current Studies and Directions for Future Research," *Human Resource Management Review* 19 (2009): 201–218, for a more recent examination of the same questions.

6. Tyler Cowen and Michelle Dawson, "What Does the Turing Test Really Mean? And How Many Human Beings (Including Turing) Could Pass?," published online 2009, https://philpapers.org/rec/COWWDT.

7. The sources here are private conversations, and also see this Twitter thread started by Auren Hoffman (@auren), "question for those that hire people: What are the best (and most novel) strategies for evaluating people to hire?," Twitter, March 23, 2019, 11:56 a.m., https://twitter.com/auren/status/1109484159389425664. For one source on the importance of childhood achievements, see Ruchir Agarwal and Patrick Gaule, "Invisible Geniuses: Could the Knowledge Frontier Advance Faster?," *American Economic Review: Insights* 2, no. 4 (2020): 409–424.

8. Peggy McKee, "How to Answer Interview Questions: 101 Tough Interview Questions," independently published, 2017.

9. Jeff Haden, "Fifteen Interview Questions to Completely Disarm Job Candidates (In a Really Good Way)," Inc.com, February 14, 2018.

10. CS 9, "Problem-Solving for the CS Technical Interview," taught autumn 2017 by Cynthia Lee and Jerry Cain. See their slides on "Teamwork and Behavior Questions: How to Prepare in Advance," https://web.stanford.edu/class/cs9/lectures/CS9Teamwork.pdf, accessed June 7, 2019, no longer online, full class background online here: https://web.stanford.edu/class/cs9/.

11. Tyler Cowen, "What Is the Most Absurd Claim You Believe?," *Marginal Revolution* (blog), March 21, 2006, https://marginalrevolution.com/marginalrevolution/2006/03/what_is_the_mos.html; see also Tyler Cowen, "The Absurd Propositions You All Believe," *Marginal Revolution*, March 22, 2006, https://marginalrevolution.com/marginalrevolution/2006/03/the_absurd_prop.html.

12. See Nicholas Carson, "15 Google Interview Questions That Made Geniuses Feel Dumb," Business Insider, November 13, 2012.

13. Adam Bryant, "In Head-Hunting, Big Data May Not Be Such a Big Deal," *The New York Times*, June 20, 2013. Jeff Bezos also attempted such questions in the early days of Amazon, though later the company abandoned the practice. See Colin Bryar and Bill Carr, *Working Backwards: Insights, Stories, and Secrets from Inside Amazon* (New York: St. Martin's Press, 2021), 32.

14. See Jessica Stillman, "The 3 Questions Self-Made Billionaire Stripe Founder Patrick Collison Asks About Every Leadership Hire," *Inc.*, November 19, 2019, https://www.inc.com/jessica-stillman/questions-to-ask-leadership-hires-from-stripes-patrick-collison.html.

3. How to Engage with People Online

1. On some of these points, see the interesting remarks by Viv Groskop, "Zoom In on Your Meeting Techniques," *Financial Times*, April 7, 2020.

2. See Spencer Kornhaber, "Celebrities Have Never Been Less Entertaining: Top Singers and Actors Are Live-Streaming from Quarantine, Appearing Equally Bored and Technologically Inept," *Atlantic*, March 21, 2020.

3. For an interesting discussion of online teaching, see Jeanne Suk Gersen, "Finding Real Life in Teaching Law Online," *The New Yorker*, April 23, 2020.

4. On celebrities, see Gal Beckerman, "What Do Famous People's Bookshelves Reveal?," *The New York Times*, April 30, 2020. On British parliamentarians, see Sebastian Payne, "Zoom with a View: The Pitfalls of Dressing for 'Virtual Parliament,'" *Financial Times*, April 29, 2020.

5. On Zoom fatigue, see Julia Sklar, "'Zoom Fatigue' Is Taxing the Brain. Here's Why That Happens," *National Geographic*, April 24, 2020, and also Kate Murphy, "Why Zoom Is Terrible," *The New York Times*, April 29, 2020.

6. See Daniel's short essay "Communication in World 2.0," April 2020, https://dcgross.com/communication-in-world-20.

7. On the history of confession, see John Cornwell, *The Dark Box: A Secret History of Confession* (New York: Basic Books, 2015), especially xiii–xiv and 44–45.

8. For one survey of views on the therapeutic couch, including some skeptical remarks, see Ahron Friedberg and Louis Linn, "The Couch as Icon," *Psychoanalytic Review* 99, no. 1 (February 2012): 35–62.

9. Alex Schultz, "How to Go on a Digital First Date," *GQ*, March 20, 2020.

10. On this point, see "Fever When You Hold Me Tight: Under Covid-19 Casual Sex Is Out. Companionship Is In," *The Economist*, May 9, 2020.

11. Lori Leibovich, "Turning the Tables on Terry Gross," Salon, June 22, 1998.

12. See Giovanni Russonello and Sarah Lyall, "In Phone Surveys, People Are Happy to Talk (and Keep Talking)," *The New York Times*, April 18, 2020.

13. On this "dressing up" phenomenon, see Schultz, "How to Go on a Digital First Date."

14. On this general point, see Jim Hollan and Scott Stornetta's seminal article "Beyond Being There," *CHI '92: Proceedings of the SIGCHI Conference on Human Factors in Computing Systems* (New York: ACM, 1992), 119–125.

4. What Is Intelligence Good For?

1. Philippe Aghion, Ufuk Akcigit, Ari Hyytinen, and Otto Toivanen, "The Social Origins of Inventors," Centre for Economic Performance discussion paper 1522, December 2017.

2. Relying on data from Finland may make these results less relevant elsewhere. For instance, in the relatively egalitarian Finnish society, environment is perhaps less likely to shape outcomes, and that will raise the influence of IQ on outcomes in a manner that might not hold for the United States, where variations in childhood environment are much greater and thus might carry greater explanatory power.

3. Miriam Gensowski, "Personality, IQ, and Lifetime Earnings," *Labour Economics* 51 (2018): 170–183.

4. See Erik Lindqvist and Roine Vestman, "The Labor Market Returns to Cognitive and Noncognitive Ability: Evidence from the Swedish Enlistment," *American Economic Journal: Applied Economics* 3 (January 2011): 101–128.

5. Sagar Shah, "The Life Story of Vladimir Akopian (2/2)," Chessbase.com, November 28, 2019, https://en.chessbase.com/post/so-near-yet-so-far-the-life-story-of-vladimir -akopian-2-2. On chess and intelligence, see Alexander P. Burgoyne, Giovanni Sala, Fernand Gobet, Brooke N. Macnamara, Guillermo Campitelli, and David Z. Hambrick, "The Relationship Between Cognitive Ability and Chess Skill: A Comprehensive Meta-analysis," *Intelligence* 59 (2016): 72–83. For an alternative perspective, and for evidence on the import of short-term visual memory, see Yu-Hsuan A. Chang and David M. Lane, "It Takes More than Practice and Experience to Become a Chess Master: Evidence from a Child Prodigy and Adult Chess Players," *Journal of Expertise* 1, no. 1 (2018): 6–34.

6. Note, by the way, that data-based studies typically do not cover enough of these very high achievers to measure their potency in a systematic way. On this point, see Harrison J. Kell and Jonathan Wai, "Right-Tail Range Restriction: A Lurking Threat to Detecting Associations Between Traits and Skill Among Experts," *Journal of Expertise* 2, no. 4 (2019): 224–242.

7. See Dunstan Prial, *The Producer: John Hammond and the Soul of American Music* (New York: Farrar, Straus and Giroux, 2006), Benson quotation from 255.

8. Garett Jones, *Hive Mind: How Your Nation's IQ Matters So Much More than Your Own* (Stanford, CA: Stanford University Press, 2016). For a meta-analysis on the value of cooperation across talented teams, see Dennis J. Devine and Jennifer L. Phillips, "Do Smarter Teams Do Better: A Meta-Analysis of Cognitive Ability and Team Performance," *Small Group Research* 32, no. 5 (2001): 507–532. See also an idea in economics called "O-ring theory"—for instance, Michael Kremer, "The O-Ring Theory of Development," *Quarterly Journal of Economics* 108, no. 3 (August 1993): 551–575.

9. It is interesting to explore *why* higher-IQ individuals tend to cooperate more in these games. One reason is that they are more likely to open (some) games with a uni-lateral act of cooperation—an act of faith, you might call it, or perhaps boldness—perhaps reflecting a greater understanding of just how beneficial cooperation can be. The second reason is that the higher-IQ individuals have a greater consistency of strategy implementation. This makes it easier and quicker for them to get into, and stay in, self-sustaining loops of greater cooperation. And that is what you likely want for your organization—namely, people who can cooperate more because of their greater capacity for strategic thinking. That said, the higher-IQ individuals are not unconditionally greater cooperators. For instance, when cooperation is not in their self-interest, they may be quicker to defect or behave in another manner. So this risk of opportunism may remain ever present, even if they are greater cooperators on average. Another interesting feature of this research is that agree-able individuals, as would be defined by personality theory in psychology, do not cooperate much more, not as much as you might think. They are more likely to cooperate in the early stages of the game, as you might expect from their agree-able natures, and they do offer more unconditional cooperation up front. But as

the games unfold, these individuals do not match the cooperative performance of the higher-IQ individuals.

10. Marc Andreessen, "How to Hire the Best People You've Ever Worked With," June 6, 2007, https://pmarchive.com/how_to_hire_the_best_people.html.

11. See Jeffrey S. Zax and Daniel I. Rees, "IQ, Academic Performance, and Earnings," *Review of Economics and Statistics* 84, no. 4 (November 2002): 600–616. You will find broadly similar results in Jay L. Zagorsky, "Do You Have to Be Smart to Be Rich? The Impact of IQ on Wealth, Income and Financial Distress," *Intelligence* 35 (2007): 489–501. When it comes to accumulated wealth rather than income, his study cannot even find a general positive correlation between wealth and IQ.

12. See John Cawley, James Heckman, and Edward Vytlacil, "Three Observations on Wages and Measured Cognitive Ability," *Labour Economics* 8 (2001): 419–442. For an overview on this issue, see Garett Jones and W. Joel Schneider, "IQ in the Production Function: Evidence from Immigrant Earnings," *Economic Inquiry* 48, no. 3 (July 2010): 743–755, this work being co-authored by an economist and psychologist who work in this area. For a more popular treatment of the same material, see also James Pethokoukis, "Is America Smart Enough? A Long-Read Q&A with Garett Jones on IQ and the 'Hive Mind,'" American Enterprise Institute, January 12, 2016, http://www.aei.org/publication/is-america-smart-enough-a-qa-with-garett-jones-on-iq-and-the-hive-mind/.

13. See Dawson McLean, Mohsen Bouaissa, Bruno Rainville, and Ludovic Auger, "Non-Cognitive Skills: How Much Do They Matter for Earnings in Canada?," *American Journal of Management* 19, no. 4 (2019): 104–124, esp. 115.

14. See Renée Adams, Matti Keloharju, and Samuli Knüpfer, "Are CEOs Born Leaders? Lessons from Traits of a Million Individuals," *Journal of Financial Economics* 30, no. 2 (November 2018): 392–408.

15. See Ken Richardson and Sarah H. Norgate, "Does IQ Really Predict Job Performance?," *Applied Developmental Science* 19, no. 3 (2015): 153–169. As for intelligence and complexity of job tasks, one well-known piece on that topic is Linda S. Gottfredson, "Where and Why g Matters: Not a Mystery," *Human Performance* 15, no. 2 (2002): 25–46. Working through this and other pieces, however, leads to the conclusion that many of the commonly repeated claims in this literature are not verified. A useful survey and interpretation of some major pieces is Eliza Byington and Will Felps, "Why Do IQ Scores Predict Job Performance? An Alternative, Sociological Examination," *Research in Organizational Behavior* 30 (2010): 175–202.

16. "The Top Attributes Employers Want to See on Resumes," National Association of Colleges and Employers, https://www.naceweb.org/about-us/press/2020/the-top-attributes-employers-want-to-see-on-resumes/, accessed June 2, 2020. See https://www.naceweb.org/talent-acquisition/candidate-selection/key-attributes-employers-want-to-see-on-students-resumes/.

5. What Is Personality Good For? Part One: The Basic Traits

1. Timothy A. Judge, Chad A. Higgins, Carl J. Thoresen, and Murray R. Barrick, "The Big Five Personality Traits, General Mental Ability, and Career Success Across the Life Span," *Personnel Psychology* 52 (1999): 621–652; on predicting career success, see 641. For a general survey of this whole literature, see Lex Borghans, Angela Lee Duckworth, James J. Heckman, and Bas ter Weel, "The Economics and Psychology of Personality Traits," *Journal of Human Resources* 43, no. 4 (2008): 972–1059.

2. See Ellen K. Nyhus and Empar Pons, "The Effects of Personality on Earnings," *Journal of Economic Psychology* 26 (2005): 363–384.

3. See Gregory J. Feist and Frank X. Barron, "Predicting Creativity from Early to Late Adulthood: Intellect, Potential, and Personality," *Journal of Research in Personality* 37 (2003): 62–88.

4. See Dawson McLean, Mohsen Bouaissa, Bruno Rainville, and Ludovic Auger, "Non-Cognitive Skills: How Much Do They Matter for Earnings in Canada?," *American Journal of Management* 19, no. 4 (2019): 104–124, esp. 116. Note that this paper adjusts for selection into occupation as a factor mediating personality traits and resulting wages.

5. See Christopher J. Soto, "How Replicable Are Links Between Personality Traits and Consequential Life Outcomes? The Life Outcomes of Personality Replication Project," *Psychological Science* 30 (2019): 711–727. On experimental replication, see Maria Cubel, Ana Nuevo-Chiquero, Santiago Sanchez-Pages, and Marian Vidal-Fernandez, "Do Personality Traits Affect Productivity? Evidence from the Lab," Institute for the Study of Labor, IZA discussion paper 8308, July 2014.

6. Murray R. Barrick, Gregory K. Patton, and Shanna N. Haugland, "Accuracy of Interviewer Judgments of Job Applicant Personality Traits," *Personnel Psychology* 53 (2000): 925–951; also Timothy G. Wingate, "Liar at First Sight? Early Impressions and Interviewer Judgments, Attributions, and False Perceptions of Faking," master's thesis, Department of Psychology, University of Calgary, August 2017.

7. See Cornelius A. Rietveld, Eric A. W. Slob, and A. Roy Thurik, "A Decade of Research on the Genetics of Entrepreneurship: A Review and View Ahead," *Small Business Economics* 57 (2021): 1303–1317.

8. See Sam Altman, "How to Invest in Start-Ups," blog post, January 13, 2020, https://blog.samaltman.com/how-to-invest-in-startups.

9. Tom Wolfe, *The Right Stuff* (New York: Picador, 2008), 23.

10. See Miriam Gensowski, "Personality, IQ, and Lifetime Earnings," *Labour Economics* 51 (2018): 170–183.

11. See Allen Hu and Song Ma, "Persuading Investors: A Video-Based Study," National Bureau of Economic Research working paper 29048, July 2021.

12. See Terhi Maczulskij and Jutta Viinkainen, "Is Personality Related to Permanent Earnings? Evidence Using a Twin Design," *Journal of Economic Psychology* 64 (2018): 116–129.

13. On the ability of childhood personality measures to predict subsequent earnings, see Judge et al., "The Big Five Personality Traits." Another relevant paper with broadly similar results is Gerrit Mueller and Erik Plug, "Estimating the Effect of Personality on Male and Female Earnings," *Industrial and Labor Relations Review* 60, no. 1 (October 2006): 3–22.

14. See Everett S. Spain, Eric Lin, and Lissa V. Young, "Early Predictors of Successful Military Careers Among West Point Cadets," *Military Psychology* 32, no. 6 (2020): 389–407.

15. Deniz S. Ones, Stephen Dilchert, Chockalilngam Viswesvaran, and Timothy A. Judge, "In Support of Personality Assessment in Organizational Settings," *Personnel Psychology* 60 (2007): 995–1027, quotation from 1006.

16. See Steven N. Kaplan and Morten Sorensen, "Are CEOs Different? Characteristics of Top Managers," 2020 working paper, https://papers.ssrn.com/sol3/papers.cfm?abstract_id=2747691. On GitHub vs. tennis players, see Margaret L. Kern, Paul X. McCarthy, Deepanjan Chakrabarty, and Marian-Andrei Rizoui, "Social Media–Predicted Personality Traits and Values Can Help Match People to Their Ideal Jobs," *Proceedings of the National Academy of Sciences* 116, no. 52 (December 16, 2019): 26459–26464. On high-reliability occupations, see Rhona Flin, "Selecting the Right Stuff: Personality and High-Reliability Occupations," in *Personality Psychology in the Workplace*, edited by Brent W. Roberts and Robert Hogan, 253–275 (Washington, DC: American Psychological Association, 2001).

17. See Gregory J. Feist and Michael E. Gorman, "The Psychology of Science: Review and Integration of a Nascent Discipline," *Review of General Psychology* 2, no. 1 (1998): 3–47.

18. See Michael Housman and Dylan Minor, "Toxic Workers," Harvard Business School working paper 16–057, 2015.

19. Eugenio Proto, Aldo Rustichini, and Andis Sofianos, "Intelligence, Personality, and Gains from Cooperation in Repeated Interactions," *Journal of Political Economy* 127, no. 3 (2019): 1351–1390. On conscientiousness mattering the most of the five factors, see Deniz S. Ones, Stephen Dilchert, Chockalilngam Viswesvaran, and Timothy A. Judge, "In Support of Personality Assessment in Organizational Settings," *Personnel Psychology* 60 (2007): 995–1027.

20. See Erik Lindqvist and Roine Vestman, "The Labor Market Returns to Cognitive and Noncognitive Ability: Evidence from the Swedish Enlistment," *American Economic Journal: Applied Economics* 3 (January 2011): 101–128.

21. See "'Obsession Kept Me Going': Writer Vikram Seth on 25 Years of *A Suitable Boy*," *Hindustan Times*, October 22, 2018.

22. The core result is this: "For males, a one-standard-deviation increase in externalizing behavior predicts a statistically significant 6.4% increase in hourly wages. . . . For females, a one-standard-deviation increase in externalizing behavior predicts a marginally significant 4.7% increase in hours worked per week, but does not significantly affect hourly wages." See Nicholas W. Papageorge, Victor Ronda, and

Yu Zheng, "The Economic Value of Breaking Bad: Misbehavior, Schooling and the Labor Market," National Bureau of Economic Research working paper 25602, February 2019, quotation from 22. Note that those results hold even after controlling for Five Factor personality traits, although such controls reduce the effect of externalizing behavior on male earnings by about 20 percent.

23. One distinction between VC firms is the degree to which they'll pursue talent working on the extreme frontier. While Andreessen Horowitz will fund speculative companies and individuals, Sequoia and Moritz seem more focused on finding projects with an obvious path to revenue. Peter Thiel seems to have been a remarkable magnet for weirdness—namely, people doing new and strange things—but nonetheless prefers strong executors doing projects with huge payoffs.

24. See James J. Heckman, Tomas Jagelka, and Timothy D. Kautz, "Some Contributions of Economics to the Study of Personality," National Bureau of Economic Research working paper 26459, August 2019.

25. See Juan Barceló and Greg Sheen, "Voluntary Adoption of Social Welfare-Enhancing Behavior: Mask-Wearing in Spain During the Covid-19 Outbreak," SocArXiv preprint at https://osf.io/preprints/socarxiv/6m85q/, accessed July 5, 2020.

26. On leaders and conscientiousness, see Leah Frazier and Adriane M. F. Saunders, "Can a Leader Be Too Conscientious? A Linear vs. Curvilinear Comparison," paper presented at the 15th Annual River Cities Industrial and Organizational Psychology Conference, 2019, https://scholar.utc.edu/rcio/2019/sessions/18/. See Michael P. Wilmot and Deniz S. Ones, "A Century of Research on Conscientiousness at Work," *Proceedings of the National Academy of Sciences* 116, no. 46 (2019): 23004–23010.

27. Robin Hanson, "Stamina Succeeds," *Overcoming Bias* (blog), September 10, 2019, http://www.overcomingbias.com/2019/09/stamina-succeeds.html. More generally, see Angela Duckworth, *Grit: The Power of Passion and Perseverance* (New York: Scribner, 2016). One example of a study stressing the importance of ongoing "zeal" is Brian Butterworth, "Mathematical Expertise," in *The Cambridge Handbook of Expertise and Expert Performance*, edited by K. Anders Ericsson, Robert R. Hoffman, Aaron Kozbelt, and A. Mark Williams, 616–633 (Cambridge: Cambridge University Press, 2018).

28. John Leen, "My Dinners with Le Carré: What I Learned About Writing, Fame and Grace When I Spent Two Weeks Showing the Master Spy Novelist Around Miami," *Washington Post*, December 30, 2020.

29. On grit and perseverance of effort, see Marcus Crede, Michael C. Tynan, and Peter D. Harms, "Much Ado About Grit: A Meta-Analytic Synthesis of the Grit Literature," *Journal of Personality and Social Psychology* 113, no. 3 (2017): 492–511. More generally on grit and intelligence, see Angela L. Duckworth, Abigail Quirk, Robert Gallop, Rick H. Hoyle, Dennis R. Kelly, and Michael D. Matthews, "Cognitive and Noncognitive Predictors of Success," *Proceedings of the National Academy of Sciences* 116, no. 47 (2019): 23499–23504.

6. What Is Personality Good For? Part Two: Some More Exotic Concepts

1. For one look at some issues related to China, see Fanny M. Cheung, Kwok Leung, Jian-Xin Zhang, Hai-Fa Sun, Yi-Qun Gan, Wei-Zhen Song, and Dong Zie, "Indigenous Chinese Personality Constructs: Is the Five-Factor Model Complete?," *Journal of Cross-Cultural Psychology* 32, no. 4 (July 2001): 407–433.

2. On the notion of useful personality concepts evolving into words, see the earlier "lexical hypothesis," defended in, for instance, Michael C. Ashton and Kibeom Lee, "A Defence of the Lexical Approach to the Study of Personality Structure," *European Journal of Personality* 19 (2005): 5–24.

3. See Sam Altman, "How to Invest in Start-Ups," blog post, January 13, 2020, https://blog.samaltman.com/how-to-invest-in-startups.

4. Malcolm Gladwell, in his *Outliers: The Story of Success* (New York: Little, Brown, 2008), stresses the returns from practice, drawing on the research of Anders Ericsson and others.

5. On the related concept of psychological hardiness, see Salvatore R. Maddi, "The Story of Hardiness: Twenty Years of Theorizing, Research, and Practice," *Consulting Psychology Journal: Practice and Research* 54, no. 3 (2002): 175–185; and Kevin J. Eschleman, Nathan A. Bowling, and Gene M. Alarcon, "A Meta-Analytic Examination of Hardiness," *International Journal of Stress Management* 17, no. 4 (2010): 277–307. On hardiness in the military, see Paul T. Bartone, Robert R. Roland, James J. Picano, and Thomas J. Williams, "Psychological Hardiness Predicts Success in US Army Special Forces Candidates," *International Journal of Selection and Assessment* 16, no. 1 (2008): 78–81.

6. See Arne Güllich et al., "Developmental Biographies of Olympic Super-Elite and Elite Athletes: A Multidisciplinary Pattern Recognition Analysis," *Journal of Expertise* 2, no. 1 (March 2019): 23–46.

7. See Scott Simon, "Let's Play Two! Remembering Chicago Cub Ernie Banks," National Public Radio, January 24, 2015, https://www.npr.org/2015/01/24/379546360/lets-play-two-remembering-chicago-cub-ernie-banks.

8. For data on scientists and publication date, see Gregory J. Feist, "The Development of Scientific Talent in Westinghouse Finalists and Members of the National Academy of Sciences," *Journal of Adult Development* 13, no. 1 (March 2006): 23–35.

9. For the study, see Ben Weidmann and David J. Deming, "Team Players: How Social Skills Improve Group Performance," National Bureau of Economic Research working paper 27071, May 2020.

10. On the related concept of achievement motivation, found in the personality psychology literature, see Leonora Risse, Lisa Farrell, and Tim R. L. Fry, "Personality and Pay: Do Gender Gaps in Confidence Explain Gender Gaps in Wages?," *Oxford Economic Papers* 70, no. 4 (2018): 919–949. See also Allan Wigfield, Jacquelynne S. Eccles, Ulrich Schiefele, Robert W. Roeser, and Pamela Davis-Kean, "Development of Achievement Motivation," in *Handbook of Childhood Psychology*, vol. III,

Social, Emotional, and Personality Development, 6th ed., edited by William Damon and Richard M. Lerner, 406–434 (New York: John Wiley, 2008).

11. "Susan Barnes has observed that Steve entered every negotiation knowing exactly what he had to get, and what his position was versus the other side." Brent Schlender, *Becoming Steve Jobs* (New York: Crown Publishing Group, 2015), 289.

7. Disability and Talent

1. On Greta's autism as a factor behind her success, see Steve Silberman, "Greta Thunberg Became a Climate Activist Not in Spite of Her Autism, but Because of It," Vox, last updated September 24, 2019.

2. Masha Gessen, "The Fifteen-Year-Old Climate Activist Who is Demanding a Different Kind of Politics," *The New Yorker*, October 2, 2018.

3. I am grateful to Michelle Dawson for discussions on this point, though she bears no liability for our concept or discussion of disabilities.

4. See Chloe Taylor, "Billionaire Richard Branson: Dyslexia Helped Me to Become Successful," CNBC, October 7, 2019, https://www.cnbc.com/2019/10/07 /billionaire-richard-branson-dyslexia-helped-me-to-become-successful.html.

5. The report is "The Value of Dyslexia: Dyslexic Strengths and the Changing World of Work," Ernst & Young Global Limited, 2018.

6. See Darcey Steinke, "My Stutter Made Me a Better Writer," *The New York Times*, June 6, 2019.

7. See James Gallagher, "Aphantasia: Ex-Pixar Chief Ed Catmull Says 'My Mind's Eye Is Blind,'" BBC News, April 9, 2019. For a broader recent survey on aphantasia, see Adam Zeman et al., "Phantasia—The Psychological Significance of Lifelong Visual Imagery Vividness Extremes," *Cortex* 130 (2020): 426–440. More broadly, see Anna Clemens, "When the Mind's Eye Is Blind," *Scientific American*, August 1, 2018.

8. Again, over time, the "Asperger's" terminology increasingly has been replaced by "autism," including in the latest version of the *DSM*, *DSM-5*. We are not committed to any particular view on this matter and are employing the terms broadly enough so that they may be consistent with varying uses of the terminology.

9. See Tony Atwood, *The Complete Guide to Asperger's Syndrome* (London: Jessica Kingsley, 2015), 27–28.

10. On the possible social intelligence of autistics, see Anton Gollwitzer, Cameron Martel, James C. McPartland, and John A. Bargh, "Autism Spectrum Traits Predict Higher Social Psychological Skill," *Proceedings of the National Academy of Sciences* 116, no. 39 (September 24, 2019): 19245–19247.

11. On Tyler and information (and autism), see his *The Age of the Infovore* (New York: Plume, 2010).

12. For a variety of perspectives on this topic, see the Behavioral and Brain Sciences symposium on social motivation in autism, led by Vikram K. Jaswal and Nameera Akhtar, "Being Versus Appearing Socially Uninterested: Challenging

Assumptions About Social Motivation in Autism," *Behavioral and Brain Sciences* 42 (2019): e82.

13. See Ellen Rosen, "Using Technology to Close the Autism Job Gap," *The New York Times*, October 24, 2019; on Microsoft, see Maitane Sardon, "How Microsoft Tapped the Autism Community for Talent," *The Wall Street Journal*, October 26, 2019.

14. See David Friedman, "Cold Houses in Warm Climates and Vice Versa: A Paradox of Rational Heating," *Journal of Political Economy* 95, no. 5 (1987): 1089–1097. You will find an online version on Friedman's home page here: http://www .daviddfriedman.com/Academic/Cold_Houses/Cold_Houses.html. Outside of economics, one source to consult is Willem E. Frankenhuis, Ethan S. Young, and Bruce J. Ellis, "The Hidden Talents Approach: Theoretical and Methodological Challenges," *Trends in Cognitive Sciences* 24, no. 7 (March 2020): 569–581.

15. See Michael Cavna, "Dav Pilkey Credits His ADHD for His Massive Success. Now He Wants Kids to Find Their Own 'Superpower,'" *The Washington Post*, October 11, 2019.

16. For one survey of these literatures, see Cowen, *The Age of the Infovore*; more recently, see Rachel Nuwer, "Finding Strengths in Autism," *Spectrum*, May 12, 2021. See also Simon Baron-Cohen, "Autism: The Emphathizing-Sympathizing (E-S) Theory," *Annals of the New York Academy of Sciences* 1156 (2009): 68–80; Francesca Happe and Pedro Vital, "What Aspects of Autism Predispose to Talent?," *Philosophical Transactions of the Royal Society of London B: Biological Sciences* 364, no. 1522 (2009): 1369–1375; Laurent Mottron, Michelle Dawson, Isabelle Soulières, Benedicte Hubert, and Jake Burack, "Enhanced Perceptual Functioning in Autism: An Update, and Eight Principles of Autistic Perception," *Journal of Autism and Developmental Disorders* 36, no. 1 (January 2006): 27–43; and Liron Rozenkrantz, Anila M. D'Mello, and John D. E. Gabrieli, "Enhanced Rationality in Autism Spectrum Disorder," *Trends in Cognitive Sciences* 25, no. 8 (August 1, 2021): P685–P696. For the Ravens results, see Michelle Dawson, Isabelle Soulieres, Morton Ann Gernsbacher, and Laurent Mottron, "The Level and Nature of Autistic Intelligence," *Psychological Science* 18, no. 8 (2007): 657–662. On genetic risk for autism and intelligence, I have drawn on Scott Alexander, "Autism and Intelligence: Much More than You Wanted to Know," SlateStarCodex, November 13, 2019, https://slatestarcodex.com/2019/11/13/autism-and-intelligence-much-more -than-you-wanted-to-know/. More specifically on that topic, see S. P. Hagenaars et al., "Shared Genetic Aetiology Between Cognitive Functions and Physical and Mental Health in UK Biobank (N =112 151) and 24 GWAS Consortia," *Molecular Psychiatry* 21 (2016): 1624–1632.

17. On autism and de novo mutations, see Scott Myers et al., "Insufficient Evidence for 'Autism-Specific' Genes," *American Journal of Human Genetics* 106, no. 5 (May 7, 2020): 587–595.

18. For Vernon on his own autism, see, for instance, his autobiography, Vernon L.

Smith, *A Life of Experimental Economics*, vol. 1, *Forty Years of Discovery* (New York: Palgrave Macmillan, 2018).

19. Temple Grandin, "Why Visual Thinking Is a Different Approach to Problem Solving," *Forbes*, October 9, 2019.

20. See Jeff Bell, "Ten-Year-Old Has Pi Memorized to 200 Digits, Speaks 4 Languages," *Times Colonist*, December 1, 2019.

21. On some of these deficits, see Mark A. Bellgrove, Alasdair Vance, and John L. Bradshaw, "Local-Global Processing in Early-Onset Schizophrenia: Evidence for an Impairment in Shifting the Spatial Scale of Attention," *Brain and Cognition* 51, no. 1 (2003): 48–65; Peter Brugger, "Testing vs. Believing Hypotheses: Magical Ideation in the Judgment of Contingencies," *Cognitive Neuropsychiatry* 2, no. 4 (1997): 251–272; Birgit Mathes et al., "Early Processing Deficits in Object Working Memory in First-Episode Schizophreniform Psychosis and Established Schizophrenia," *Psychological Medicine* 35 (2005): 1053–1062; and Diego Pizzagalli et al., "Brain Electric Correlates of Strong Belief in Paranormal Phenomena: Intracerebral EEG Source and Regional Omega Complexity Analyses," *Psychiatry Research: Neuroimaging Section* 100, no. 3 (2000): 139–154. On the question of how bipolar individuals differ, see M. F. Green, "Cognitive Impairment and Functional Outcome in Schizophrenia and Bipolar Disorder," *Journal of Clinical Psychiatry* 67, suppl. 9 (December 31, 2005): 3–8.

22. For one look at an extensive literature, see Sara Weinstein and Roger E. Graves, "Are Creativity and Schizotypy Products of a Right Hemisphere Bias?," *Brain and Cognition* 49 (2002): 138–151, quotations from 138. See also Selcuk Acar and Sedat Sen, "A Multilevel Meta-Analysis of the Relationship Between Creativity and Schizotypy," *Psychology of Aesthetics, Creativity, and the Arts* 7, no. 3 (2013): 214–228; Andreas Fink et al., "Creativity and Schizotypy from the Neuroscience Perspective," *Cognitive, Affective, and Behavioral Neuroscience* 14, no. 1 (March 2014): 378–387; Mark Batey and Adrian Furnham, "The Relationship Between Measures of Creativity and Schizotypy," *Personality and Individual Differences* 45 (2008): 816–821; and Daniel Nettle, "Schizotypy and Mental Health Amongst Poets, Visual Artists, and Mathematicians," *Journal of Research in Personality* 40, no. 6 (December 2006): 876–890. On relatives, see Diana I. Simeonova, Kiki D. Chang, Connie Strong, and Terence A. Ketter, "Creativity in Familial Bipolar Disorder," *Journal of Psychiatric Research* 39 (2005): 623–631. On polygenic risk scores predicting creativity, see Robert A. Power et al., "Polygenic Risk Scores for Schizophrenia and Bipolar Disorder Predict Creativity," *Nature Neuroscience* 18, no. 7 (July 2015): 953–956. On the genetics of schizophrenia and education, see Perline A. Demange et al., "Investigating the Genetic Architecture of Non-Cognitive Skills Using GWAS-by-Subtraction," bioRxiv, January 15, 2020.

23. The cited lyrics are from the Kanye West song "Yikes," from his 2018 album *Ye*.

24. On the Kanye episode, see Wessel de Cock, "Kanye West's Bipolar Disorder as a

'Superpower' and the Role of Celebrities in the Rethinking of Mental Disorders," http://rethinkingdisability.net/kanye-wests-bipolar-disorder-as-a-superpower-and -the-role-of-celebrities-in-the-rethinking-of-mental-disorders/, accessed July 7, 2020.

25. For one look at these features of schizophrenia and schizotypy, see Bernard Crespi and Christopher Badcock, "Psychosis and Autism as Diametrical Disorders of the Social Brain," *Behavioral and Brain Sciences* 31, no. 3 (2008): 241–260; in particular, the relevant literature more broadly is cited on 253–254.

26. On how schizophrenics may have exaggerated theory of mind, see Ahmad Aku-Abel, "Impaired Theory of Mind in Schizophrenia," *Pragmatics and Cognition* 7, no. 2 (January 1999): 247–282. For a more general look at schizophrenia and theory of mind, see Mirjam Spring et al., "Theory of Mind in Schizophrenia: Meta-analysis," *British Journal of Psychiatry* 191 (2007): 5–13.

8. Why Talented Women and Minorities Are Still Undervalued

1. From "Clementine Jacoby," *Forbes* profile, https://www.forbes.com/profile /clementine-jacoby/?sh=3b852e72a654, and also the Recidiviz home page, https:// www.recidiviz.org/team/cjacoby.

2. "Clementine Jacoby," *Forbes* profile.

3. See Gerrit Mueller and Erik Plug, "Estimating the Effect of Personality on Male and Female Earnings," *Industrial and Labor Relations Review* 60, no. 1 (October 2006): 3–22.

4. See Tim Kaiser and Marco Del Giudice, "Global Sex Differences in Personality: Replication with an Open Online Dataset," *Journal of Personality* 88, no. 3 (June 2020): 415–429. See also Marco Del Giudice, "Measuring Sex Differences and Similarities," in *Gender and Sexuality Development: Contemporary Theory and Research*, edited by D. P. VanderLaan and W. I. Wong (New York: Springer, forthcoming). On variance in agreeableness and extraversion, see Richard A. Lippa, "Sex Differences in Personality Traits and Gender-Related Occupational Preferences Across 53 Nations: Testing Evolutionary and Social-Environmental Theories," *Archives of Sexual Behavior* 39, no. 3 (2010): 619–636. For a useful survey of these literatures, see Scott Barry Kaufman, "Taking Sex Differences in Personality Seriously," *Scientific American*, December 12, 2019.

5. See Ellen K. Nyhus and Empar Pons, "The Effects of Personality on Earnings," *Journal of Economic Psychology* 26 (2005): 363–384. On emotional stability and extraversion, see SunYoun Lee and Fumio Ohtake, "The Effect of Personality Traits and Behavioral Characteristics on Schooling, Earnings and Career Promotion," *Journal of Behavioral Economics and Finance* 5 (2012): 231–238. See also Miriam Gensowski, "Personality, IQ, and Lifetime Earnings," *Labour Economics* 51 (2018): 170–183. On the Canadian data, see Dawson McLean, Mohsen Bouaissa, Bruno Rainville, and Ludovic Auger, "Non-Cognitive Skills: How Much Do They Matter for Earnings in Canada?," *American Journal of Management* 19, no. 4 (2019):104–124, esp. 116.

6. See Melissa Osborne Groves, "How Important Is Your Personality? Labor Market Returns to Personality for Women in the US and UK," *Journal of Economic Psychology* 26 (2005): 827–841. See also her dissertation, "The Power of Personality: Labor Market Rewards and the Transmission of Earnings," University of Massachusetts, Amherst, 2000.

7. See Groves, "The Power of Personality," 44–45.

8. See Martin Abel, "Do Workers Discriminate Against Female Bosses?," Institute for the Study of Labor, IZA working paper 12611, September 2019, https://www.iza .org/publications/dp/12611/do-workers-discriminate-against-female-bosses.

9. See David Robson, "The Reason Why Women's Voices Are Deeper Today," BBC Worklife, June 12, 2018. On vocal pitch, one study is Cecilia Pemberton, Paul McCormack, and Alison Russell, "Have Women's Voices Lowered Across Time? A Cross Sectional Study of Australian Women's Voices," *Journal of Voice* 12, no. 2 (1998): 208–213. On male use of voice to project dominance, see David Andrew Puts, Carolyn R. Hodges, Rodrigo A. Cárdenas, and Steven J. C. Gaulin, "Men's Voices as Dominance Signals: Vocal Fundamental and Formant Frequencies Influence Dominance Attributions Among Men," *Evolution and Human Behavior* 28, no. 5 (September 2007): 340–344.

10. On these differences, see Rachel Croson and Uri Gneezy, "Gender Differences in Preferences," *Journal of Economic Literature* 47, no. 2 (June 2009): 448–474; Thomas Buser, Muriel Niederle, and Hessel Oosterbeek, "Gender Competitiveness and Career Choices," *Quarterly Journal of Economics* 129, no. 3 (August 2014): 1409–1447; and Muriel Niederle and Lise Vesterlund, "Do Women Shy Away from Competition? Do Men Compete Too Much?," *Quarterly Journal of Economics* 122, no. 3 (August 2007): 1067–1101, among many other papers. By the way, these same research studies do *not* assess whether these are innate biological differences or brought on by gender socialization. In any case, from your vantage point as a talent scout, that is not the major issue. Instead, the question is how you might use this information to make better hires and find and mobilize more talented women.

11. See Christine L. Exley and Judd B. Kessler, "The Gender Gap in Self-Promotion," working paper, 2019, https://www.hbs.edu/faculty/Pages/item.aspx?num=57092.

12. See Julian Kolev, Yuly Fuentes-Medel, and Fiona Murray, "Is Blinded Review Enough? How Gendered Outcomes Arise Even Under Anonymous Evaluation," National Bureau of Economic Research working paper 25759, April 2019.

13. See Sarah Cattan, "Psychological Traits and the Gender Wage Gap," Institute for Fiscal Studies working paper, 2013; Francine D. Blau and Lawrence M. Kahn, "The Gender Wage Gap: Extent, Trends, and Explanations," National Bureau of Economic Research working paper 21913, January 2016. For a significant follow-up study, see Leonora Risse, Lisa Farrell, and Tim R. L. Fry, "Personality and Pay: Do Gender Gaps in Confidence Explain Gender Gaps in Wages?," *Oxford Economic Papers* 70, no. 4 (2018): 919–949; see also Adina D. Sterling et al., "The

Confidence Gap Predicts the Gender Pay Gap Among STEM Graduates," *Proceedings of the National Academy of Sciences* 117, no. 48 (December 1, 2020): 30303–30308. For evidence on the confidence gap and how stereotyping may contribute to it, see Pedro Bordalo, Katherine Coffman, Nicola Gennaioli, and Andrei Shleifer, "Beliefs About Gender," *American Economic Review* 109, no. 3 (March 2019): 739–773, https://scholar.harvard.edu/files/shleifer/files/beliefsaboutgender2.2019.pdf.

14. See Angela Cools, Raquel Fernandez, and Eleonora Patacchini, "Girls, Boys, and High Achievers," National Bureau of Economic Research working paper 25763, April 2019. For evidence that the confidence gap helps explain why boys more aggressively ask for regrading in school, see Cher Hsuehhsiang Li and Basit Zafar, "Ask and You Shall Receive? Gender Differences in Regrades in College," National Bureau of Economic Research working paper 26703, January 2020.

15. For one piece of evidence that women may be the more rational traders, see Catherine C. Eckel and Sascha C. Füllbrunn, "Thar SHE Blows? Gender, Competition, and Bubbles in Experimental Asset Markets," *American Economic Review* 105, no. 2 (2015): 906–920. On the confidence gap in economics, see Heather Sarsons and Guo Xu, "Confidence Men? Evidence on Confidence and Gender Among Top Economists," *AEA Papers and Proceedings* 111 (2021): 65–68.

16. For the tournament study, see Joyce He, Sonia Kang, and Nicola Lacetera, "Leaning In or Not Leaning Out? Opt-Out Choice Framing Attenuates Gender Differences in the Decision to Compete," National Bureau of Economic Research working paper 26484, November 2019.

17. Jennifer Hunt, Jean-Philippe Garant, Hannah Herman, and David J. Munroe, "Why Don't Women Patent?," National Bureau of Economic Research working paper 17888, March 2012.

18. See Sabrina T. Howell and Ramana Nanda, "Networking Frictions in Venture Capital, and the Gender Gap in Entrepreneurship," National Bureau of Economic Research working paper 26449, November 2019.

19. For one series of anecdotal accounts, see Susan Chira, "Why Women Aren't C.E.O.s, According to Women Who Almost Were," *The New York Times*, July 21, 2017.

20. See Allen Hu and Song Ma, "Persuading Investors: A Video-Based Study, National Bureau of Economic Research working paper 29048, July 2021.

21. Raffi Khatchadourian, "N. K. Jemisin's Dream Worlds," *The New Yorker*, January 27, 2020.

22. See Frank Bruni, "Sister Wendy, Cloistered," *The New York Times*, September 30, 1997, and also her Wikipedia page, https://en.wikipedia.org/wiki/Wendy_Beckett.

23. Interestingly, in this paper attractiveness and smarts are not correlated. It is also interesting to see what people judge as smart. For instance, those men judged as smart on average have somewhat elongated faces, with a broader distance between the eyes, a larger nose, a slight upturn to the corners of the mouth, and a sharper, less rounded chin. Yet those same traits, when measured directly, do not predict

intelligence at all. Therefore it seems there is an incorrect stereotypical set of intelligence judgments layered upon some partially correct intuitions. The paper is Karel Kleisner, Veronika Chvátalová, and Jaroslav Flegr, "Perceived Intelligence is Associated with Measured Intelligence in Men but Not Women," *PLoS ONE* 9, no. 3 (2014): e81237.

24. See Xingjie Wei and David Stillwell, "How Smart Does Your Profile Image Look? Intelligence Estimation from Social Network Profile Images," December 11, 2016, https://arxiv.org/abs/1606.09264.

9. The Search for Talent in Beauty, Sports, and Gaming, or How to Make Scouts Work for You

1. See Alexei Barrionuevo, "Off Runway, Brazilian Beauty Goes Beyond Blond," *The New York Times*, June 8, 2010.

2. See Gisele Bündchen, *Lessons: My Path to a Meaningful Life* (New York: Penguin Random House, 2018), 2. On the absence of modeling school in the backgrounds of the top supermodels, see Ian Halperin, *Bad and Beautiful: Inside the Dazzling and Deadly World of Supermodels* (New York: Citadel Press, 2001), 161. On Brinkley, see Alexa Tietjen, "Christie Brinkley on Aging, Healthy Living and How a Sick Puppy Started Her Career," *WWD*, June 21, 2017, https://wwd.com/eye/people/christie-brinkley-ageism-and-healthy-living-10922910/. On Claudia Schiffer, see Michael Gross, *Model: The Ugly Business of Beautiful Women* (New York: William Morrow, 1995), 475. Perhaps most useful is Erica Gonzales, Chelsey Sanchez, and Isabel Greenberg, "How 40 of Your Favorite Models Got Discovered," *Harper's Bazaar*, August 14, 2019, which covers the story of Kate Moss and also numerous other stories of spontaneous discovery. For the story of Janice Dickinson's discovery, see Janice Dickinson, *No Lifeguard on Duty: The Accidental Life of the World's First Supermodel* (New York: HarperCollins, 2002), esp. 63. On Behati Prinsloo, see Britt Aboutaleb, "Life with Behati Prinsloo," Fashionista, April 8, 2014; on Naomi Campbell, see "Naomi Campbell: 'At an Early Age, I Understood What It Meant to Be Black. You Had to Be Twice as Good,'" *The Guardian*, March 19, 2016.

3. On the variety of scouts, see Gross, *Model*, 475. On finding, recruiting, and maintaining models, see Ashley Mears, *Pricing Beauty: The Making of a Fashion Model* (Berkeley: University of California Press, 2011), esp. 77–78.

4. See Olga Khazan, "The Midwest, Home of the Supermodel: What a Scout's Success in the Heartland Says About the Modeling Industry," *Atlantic*, August 13, 2015.

5. Dalya Alberge, "Opera's Newest Star Taught Herself to Sing by Copying Divas on DVDs," *The Guardian*, August 31, 2019. See also Kim Cloete, "A New Opera Star Emerges from the 'Vocal Breadbasket' of South Africa," *The World*, October 21, 2016.

6. See Ben Golliver, "Like Father, Like Son: Bronny James, LeBron's Kid, Is the Biggest Draw in High School Hoops," *The New York Times*, December 6, 2019.

7. Tyler Conroy, *Taylor Swift: This Is Our Song* (New York: Simon and Schuster, 2016), quotation from 43.

8. See Ben Casnocha, "Venture Capital Scout Programs: FAQs," blog post, October 29, 2019, https://casnocha.com/2019/10/venture-capital-programs.html. See also Elad Gil, "Founder Investors & Scout Programs," blog post, April 1, 2019, http://blog.eladgil.com/2019/04/founder-investors-scout-programs.html.

9. See Cade Massey and Richard H. Thaler, "The Loser's Curse: Decision Making and Market Efficiency in the National Football League Draft," *Management Science* 59, no. 7 (July 2013): 1479–1495. There is also a concrete way of showing that the early picks often are mistakes. By the sixth year of NFL play, there is an open market in trading these players, and that market can be used as an estimate of eventual value. It turns out that the very high draft picks, when they are traded, do not bring nearly as much value as their high early draft status might indicate. Massey and Thaler write: "Surplus value of the picks during the first round actually increases throughout most of the round: the player selected with the final pick in the first round, on average, produces more surplus to his team than the first pick!" (1480).

10. See Ben Lindbergh and Travis Sawchik, *The MVP Machine: How Baseball's New Nonconformists Are Using Data to Build Better Players* (New York: Basic Books, 2019), esp. 191.

11. On Heidi Klum, see Rainer Zitelmann, *Dare to be Different and Grow Rich* (London: LID Publishing, 2020), 196.

12. On the value of scout communication, see Christopher J. Phillips, *Scouting and Scoring: How We Know What We Know About Baseball* (Princeton, NJ: Princeton University Press, 2019), 138–139.

13. Lindbergh and Sawchik, *The MVP Machine*, 171–172.

14. All of this is from Tony Kulesa, "Tyler Cowen Is the Best Curator of Talent in the World," from his Substack, https://kulesa.substack.com/p/tyler-cowen-is-the-best-curator-of, August 31, 2021.

15. See Aretha Franklin and David Ritz, *Aretha: From These Roots* (New York: Villard, 1999), and also David Ritz, *Respect: The Life of Aretha Franklin* (New York: Back Bay Books, 2015).

16. This discussion draws in part upon some tweets by Erik Torenberg of Village Global (@eriktorenberg), for instance, ".@rabois has been talking about getting a monopoly on talent for the last decade(s). What's the most clever approach you've seen or considered in this vein?," February 24, 2019, 4:22 p.m., https://twitter.com/eriktorenberg/status/1099781696860282885.

10. How to Convince Talent to Join Your Cause

1. See George Eliot, *Daniel Deronda* (New York: Penguin Books, 1995 [1876]), 430. See also Michal Nielsen's Facebook post on what he calls "volitional philanthropy," https://www.facebook.com/permalink.php?story_fbid=224735391342335&id=100014176268390.

2. See Audie Cornish, "Rare National Buzz Tipped Obama's Decision to Run," *All Things Considered*, National Public Radio, November 19, 2007, https://www.npr .org/templates/story/story.php?storyId=16364560.

3. On this process of how the mentee comes to see a different and more ambitious future, see, for instance, Cathy Freeman, "The Crystallizing Experience: A Study in Musical Precocity," *Gifted Child Quarterly* 43, no. 2 (Spring 1999): 75–85, and Patricia A. Cameron, Carol J. Mills, and Thomas E. Heinzen, "The Social Context and Developmental Pattern of Crystallizing Experiences Among Academically Talented Youth," *Roeper Review* 17, no. 3 (February 1995): 197–200.

4. See, for instance, Seth Gershenson, Cassandra M. D. Hart, Joshua Hyman, Constance Lindsay, and Nicholas W. Papageorge, " The Long-Run Impacts of Same-Race Teachers," National Bureau of Economic Research working paper 25254, November 2018.

5. See Abhijit Banerjee, Esther Duflo, et al., "A Multifaceted Program Causes Lasting Progress for the Very Poor: Evidence from Six Countries," *Science* 348, no. 6236 (May 15, 2015). The quotation is from the podcast *Conversations with Tyler*, Abhijit Banerjee episode, released December 30, 2019, https://medium.com/@mercatus/abhijit-banerjee-tyler-cowen-economics-markets-ceda4b520b62?.

6. Daniel Gross, "Introducing Pioneer," Medium, August 10, 2018, https://medium .com/pioneerdotapp/introducing-pioneer-e18769d2e4d0.

INDEX